THE TAO GALS' GUIDE TO REAL ESTATE

ALSO BY BERNADETTE MURPHY
The Knitter's Gift (editor)
Zen and the Art of Knitting

ALSO BY MICHELLE HUNEVEN
Jamesland
Round Rock

The Tao Gals' Guide to Real Estate

Six Modern Women Discover the Ancient Art of Finding, Owning, and Making a Home

Bernadette Murphy and Michelle Huneven

BLOOMSBURY

Published by Bloomsbury Publishing, New York and London
Distributed to the trade by Holtzbrinck Publishers

All papers used by Bloomsbury Publishing are natural, recyclable products made from wood grown in well-managed forests. The manufacturing processes conform to the environmental regulations of the country of origin.

Library of Congress Cataloging-in-Publication Data

Murphy, Bernadette M. (Bernadette Mary), 1963–
     The Tao gals' guide to real estate : six modern women discover the ancient art of finding, owning, and making a home / by Bernadette Murphy and Michelle Huneven.—1st U.S. ed.
     p. cm
     ISBN-13: 978-1-58234-561-1 (pbk. : alk. paper)
     ISBN-10: 1-58234-561-9 (pbk. : alk. paper)
     1. House buying—United States.   2. Residential real estate—Purchasing—United States.   3. Mortgage loans— United States.   4. Spiritual life—Taoism.   I. Huneven, Michelle, 1953–   II. Title.

HD259.M87   2005
643′.12′0973—dc22

                                                         2005016177

First U.S. Edition 2006

1 3 5 7 9 10 8 6 4 2

Typeset by Westchester Book Group
Printed in the United States of America by Quebecor World Fairfield

CONTENTS

BY WAY OF INTRODUCTION

THE TAO GALS are a group of six women who meet on Tuesday nights to reflect on spiritual principles and how to implement them in our lives. We "fell into" the Tao when we agreed to anchor each meeting with a period of reading and writing. The Tao Te Ching (a spiritual text of eighty-one short verses written twenty-five centuries ago in China by the wise man Lao-tzu) was suggested as a text. We used the translation by Stephen Mitchell, published by HarperPerennial. Each of us, it turned out, had previously encountered at least excerpts from this slim, intriguing document, and all were equally drawn to explore it more systematically. Practically, its format of short poem—shaped chapters perfectly suited our purposes.

We Gals hail from varied religious backgrounds (Catholic, Jewish, Baptist, Unitarian Universalist), yet, to a woman, we found in the Tao Te Ching concrete, practical help in steering—or better yet, not steering—our personal and professional lives. We've learned to weaken our ambition and strengthen our resolve—only to find long-standing goals quietly attained. We've learned to do our work and move on without waiting for approbation—and are amazed at how much more we accomplish. We've learned to temper our expectations—and find our disappointments sizably reduced. We've learned to relate to and trust the powerful, invisible, endlessly replenished, unknowable source "older than god"—and find we navigate our lives with more facility and brio.

Meeting, reading, writing, then discussing the problems and

issues of our lives as seen through the lens of the Tao has car-
ried us through many a threshold—literally. For, over the six
years we've been gathering, one common thread has arisen
over and over: our individual struggles with home—finding
one, making one, and owning one. Or not owning one, as the
case may be.

Living in Los Angeles during a peaking real estate market
has been especially challenging. Together, we have learned
firsthand what it's like to be women buying real estate in cut-
throat circumstances. Through each other's examples, we now
know that it's possible to keep your sanity and equanimity
when the market has lost its head. We've seen that real inner
security is not something that can be purchased—and also that
it's equally possible to lose the real estate game and still come
out ahead in life, with a deep sense of contentment and a true
sense of being home.

Buying a house, we've also discovered, isn't simply buying a
house, but a statement about where we think we belong in the
world, how we see ourselves, and how we imagine others will
see us. So much more is involved than simply finding suitable
living quarters and signing the contract. Indeed, to be fully
alive and conscious as a first-time home buyer, a certain
amount of emotional prep work is required; there must be a
willingness to look at old assumptions, unexamined beliefs,
and entrenched prejudices about who gets to own a home, and
where, and what kind of a home it will be. As with all growth,
first-time home buying can be a painful—if revelatory—
process, and how we handle it tells us a lot about how we handle life in general.

On a typical Tuesday night, we'll read aloud a chapter of

the Tao Te Ching, then silently reflect and write for about twenty minutes on how some part of that section applies to our lives. In the writing, we make a point of telling stories— stories full of specific detail based on our own experience. When everyone's pen has come to rest, we'll take turns reading aloud what we've written. Sometimes, we sit in silence listening to each other, nodding in agreement; other times, we might add a word of encouragement or toss out comments. We laugh a lot—maybe even as much as we weep. Again and again, we see the old text come to life through the mirror of our own experiences. The Tao's wisdom, we've found, is inexhaustible. It doesn't compete with other theologies, doesn't insist on being preeminent; anyone, we've discovered, can enter its calm waters and gain a new perspective on life.

By participating in this group, we've found strengths we had no idea we possessed. We've often divided up a burden one of us is carrying, each woman taking a piece of the load—a task, a bit of research, a series of daily, hand-holding phone calls. We've shared our struggles and triumphs, looking to the Tao for clues not only on how to handle the lows and the highs, but also the vast, often-dull middle ground of life. In this group, we've come to see how spiritual principles, like those in the Tao, can guide a life and make even the most roller coaster times navigable.

As for us, we are six quite disparate women, each intelligent, educated, and possessing extensive expertise in our own fields. Yet when it came to dealing with real estate, we all felt on shaky ground—and discovered that many of our insecurities had to do with being women in the home marketplace. In all of our families of origin, our fathers had exclusively handled the real estate transactions, so the arena of home buying seemed well outside our realm of expertise and experience.

Two of us—the coauthors of the book—will tell our stories directly.

MICHELLE

I'm the novelist of the group and a freelance journalist. As a single woman, I had never thought seriously about buying my own home until the eviction notice arrived. My experience—the ups and downs—will be explored here.

BERNADETTE

I'm a writer, creative writing teacher at the UCLA Extension Writers Program, and literary critic for the *Los Angeles Times*. I'm a married mother of three whose previous foray into real estate ended badly—very badly. Can you spell *foreclosure?*

THROUGHOUT THE BOOK, we'll share our stories as well as those of the other Tao Gals, who offered practical advice and emotional support during our moments of real estate–inspired panic and who shared their experience, strength, and hope with us as we walked our own paths. To protect the privacy of these women and to allow their stories to be told honestly and without fear of reprisal, we've changed their names.

Marie is a married stock market–financial administrator whose house depreciated after the real estate boom of 1990, but she hung on and made improvements, taking out loans beyond the equity value in her home, trusting that it would all work out—and it did. Marie was stellar in convincing us we could actually buy a house, and she can generate loan schedules at a moment's notice—so if we want to see what 5 percent interest on $200,000 looks like over fifteen years, she's the person we call.

Rose, a three-time track-and-field Olympian, is single and had been quite content living in her little rental home in the hills before Michelle bought her house and convinced Rose to give home ownership a try. (Home owning, we discovered, is dangerously contagious!) Gayle, who works as a researcher for the *LA Times,* is a single mom who is just now allowing herself to dream of buying a home for herself and her twelve-year-old daughter, Sophie. For the time being, however, she believes that renting still may be her best choice. Colleen is a deputy district attorney working on some of the toughest cases being prosecuted in downtown LA. Over the course of our six years together as a group, Colleen gave birth to two spirited boys and divorced her husband, and thus lost the house they'd shared. With bolstering from the Tao Gals, she bought her own home and established a new life there as a single mother.

As a group, we have each influenced one another on our individual paths toward and away from home ownership. "We couldn't have made our way without the Tao Gals," we assert. "And it's not just the moral support; these women are a wealth of practical information, know-how, and hands-on help."

Though we all live in Los Angeles, we've found that our experiences are mirrored in other large urban areas where real estate has skyrocketed, leaving potential buyers with shaky knees: New York City, San Francisco, Chicago, Boston, and elsewhere. The stories we tell, though centered on Los Angeles, are not endemic to this region.

What we hope to give our readers is that wealth of experience and expertise so missing from our own lives when we set out to buy homes. Through our stories, we want to familiarize you not only with the lingo, or "real estate speak," and the various processes (finding a Realtor, prequalifying for a loan, establishing an escrow account, etc.), but also with the fears and impulsiveness and, indeed, the whole range of emotions and feelings that are so typical and possible in any real estate transaction.

In this book, each chapter on a specific element of the real estate process—making the decision to buy, finding a Realtor, etc.—includes a Tao-based worksheet to help you reflect on what you want in terms of both home and real estate. You could even form your own Tao group by hooking up with others on the same path. Also, we've included sidebars to help you sort out all the information, as well as an extensive glossary defining terms that may be unfamiliar.

Along the way to home ownership, we've all learned difficult lessons. Lessons like don't count yourself out of the housing market no matter how unusual your financial situation is; at the same time, don't push when it's not happening. Trust things to unfold. Make decisions based on the information you have now and be able to change those decisions as more information becomes available. Be patient; just because you can't buy a house today doesn't mean you won't buy one tomorrow. Ask for help—open yourself up to assistance, and you may be surprised where it comes from. The key lesson we've gleaned from the Tao has been just this: "Do your work, then step back. The only path to serenity."

So, walk with us along the Tao—"The Way," as it is often translated—to see how your real estate dreams may come true, or not, without a sense of helplessness, dire struggle, and undue tension. Perhaps you'll find, as we sometimes did, that what you dream of is the life you already have.

CHAPTER ONE

TAO GAL QUALIFIES FOR HOME OWNERSHIP

The Tao doesn't take sides;
it gives birth to both good and evil.
The Master doesn't take sides;
she welcomes both saints and sinners.

MICHELLE

I NEVER DREAMED I could buy a house.

I was prejudiced against the whole idea.

I began my career as a freelance writer with no savings and an unsteady source of income. Over time, I began to make a decent living, but my income was still unpredictable, arriving as it did in big bursts and small bits. Even when I inherited enough for a small down payment, I was sure that nobody would trust me with a mortgage—though what exactly a mortgage entailed, I couldn't quite tell you.

My reluctance to buy a house wasn't just about money.

I was a single woman, living alone. Houses were what couples bought—couples who planned to have children. My sister, at a time when she was also single, once asked my father for advice and help in buying a flat in London, where she lived. (My father made part of his living carrying second mortgages.) He advised her against buying a flat. "Single women are bad risks," he explained, and refused her a loan. My sister, I should point out, was also self-employed, but incredibly disciplined and frugal. She was and is so frugal, in fact, she makes car payments into a savings account and only buys a new car when she has the cash in hand. This is the person my father labeled a bad risk. But he was our father, and he knew about mortgages, and for a while, at least, we couldn't help but take his opinion to heart.

If my sister was a bad risk, I was an appalling, unspeakable risk. I never really balanced my checkbook or regularly put money into any account, not even my checking account. I splurged on clothes and shoes and books and gardening supplies. And as a restaurant critic, I was notoriously slow in filing my expense reports.

All things financial both frightened and bored me. I could not look at a bank statement without immediately wanting to take a nap, no matter how rosy or grim the numbers were. I would've happily sacrificed all refunds in exchange for not having to file tax returns, except that I was terrified the IRS would swoop down and punish me. Back in the mid-eighties, when I went out on my own as a freelancer and no longer had an employer who deducted taxes, I found myself at a loss regarding financial doings and froze. Come tax time, I had a zillion scraps of paper from a zillion different sources and no idea what to do with them. Somebody told me that I should be paying money to the IRS and state every three months—all of which seemed like such a big awful mystery that I just ignored my taxes for a couple of years. Of course, my terror of the IRS grew proportionately. Then, somebody else suggested I just needed an accountant. Actually, what she said was "I'm sick of hearing you fret about your taxes. Just go to an accountant and get them done." I was flabbergasted. Me and my pathetic dribbling income required an *accountant?* Who could've guessed? And how did she know? Are some people just born with the knowledge that at a certain point they should go to an accountant?

You can see why home owning didn't occur to me then, or later. Home owning was too big, too much responsibility, too much about finances for a single woman like myself, a single woman who ran a loose ship, who was sorely undereducated in such matters.

For who knew how to buy a house? Even once I had that nice little down payment languishing in my checking account, I had no idea what to do with it, what steps to take to pledge it to a home. The whole process of home buying had an aura of such complication and difficulty that I felt automatically excluded—or, I automatically excluded myself. Meanwhile, I watched my best friend, Jan, go through the process with her husband. Jan had inherited money and property and was a freelancer like I was. When she got married, she and her husband, also a freelance writer, decided to buy a house. For months, they looked, and when they finally found something— it was not quite in the lowest tier of the market but maybe half a step up from the lowest tier—they were able to pay more than 50 percent down, which you'd think might've made things easy for them. But no. For two to three months, every time I phoned her, Jan was filling out this and that form or application for the bank, or she was frantically looking for one of last year's bank statements, or faxing two years' worth of statements to the bank, then two or three years' worth of rent checks—both hers and her husband's—and then there were inspectors and geologists and more inspectors and more documents required by the bank. From the sidelines, it seemed like a form of hell, an abyss of uncertainty, not to mention a suffocating haystack of paperwork. And this was a couple! With two incomes! With a huge down payment! Buying pretty damn near the bottom of the market! Their new home was one step up from a shack!

How could I, with my tiny nest egg, ever hope to take part in such a process? I, who was a rotten risk. I, a paperwork-phobic. I could never qualify. My own father wouldn't lend me the money, let alone any bank. Clearly—and I would be the first to tell you—I did not deserve a home of my own.

And there were still deeper issues at work, more half-baked ideas and assumptions lurking in the dim zones just under consciousness where they flourished and essentially ran my life.

My friend Claire, a longtime spiritual adviser and mentor, went out house hunting. She was single at the time she set out to buy a house, but she had a steady job as a construction supervisor. She wanted company in the search for a house and—curiously—she wanted me to buy a house too. Claire didn't question my ability to buy and pay for a house and she quickly dismissed my fears. She knew me and my finances as well as anybody and she essentially gave me permission to buy a house. But I still resisted. While she knocked on walls and cranked open windows and wrinkled her nose at this and that, I entered prospective homes like a skittish cat, never quite believing I had the right to be there. I didn't dare like any house, even for her. I was scared for her as well. Buying a house on one's own, I realized, was about more than money. It seemed like giving up. Like saying, okay, this is it. I'm not getting the spouse. I'm not getting the family. I'm setting up alone.

In fact, when I thought about living in my own home, I thought about one single woman in particular. She'd bought a house and made it perfect in every detail. Off-white walls. Off-white furniture. Off-white rugs. A breakfront filled with matching china and silver. A sparkling kitchen. Three coddled cats. No wet towels on any floor, no dishes ever in the sink. Her house broadcast such an entrenched, perfected, airtight, impenetrable femininity, it all but forbade the possibility of any man or child inhabiting it. It was a fortress and I wanted no part of such a place. I liked a mess, and a lot of company.

What's more, renting was fine for me. Renting was tentative, uncommitted. Renting left me ready for adventure. Never mind that I'd been in the same place for eight years—with a thirty-day notice I could, at any time, opt out for a whole new life. I wrote one check a month, made a phone call when the furnace blew out. Nobody asked to see my tax returns or bank statements. Nobody talked of interest and equity and, heaven forbid, property tax. I didn't have to decorate, let alone reroof.

So leave home ownership to the predictably employed, the responsible, the settled, the defeated. In terms of finances, home repair, and human connections—I was not fit for home ownership.

Thus was I prejudiced against buying a house.

One definition of *prejudice,* however, is "an opinion or leaning adverse to anything without just grounds or sufficient knowledge." And if you look at it, my home-owning aversion was really just based on a few anecdotes, a dearth of information, and a big dose of fear and shame—a bunch of straw dogs, false fronts. However baseless, all of these elements were still deeply entrenched, and they might never have gone unchallenged, except that heaven and earth have no such opinions about the housing market and who qualifies—or anything else—and the time came when a reality greater than that existing in my own mind opened up before me.

What happened was, after nine years renting a small house in Atwater Village, I was evicted. My landlord wanted the place back in order to make the extensive renovations necessary to rent it to someone else for twice the pittance he charged me. But no hurry, he said. I could have five months to find someplace else to live.

Naturally, I brought this crisis to the Tao Gals. "I have to find a new place to live," I wailed. "With a yappy terrier, an ancient cat, and a screaming parrot! Nobody will rent to me."

"Why don't you buy?" asked Marie. She's married and has owned her home forever. She also worked for real estate lawyers, and in the real estate arm of a big storage company buying and selling properties.

"I can't buy a house," I said. "I'd never qualify."

"Are you sure?" she asked. "How much did you earn last year?"

I hemmed and hawed, insisted I was too flaky, too poor. But Marie, like heaven and earth had no opinion—at least about my ability to buy a house—and somehow I agreed to meet her and her calculator and an amortization table for breakfast on Saturday morning. She asked me only for a few very basic figures: my yearly income, how much rent I paid, how much money I could put down. Even I could handle that.

I showed up with my paltry sheet of paper. She took the figures, punched some numbers on her calculator, consulted some long rows of numbers in her little book, and gave me the price range of homes I could afford. I was stunned: The figure (which I needn't bother putting in here, given that it has already become so ridiculously outdated) was already a good $100,000 more than I ever dreamed I could pay. Patiently, she showed me that, with my down payment, my monthly payments would still be below most of the rent prices I could find.

In short, I could afford to buy a home.

"Start looking," she said.

What Can You Afford?

List your monthly income (before taxes) from all sources:

_____

Subtract your current monthly debt:

Car payment   _____

Credit cards   _____

Student loan   _____

Department store charge cards   _____

Child or spousal support   _____

Other personal debt   _____

Homeowners Association fees you will be charged for
new property (check with your real estate agent)   _____

Total remaining   _____

Multiply the total remaining amount by .38 to get
your maximum monthly mortgage payment, including
principal, interest, property taxes, and insurance   _____

Note: While this formula is a general guideline, many lenders have different or looser interpretations and may be willing to allow you to borrow more.

Learn the 6, 7, 8 Rule

To calculate your expected housing costs—including the cost of capital used in your down payment—here's an easy rule of thumb you can follow.

- To figure the approximate monthly mortgage cost (principal and interest), multiply the purchase price (reduced to thousand-dollar increments) by 6. (For a $500,000 house, you'd multiply $500 \times 6 = \$3,000$ a month.) This approximates the carrying cost of both the mortgage and down payment amounts.

- To figure the monthly mortgage payment plus interest and taxes, multiply the purchase price (reduced to thousand-dollar increments) by 7. (For a $500,000 house, you'd multiply $500 \times 7 = \$3,500$ a month.)

- To figure your total monthly costs—mortgage payment, insurance and taxes, as well as maintenance and utilities, multiply the purchase price (reduced to thousand-dollar increments) by 8. (For a $500,000 house, you'd multiply $500 \times 8 = \$4,000$ a month.)

Note: This rule takes into consideration that your down payment in reality costs you interest. In other words, your 10 percent or 20 percent down payment could be working in other ways, e.g., stock market returns or other investments. Thus, the calculations are based on a 0 percent down payment. Even if you have a sizable down payment to bring to the table, this rule still takes into consideration the ways that your down payment money might have been working for you in other ways: earning interest in the bank, lessening your consumer debt by allowing you to pay down credit cards, or lowering your mortgage debt.

Tax Benefit of Buying a Home

If this home is for your primary or secondary residence, you will likely have a home interest deduction against your income. For the first 5 years of a 30-year mortgage, interest is almost the entire mortgage payment. For a $500,000 house, this would be about $3,000 in interest per month. If you are in the 25 percent tax bracket, you can take an interest deduction providing a tax credit of approximately 25 percent × $3,000 per month, or $750 per month! This reduces your $4,000 per month cost by $750 to yield about $3,250 per month after taxes.

Your costs may not be this high, but it's a good way to figure out what the bottom line could very well be. This formula is used by many who buy properties as investments to figure out if the rents they charge will cover their costs and allow them to make a profit.

"I HAVE TO start looking for a house—to buy," I told my friend Michele. She and I had been friends—"the two Michelles"—since high school.

"The one behind us is for sale," Michele said. "It's on a flag lot—in the middle of the block. The house itself is awful, but it's a great big beautiful piece of property. We almost bought it as a rental, but decided we couldn't. Wanna go see?"

"Sure," I said, though I already knew I didn't want an awful house. I *wanted* a house like Michele had, a historically significant Spanish-style home on an acre of gardens, which her husband, a landscape architect, had made lush, balanced, and serene. Of course I couldn't afford Michele's house, but I hoped to do better than *awful*. Also, I'd grown up in Altadena—a small, unincorporated town—a mile due west of that very house. I had no interest in returning to the scene of my childhood. But no harm in looking.

We considered hopping the fence in her backyard, then walked around the corner and down a long driveway to a white stucco house with ugly blue shutters and bars on the windows. Positioned right on the front property line of its large rectangular lot, the house had no front yard, merely faced a wide asphalt driveway and, a few yards away, another, identical house.

The seller allowed us inside, and the house *was* awful, a claustrophobic, '50s stucco cube inhabited by heavy smokers and three dogs. The bathrooms were depressing; the kitchen cabinets were a soft composition board, that fake wood made of sawdust; in this case, it blistered where it had gotten wet.

But Michele danced around the kitchen. "You could knock out these walls, open it up to the back. Mount more cabinets over there . . ."

I saw her point. The house could be nice, if you poured buckets of money into it.

When we tried to go into the backyard, the dogs barked and growled at us. "They won't hurt you," the owner said, but they indicated differently. The yard was dirt and weeds, anyway, with a few small fruit trees.

"How much are you asking?" I said. Given the flag lot, the dereliction, the smell, I was certain it wouldn't be much.

Wordlessly, the man handed me a flyer, and I saw why he dared not speak the sum. It was huge. Flagrantly, depressingly, shockingly expensive. He was asking close to twice what Michele had paid for her gracious and elegant home eight years before. He was asking $70,000 more than my friend Claire paid for a much better house four years ago.

We walked back down the driveway. "He's not living in reality," I said.

Michele agreed. "That's why it's been on the market over a year. But house prices are rising," she added, words that would become the understatement of the decade. Who knew that this was to be the year the market exploded? Who knew that this would be the least expensive house I would look at?

THUS BEGAN MY house hunting, which proved to be a complex process in every way possible: financially, emotionally, socially, spiritually.

Luckily, I had the Tao Gals, who reminded me not to get overly attached to any one idea, to remain open, to do the necessary footwork, to pause, to check in with them whenever confusion and fear threatened to overwhelm me.

Luckily, too, I'd read *Independence Day*, by Richard Ford, the Pulitzer Prize–winning novel whose protagonist, Frank Bascombe, is a real estate agent. The novel, among other things, offers an extended meditation on the nature of home and belonging. There's always some conflict, the book seems to say, between where we think we deserve to live versus where market forces and our own incomes and credit ratings allow us to live.

House hunting, then, is a reality check, and always a bit of a rude awakening. I like to think that, unlike many of Frank Bascombe's finicky clients, I did not have unrealistic expectations. And I was open to anything, with only a few basic wants as guidelines.

I wanted at least a thousand square feet and at least two bedrooms, since I worked at home and needed an office. I wanted some yard, as I am an avid gardener.

Then, the night after I saw the house with Michele, I had a dream.

I dreamed I lived next door to Michele, only the house was not some awful midcentury, small-roomed, tract-type thing set awkwardly on a flat piece of dirt, but a graceful airy home with doors open to the outside, light and air, and a Provençal-style courtyard and gardens with reflecting pools. I woke up awash with yearning—for beauty.

The rental house I was leaving was not beautiful. When I moved in eight years before, from a charming but too tiny courtyard rental cottage in Pasadena, I had been shocked and benumbed by the general lack of beauty in my new dwelling, its property, the street and block. The house had good features, including a large fenced yard, two bedrooms, and a certain '30s flavor, but I was more affected than I'd anticipated by the harsh treelessness of the neighborhood, the urban armor—hurricane fences, bars on windows, the incessant chirping and screaming of car alarms—and the fact that not one window in my home offered a pleasing sight. On the floor, the cheap sheet linoleum was so thin you could tear it with a fingernail. The plumbing was installed by an amateur and highly imperfect. The tiny water heater allowed three-minute showers and washed half a dinner party's dishes. The new but halfhearted exterior paint job peeled in a year. All these imperfections soon produced an overall palpable shabbiness. I made the house sweet enough, hanging curtains and scrims to soften a view of one neighbor's corrugated plastic fence and another neighbor's sloppily built cinder block wall. I replastered the rotting bathroom, and I installed good linoleum, at my own expense. But these were Band-Aids, ameliorations. They were not beauty. And I yearned for beauty. My dream gave voice to that yearning, which was strong, almost heartbreaking in its intensity. I had to pay attention.

It's hard—for women, especially—to have and articulate a dream, a vision, a desire. There's a sense, a superstition, that if we speak of a desire or even admit to one, we'll jinx it. When it comes to home owning, ignoring our dreams is a mistake—as much of a mistake as insisting on unrealistic standards. It is important to listen to one's yearnings, to be guided by them, to respect them, because ignoring them is what leads to chronic general unhappiness and low-grade depression. I know.

I should say that by *beauty* I didn't mean grand. Earlier in my life, I'd lived in a hideous, kitschy, '60s A-frame cabin, but it sat on a Sierran slope with a panorama of big trees and mountains through the Thermopane. I'd also once lived in a bland, one-bedroom stucco cube in the foothills of the Sierra, on the banks of the Tule River with another vista of rolling, grassy hills and snow-capped peaks—*and* the property had a swimming hole. In graduate school in Iowa, I'd lived on a disagreeably busy road in a lovely old Victorian with a fifty-foot-long peony bed that stopped traffic when the flowers bloomed. Whether beauty was in the yard, the view, or the architecture wasn't important. I would settle for a modest-size house, a friendly degree of ramshackleness; I'd happily go for simple and out-of-the-way, not the very best neighborhood, so long as beauty was a factor.

So much for dreams.

Now for practicalities. I started driving around neighborhoods. Because so few houses were on the market in Southern California, I was determined to cast a wide net, from Silver Lake to Monrovia, La Crescenta to Alhambra. I'd stop at FOR SALE signs of houses that appealed to me and call the real estate agent's number. I talked to all sorts of real estate agents that way.

One real estate agent, Raoul, met me at a property I'd called about. A gentlemanly, calm person and a good listener, he asked for my number and called whenever he had at least two houses to show me. Last year at this time, he said, there were two-hundred-plus houses on the market in Glendale alone. Now there were thirty-two. Raoul approved of my wide-net approach, took pleasure in scouting out potential homes in all sorts of far-flung suburbs.

"First of all, let's get you prequalified for a loan," he said. By which he meant that I should get a letter from a bank or mortgage broker attesting to my ability to take out a loan for a specified amount. "You need one to make an offer on a house." I obtained one fairly easily—by finding and simply talking to Michele's mortgage broker.

Armed with my prequal letter, we looked at a rustic 600-square-foot hideaway on a 4,000-square-foot lot up in the La Canada hills—La Canada being a tony, residential suburb. It was beautiful—and too tiny to turn around in.

We looked at a house bought and fixed up by a contractor who had about the same taste and construction values as my landlord.

We looked at a small, well-located, two-bedroom '30s home where every room had been overdone: marble and stone floors, expensive tile work, gold fixtures, multiple layers of curtains. Suffocating!

I knew, in a way, I was being overly critical. I took personal offense at cheap faucets and gold faucets alike, ugly new linoleum and garish marble floors. I began to feel sympathy with some of Frank Bascombe's reluctant, picky clients in the Ford novel; it's difficult and scary to make such a big decision, and our defenses automatically rise into play.

We looked at a house at the very top of my price range—well, $10,000 more than the top of my price range, but I could've made a credible offer. The house had a great room with a fireplace, and two large bedrooms. If the lot was small and steep, it also backed up onto wilderness, a grassy ridge with mature, graceful oaks. I could've set out the back door and hiked for hours. All the buzzwords applied: copper plumbing, crown molding, forced air. The old kitchen cabinets had been installed in the garage, so there was lots of tidy storage. I could've lived there easily and happily.

"Let's make an offer," said Raoul.

I just couldn't go that far. I wasn't done looking. For the moment, anyway, it seemed like enough just to know that there were houses out there that I could live in happily.

I began to relax. I began to enjoy looking. I was in no hurry to make a decision.

Some time after this, I visited Michele. She was in the yard talking to the real estate agent who was offering the house behind her. "Why didn't you like it?" he asked.

"Not my style," I said.

"Let's go see it again," he said.

"That's okay," I said.

Michele said, "Come on, why not?"

I shrugged and agreed, so as not to hurt the real estate agent's feelings. (This was before I knew that real estate agents' feelings shouldn't really enter into the picture. Assuming that any of them actually have feelings.)

He corralled the dogs—not easy, considering there were now six puppies as well—while Michele and I walked around the 16,000-square-foot property. Two huge—eighty- and a hundred-foot—eucalyptus trees in the neighbor's yard presided over all.

There was a basketball court, a half dozen fruit trees, a lot of dog poop. Chickens clucked and crowed nearby. Mountains peeked through the trees. From the backyard I couldn't see another house, only a varied, lush treescape. I shrugged. "If they'd take $30,000 less than their asking price, I might be interested," I told Michele.

"Make an offer, make an offer!" she said. "It would be so much fun if you lived here." When we got back to the real estate agent, she said, "She wants to make an offer!"

"Well, kind of," I said, and reported what I'd be willing to pay.

The real estate agent shook his head—as I knew he would. "I'm not even going to write that up," he said. "The seller would take it as an insult."

Fine. I hadn't wanted the house anyway. Still, something had happened. I'd made my first offer, however tentative, overly cautious, and intentionally implausible. As such, I'd dipped my toe in the water. And lived to tell the tale. This house was becoming my practice house: the first one I'd seen, the first I'd made an offer on.

Soon enough, I'd be making a real offer on a house I actually wanted.

Slowly, thanks to Raoul and many days of open houses, I got a sense of what was available to me. I had looked enough and I began to see what was essentially the same house over and over again: not quite the bottom of the market, but by no means high-end. Nice starter homes. Two bedrooms, 1 to 1.75 baths. Many had a little extra something, like a closed-in back porch (unpermitted, uninsulated) or a garage fixed up as an office. Just as often, as if to compensate for the extras, something else would be lacking: the yard was teeny, or paved over, or full of spiky yuccas, undesirable trees. Over and over, I wandered through nice, postwar, late-'40s, small family homes, homes built for returning GIs, the birthplaces of baby boomers. Wood floors, wood-sash windows, prettily tiled bathrooms and kitchens, sometimes a fireplace—all things I liked. Most had garden potential. All were about forty to sixty thousand dollars more than the awful house behind Michele's. But I was getting used to the prices.

Amazing what you can get used to.

I looked at a small cabin in Echo Park nicely perched on a hill and freshly painted in a fancy way by some off-work set dresser; it had all the charm of a fairy tale and an equally unrealistic price tag. "We'll lower the price," the real estate agent said, "if you're interested." I wasn't, not really. Too tiny and too cute.

Then Raoul drove me to an architect-built 900-square-foot home on a deep, skinny lot whose beauty quotient was sky-high. Yet, in what could've been a page right out of Richard Ford's novel—Frank Bascombe had some truly difficult clients—I found myself bothered by the power station next door: a row of fifty-foot towers and an acre of squat, intricately strung trans-formers. "Before we moved in," the sellers said, "we researched all the potential health hazards and found none."

The price was a bargain.

"This is your house," Raoul told me.

Indeed, it looked like my house. Painted wood walls. Light streaming in clerestories. An office overlooking the calm, tended garden. Raised vegetable beds. A bubbling fountain. A wood fence overgrown with trumpet vine. And . . . just beyond that . . . transformers.

"I'll think about it," I said.

When I went back for a second look a few days later, the house had been sold. I wasn't sorry.

One day, a month into my search, I got a phone call from the real estate agent handling the house behind Michele's. "Somebody else is very interested," he said. "If you want to make a better offer, you should do it today, and I'll get it accepted."

"I don't think so," I said.

I got off the phone and began to feel uneasy. Basically, I didn't like having my options disappear. I had liked to think about that huge lot, with its lovely, private treescape—all other lots had looked diminutive compared to that one. But the house . . .

I called the real estate agent back. "I guess I'll go look at it one more time." I already knew I wouldn't want it. But the decision had to be mine, and not made by default, by someone else buying it. I didn't want to regret anything. I didn't want to rue "the one that got away."

Walking into the house, I asked myself, Could I live here? The smell of cigarette smoke had been sprayed over with a strong, chemical perfume. The porch reeked of puppy pee. Plastic vertical blinds clattered in the windows. All that, of course, could be worked around. There *were* wood floors, and wood-sash windows at least—the house's only accessions to charm.

Most important, I asked myself, Could I work here? I walked into the back bedroom that would most likely serve as an office. Through the window, a big shaggy oleander was in full white bloom, as effusive as a wedding dress. An orange tree was bearing fruit and blossoms at the same time.

I could write here, I thought.

And the yard—after looking at some forty-odd lots ranging

in size from 4,000 to 8,000 square feet, this one seemed gargantuan. And private. A possible refuge.

All told, even at its asking price, this was still the least expensive house I'd looked at. I went through the kitchen and noted the walls that I could knock out. With the $30,000 or $40,000 price differential between this and all the other houses I looked at, I could afford to do the work.

Then, I had one of those life-changing conversations with myself, in which I made a series of promises.

I'll make it beautiful, I promised myself. And I'll do it right away, before I have a chance to get too settled in, before inertia takes hold and I find myself living in another ugly home.

If I hated the place after a couple years, I could always move. That was another promise I made that day. If I really didn't like it, I wouldn't have to stay.

"Okay," I said to the real estate agent, and named a sum $12,000 below asking price. We sat down and filled out a mountain of paperwork, including a purchase agreement (also called a sales agreement), and listed contingencies on the sale, i.e., what both the owner and I would have to do before the sale was final.

I knew at the time that—in allowing the seller's real estate agent to serve as my real estate agent, I was doing an ill-advised thing. I also felt bad that Raoul, after all the time he took with me, wasn't going to be in on the deal—though not bad enough to hang back. And I might not get the house anyway. This might simply be another practice drill.

If I got the house, I decided, the deal would make the risk worthwhile. If the seller didn't accept the offer, I was saved from having made an ill-advised decision.

I did the paperwork, then let go.

Later that night, when I was out on a date, I phoned to get my messages.

Offer accepted.

Tao Worksheet

Write a response to the following questions. As you write, try to tell a story. Illustrate your thoughts with specific examples. Be fearless. Tell the truth.

1. What are your prejudices concerning real estate? Where did they come from? How do they rule your life?

2. What are your fears? Where do they come from? What do they prevent you from doing?

3. Where does Michelle's story make you hopeful? Why?

4. Where does Michelle's story make you doubtful or afraid? Why?

5. Are you willing to settle for something less than perfect the first time around?

6. What friend has bought a home recently? What have you observed about her process? Ask that friend to tell you about the process, then jot down what you learned from her.

CHAPTER TWO

WOMEN AND REAL ESTATE— NEW, SCARY TERRITORY

Seeing into darkness is clarity.
Knowing how to yield is strength.
Use your own light
and return to the source of light.

U NDER THE HEADLINE SOLO PERFORMANCES, the bold-faced words from the *LA Times* real estate section of August 1, 2004, practically scream across the page: "Single women now make up the second-largest segment of home buyers." On the front page of the section, we see a photo of a pretty young violinist, studiously practicing in her new condo, the home and refuge she's purchased by herself. Here's a woman, accomplished and strong, the story tells us, who set out to do what most women of earlier generations never dared dream: own her own place.

That women are buying real estate at a record-breaking pace doesn't come as a shock to the Tao Gals; our experience alone tells us this is true. But why does this fact warrant such coverage? Haven't we, as women, always been concerned about the needs of making a home—perhaps not in the traditionalist mode of "a woman's place is in the home," but more in tune with Virginia Woolf's ideal of "a room of one's own"? Psychologists tell us that women tend to define themselves by their sense of belonging and the community they share with each other and their loved ones. If this is true, it seems logical that belonging to a place—a building, a room, a city, a particular street—defines us in crucial ways as well. Making a "home," perhaps, is truly—if not exclusively—a female thing.

We know, though, that in generations past, women who bought property on their own were rare. Think about it: How many women do you know of your mother's generation who bought their own homes?

In the *Times* article, the reporter credits the higher salaries women now command as paving the way for our increasing ability to buy homes without husbands. While salaries are a contributing factor, we also believe that the concept of home profoundly matters to women; now that we are finally in a position to buy, we're doing so with unrivaled enthusiasm. After all, women continue to earn around 30 percent less on the dollar than their male colleagues, yet single women purchase real property at a rate that far outstrips their single male counterparts. According to the National Association of Realtors, single women accounted for 21 percent of home purchases in 2003, trailing married couples (who made up 59 percent) but well ahead of single men at 11 percent. To most women, even single women, home is more than an investment.

We want a place of our own to shelter ourselves and those we love, a space in which we can express our personalities, have some control, forget about landlords, and enjoy the assurance, no matter how tenuous, that we can stay there a while. For what may be the first time in history, the satisfaction of these desires is not generally dependent on some man (father or husband) paying the bills.

Though, to be honest, many of us single women would prefer to walk through the home-creation process with a partner. Everything's more fun (and occasionally easier) when we have someone to share it with, but we don't always have that option. According to Fannie Mae, one of the nation's largest providers of mortgage financing, the number of households headed by women has grown fourfold since the 1950s, with no sign of this trend abating. Thus, partnered or not, we women are learning how to plot a course through what is traditionally unfamiliar territory.

As the first generation to realize in a large way that home-ownership is within our grasp, we are pioneers in a world that we weren't raised to know. In our childhoods, our fathers most likely made the real estate decisions, signed the loan documents, provided the income record and credit report. Our mothers—even working mothers—may have picked out the house or chosen the neighborhood, but our fathers usually handled the contractual and financial matters.

If we don't have our mothers to look toward for inspiration, then we must rely on the stories we tell each other. "I never dreamed I could buy a house" begins Rose's story. "I've never been more content" ends Michelle's. And Bernadette laments, "We lost every cent." In between are tales from the trenches featuring terrific Realtors and also lazy ones, ingenious loan makers and shifty ones, moments of euphoria and of terror and despair. We tell these stories to map the territory for others.

Even if we buy alone, we don't have to be alone through the

often-scary, new process. We can rely on our friends and loved ones to help us along the way.

Fannie Mae estimates that by 2010, the number of households headed by an unpartnered woman will increase to 31 million, or about 28 percent of all households in the country. In response to this trend, many mortgage lenders and marketing companies are targeting single and divorced women for home loans, a strategy that makes good business sense, since, collectively, women earn more than $1 trillion annually and influence $2.4 trillion—80 percent—of the $3 trillion in annual consumer sales, according to the Women's Mortgage Industry Network, an industry educational group (as reported in *LA Times*).

Though all these factors point in a positive direction for female home buyers, there are still hurdles to be overcome. The number-one problem is a lack of information about the home-buying process. As women, we need to familiarize ourselves with the process. We need to hear and tell the stories of women who have bought houses.

ROSE AND HER "FORCIBLE SAVINGS PLAN"

The Olympian in the group, Rose bought a house two years ago and her decision to do so surprised even her. For as long as she could remember, she'd never harbored any intention of buying a house. Her seasonal work as a college track coach paid little but provided a lot of personal satisfaction; her personal training of wealthy patrons and celebrities on the Westside of Los Angeles was financially remunerative but could also be unpredictable.

Fifty years old, tall with short, reddish hair, Rose moves with an athlete's long-limbed grace. She laughs frequently—her sense of humor is contagious—but she'll also look right at you and ask a probing, direct question: *Why isn't the new book going well? Why don't you look for another job? Did you make the dreaded phone call? So what happened?* A cancer survivor and recovering alcoholic, she also knows how short life can be and tries to be as awake and conscious as possible. Her candor sometimes takes a person off guard, but her honesty is refreshing and direct, and she can take as good as she gives. "I wish people would ask *me* direct questions!" she says.

For decades, Rose had justified *not* buying a house by claiming she didn't want the hassles, the commitment: "I was convinced it was easier to rent. If you have a problem with a rental, you call the landlord, they fix it. You don't have to worry about the plumbing, the fuses." She'd been very happy and at home in her little hilltop rental. "I was there for eighteen years. The landlord said she might want to retire there, but why worry until then?" she says.

Rose's hesitation to enter the home market was never, she thought, based on gender issues. After all, she'd excelled and made a name for herself in a male-dominated sport. Growing up, she'd seen her mother handle all the family's money matters. "For me, it was more a lack of intelligence about money," she says. "I had an amateur-athlete mentality. We joked about it, some of us athletes. It's kind of a Peter Pan thing: We're going to be young, indestructible, and carefree forever. It's very immature—but there's a lack of financial responsibility implicit in amateurism. You do the sport for love, not for money." Indeed, as serious an athlete as she was (and her U.S. record remains unbroken some twenty years later), Rose never had to deal with the professional athlete's financial and contractual arrangements.

At the Tao group, Rose listened to Michelle talk about buying a home and wondered why, even after she'd become a mature, self-sufficient adult in so many ways, she still had no great desire to own a house. The question lingered in her mind. Then she went to her parents' house for a family dinner.

Her parents live on the Westside of town, in Pacific Palisades, in an exclusive neighborhood by the ocean. "They call it Shangri-La," says Rose. "It's the American dream writ large, what my father worked his whole life to have. My oldest sister had done the same thing my parents had. She has a gorgeous house in Washington state—never mind that my brother-in-law has worked eighteen hours a day, seven days a week for thirty years so that they can have that home. They have the exact life my parents have: the church, the bell choir, the kids, every single thing. In my family all that was just assumed—the college education, having a family, finding a steady corporate job, and buying a home regardless of how you might feel about it."

Rose's athleticism and Olympic career had long since taken her on a decisively different path. But as much as she didn't want to be just like her parents and siblings, she didn't feel very good about being different, either. In fact, being different felt exactly like being defective.

Around her parents, Rose reported back to the Tao Gals, she was flooded with a sense of "not being good enough" in most every department. This was a very old, familiar feeling to her. "They're all about stuff and how things look and the neighborhood. And either I have lived my entire life in reaction to those values or I sincerely don't share them. Whichever it is, I have a lot shame about it."

To see Rose in action, one would never guess there were areas of her life where she doesn't feel good enough. She comes across as strong and whole, happy in herself. Once again we Tao gals were privileged to glimpse how feelings about real estate can tap into whole subterranean areas in the psyche. No matter how mature we've become, how many years of therapy we've undergone, how self-empowered we feel, sometimes it's hard to shake the deep-seated fear that we won't stack up in our parents' eyes. Even parents who are dead or estranged from us can still hold sway over the big decisions in our lives. And buying property is nothing if not a big life decision.

That shame and the not-good-enough feeling—and her rebellion against such feelings—made Rose feel both guilty and self-righteous about not owning a home. At the same time, she also paid dirt-cheap rent, she reasoned, and therefore could save large sums of money for the future. Except that she wasn't. She had some money in mutual funds and stocks, but those had declined in value. She had no other nest egg, nothing for retirement, and no equity. Sooner or later, she'd have to do something to shore up her finances.

She needed a "forcible savings plan," and it occurred to her that paying a monthly mortgage could be just the ticket.

Meanwhile, friends, even those fellow athletes who had earlier repudiated the American dream, were now buying houses.

Then there was the heating-up real estate market. "The pressure! I was watching, watching, watching for a couple of years as my friends bought. I saw the prices getting higher and higher, and people having a harder and harder time on their first purchase, and I thought I better hurry up and get to it."

And then the final straw: Michelle bought her house. "I felt like, if Michelle could do it, I could do it." If Rose was going to take this huge and terrifying leap, now was the time, when Michelle's experience and references would be fresh and relevant. "What to do about escrow? Who to call as a handyman?" Michelle could offer a wealth of up-to-the-minute information and resources.

"All of a sudden, I was determined to buy a house."

Once a Tao Gal made the decision that she was ready to at least look, if not actually buy, she found it vital to figure out her priorities. In deciding what she wanted in a house, it was equally important to decide what she didn't want. Rose found she didn't want anything that had major problems or potential problems that would require a lot of money down the line. She wanted something "move-in-able," that had good bones, the right amount of space, a dining room, and, ideally, a view. One of her highest priorities was easy access to the front door from the car, because she was in and out of the car all day—no steps, no curving path. Rose turned down three or four perfectly good houses where the walk from the car to the door was too long and/or complicated.

She looked at a few architecturally significant homes in her price range, but they all had big problems, like major cracks in the foundation or sagging ceiling joists. "I quickly became aware I wasn't going to have a California bungalow or a Crafts-man."

She made an offer on a house in Altadena, but a higher offer bumped her out of the running. She made another offer, and again she was beaten out.

Rose wanted to live in a mixed neighborhood and close to the college where she coached. "I know how uncomfortable I am in places like Orange County," she says of the suburban area just south of Los Angeles. "The houses all look alike, everybody's white, everybody's Republican. I can't handle that."

Then she found a place. Two miles from the college in an iffy neighborhood. "When the students I coach find out where I live, they're scandalized," she says, laughing.

But when she walked into the house, she adored the woman who lived there, Señora García. It was a hot day and the room was really cool, air-conditioned. There was ugly carpet. The living room had padded vinyl on the wall, like station wagon upholstery. "Still, I walked in and thought, 'I could live here.'"

Rose made an offer and learned there was a previous offer on the house. "I had to wait to see if that first offer was going to go through. It didn't, and the house fell on me."

"'To me,'" Michelle corrects.

"No. More like 'on me,'" says Rose.

What did she feel when her offer was accepted?

"Terror," she says. "Nothing but terrified. Like jumping off the cliff."

"No wonder you didn't do it earlier," Bernadette says.

But Rose shakes her head. "When would I not have had fear? Doesn't anyone else have it?"

The Gals all nod.

Once her offer was accepted, she had to deal with getting a mortgage.

"It's a lonely process," Rose says quietly. If there had been somebody else to walk through it with her—a roommate, a husband, anybody else—it would have been different, she thinks, better somehow. Another person adds knowledge, energy.

She also believes it's an exciting time to be a woman buying property alone. "We're the first generation, really, who've lived in this era of single women knowing how to take care of themselves. Of course we're the children of the last generation where that wasn't so." Then again, she thinks, her mother's influence may have stopped her from taking this step before now. "There might have been, in the back of my head all this time, the thought that somebody, some man, would come along and do this for me, and maybe that created my inertia to do it for myself."

So maybe old gender roles came into play after all.

Today, the walls of Rose's house in Highland Park on the Eastside of Los Angeles are painted alluring, saturated shades of green and purple. Her furniture is big and comfortable to accommodate both her Olympian stature and vital need for relaxation in those precious few hours of leisure she gets to spend at home. Her tiny front yard is a charming mix of roses and cacti. Her dogs, Bella and Harry, exuberantly greet visitors, then resume their eternal playful tussling. In short, this is the most Rose-like place one could imagine.

Yet, it's not the kind of house her family would have wanted for her. It's not the house the Tao Gals would have wanted for her, either. Michelle, in fact, took her aside during escrow and told her—in no uncertain terms—that buying this house was a mistake. Never mind that, from the curb, the house was an ugly little box, Michelle told her. The neighborhood was shaky. Bars on too many windows, too much gang graffiti and tagging, and the parking situation was execrable—visitors will be frustrated. And besides that, Michelle went on, the house itself, an old cottage with many unpermitted add-ons, seemed unsound, with its variously sloping floors and walls so flimsy you could poke a pencil through them. "I had to say something," Michelle went on, "but if you buy it, I'll support you and help you in any way I can."

Rose's best friend, Julie, was less specific but no less

adamant about Rose's choice: "The house is appalling." She also promised to support Rose in any final decision.

Rose had her own reasons for liking the house, specifically its size (the add-ons, however shoddy, did provide a lot of square footage for the price), its hillside perch and spectacular panoramic views of northeastern Los Angeles, the three-minute drive to coaching.

And Rose has never been one for doing what other people think she should.

Since buying, Rose has done a great deal of work on the property and made the place not only prettier and far more appealing but also thoroughly and convincingly *her* home.

She admits to the Tao Gals, however, that owning a home hasn't given her all the psychic boosts she'd hoped. "I don't swell with pride walking up my driveway. I don't feel much more secure or settled than I did in my old rental. I do wake up lots of mornings being very, very happy about being in that space, and lots of mornings I still feel terrified that it's going to leak or fall down and that I can't possibly take care of myself," she says.

But has owning a home at least vanquished the sense of shame? we Tao Gals ask.

"Not really," Rose says, laughing. "Outside the family, in public, I've elevated myself a little bit as a homeowner. But I don't think I'll ever vanquish the shame my family puts on me. They need me to be the goof. It's pretty entrenched. Now that I have a house, the shame has just been attached to other factors, like the house I bought isn't upscale or good enough!" She laughs again, more quietly. "No, buying a house doesn't solve everything. But I needed something for when I'm too old to teach exercise and this is the only way I was going to be able to do it." She is thoughtful for a moment, then adds, "And I was never going to do it, except for you guys nudging me every step of the way."

Down Payments

In the old days, the minimum down payment was 10 percent of the purchase price, and if buyers wanted to avoid paying private mortgage insurance (PMI)—a type of insurance that helps the lender cover its losses if you default, though you pay for the insurance—they needed to bring 20 percent to the table. Looking at the costs of housing in LA and other hot markets, that can add up to quite a chunk—$100,000 or more!

Many lenders have loosened their requirements so that loans are now available with 3 or even 0 percent down. The less you put down, though, the less you have invested in the property, and, the thinking goes, the more likely you are to default. Lenders are aware of this and work to cover their risks by charging a high interest rate or making sure you're covered with PMI. Some lenders may suggest that you take out a second mortgage with another lender so that your total down payment equals 20 percent, thus eliminating the need for PMI.

A Gift

Some borrowers use gifts from relatives in order to finance their down payment. If you suddenly have a large amount of cash showing up in your savings account, your lender will want to know where that money came from. Below is a sample gift letter that may answer the lender's concerns:

I, Bernadette Murphy, the mother of Hope Murphy, do freely give Hope $50,000 in the form of a certificate of deposit (number 1234567) from the Bank of Glendale. I do not expect repayment of this gift. It is given free and clear. If you need to look into my financial history, please contact my accountant, Bob James, at (818) 241-1112.

COLLEEN, DECIDING FROM THE HEART

Two years ago, Colleen, a forty-year-old deputy district attorney in Los Angeles, mother of two sons, and devoted Tao Gal, asked for a divorce. Rick, the boys' father, didn't make things easy. Since he'd owned the family home before marrying Colleen, he intended to keep it outright in the settlement. He also made it clear he wouldn't pay spousal support—she was gainfully employed, after all. The divorce soon became a drawn-out and extremely unpleasant struggle. Colleen started looking for a place to move as soon as the proceedings began, even though she was strapped for cash (she was still paying off law school loans) and her prospects for support from Rick were dim.

The house she was leaving was a large, glass, concrete, and wood, modern anomaly tucked into the foothills of the San Gabriel Mountains. The south walls were all window, and skylights provided more natural light from above. A paddock for Colleen's horses sat across the driveway, and there was a pool for the kids in the yard. In many ways, it was a dream house, much nicer than anything the other Tao Gals lived in, yet unusual and engagingly hip.

Colleen had few regrets about leaving it. The price of living there with the divorce pending had grown too high, and she'd never been deeply attached to the place. "When I moved in, it was already *crammed* with his stuff. I had to dig out my own little places. It never, ever felt like it was mine," she said.

Buying a house was the last thing on Colleen's mind. The divorce was enough upheaval and negotiation, and her job was overwhelming at the time. As a district attorney, she was handling line prosecutions, which meant everything from drug cases to those involving kidnapping, robbery, and murder.

She just wanted to rent. And catch her breath. And enjoy her boys. And rest.

But there was nothing easy about finding a rental, not when a person has two dogs, two young children, and a fierce determination to live in a safe neighborhood. "Anything remotely decent started at about $2,500 a month. And that's a mortgage payment!" she exclaimed to the Tao Gals.

"I'll help you look for a house!" Michelle gleefully volunteered.

Colleen looked like she'd seen a ghost. For it was not just the divorce or her overwork that made the thought of buying untenable, she admitted. Actually, a previous brush with home-ownership also had left a bad taste in her mouth.

A previous brush?

Ah, the truth came out! Colleen had moved to the Los Angeles area from Minneapolis in 1987 with the boyfriend who would become her first husband. They'd been "shocked senseless," she said, by the high cost of housing and rented until they married. Then, in 1989, they bought a house. Neither enterprise—marriage or home buying—she told the Tao Gals, ended well then, either. Was she ever, she wondered, ever going to learn from her past mistakes?

"We bought in the Atwater Village of Los Angeles," she went on. "Both of our parents went in on the down payment. I borrowed $10,000 from my father, he borrowed $10,000 from his father, and that was enough to get in." She squawked at how easy it was. In today's market it would take so much more to even consider buying a house. How quickly things have changed!

The house was a very small, two-bedroom, one-bath, typical

California bungalow in an area adjacent to Silver Lake, near Griffith Park and the Los Angeles River, that has recently become very trendy and highly overpriced. "The lot was very deep, with the equivalent of three separate yards and many fruit trees," she said.

The Tao Gals collectively moaned—the house sounded like the Promised Land, a place that has since disappeared off the face of the earth, what, with spiking real estate costs and a great shortage of inventory.

"We paid around $165,000," she adds.

There was a collective intake of breath.

"I didn't like owning it," Colleen said. Maintenance, for one, had been very intimidating, even though her first husband had been a contractor. "The roof was leaking, water would seep into the walls. The electricity was all old and bad. We had to re-pipe with copper. I just thought 'This is *so* not worth it.' "

They refinanced in the early '90s at $230,000 and used most of the money to fix up the place. At that point, with equity growing in leaps and bounds, the young couple's financial future looked secure.

Then life, as it has a tendency to do, changed the rules of the game.

The real estate market fell. The marriage failed. When they were divorcing, the house—with all its improvements—was valued at $160,000, and their monthly payments were $2,300. "We were completely upside down, owing more than the house was worth," Colleen said. "It really didn't make sense to sell in that soft market."

Her ex-husband wanted to keep the house, and Colleen

didn't mind, except the mortgage company, knowing the loan was bad, refused to take her name off the paperwork.

She took a chance and let her ex keep the house. Two years later, when the value still hadn't risen enough to make it a worthwhile investment, he did a "short sale" on the property. (A short sale is when the bank agrees to take whatever a new buyer will pay for the house—usually close to the amount still owed on the mortgage—in exchange for letting the original owner out of the deal. With a short sale, the owner loses the down payment and any money invested in the property but keeps his or her credit clean.) That little foray into home ownership was nothing but a financial liability to Colleen and her ex. Losing it—even after the marriage and without a blotch on their credit—was deeply traumatic.

"I decided then, that was it. I was never, ever, ever going to own a home. Never."

During Colleen's new housing search, the Tao Gals began to talk a lot about the concept of "home"—what we look for in a home, where we feel at home. Surely, home is more than four walls and a set number of bedrooms. As Colleen faced finding a new place, she continued to bring up the subject at meetings. Home was always a very emotional concept for her. Her childhood home was once very secure and loving, but that ceased when her mother fell ill with Hodgkin's disease when Colleen was three years old.

"She believed she was sick after the birth of my brother, who's three years younger than me," Colleen told the Gals one evening. "The doctors said that she was having 'young mother's syndrome' and nothing was done."

"Young mother's syndrome?" the Tao Gals asked. "Huh?"

"Along the lines of hysteria."

"Oh."

Eventually, Colleen's mother was correctly diagnosed and began treatments, but they did not go well. She spent most of the next three years in the hospital and died when Colleen was seven.

Colleen retained only faint memories of her mother. "But I do have a strong feeling that she had created a 'home' environment," she said. Her father, who did not know how to create or maintain a welcoming, safe haven for his children, let things slip. "It felt like living in an empty house," Colleen said.

The Tao Gals were silent, stunned.

"That whole motherless-child thing is very real," she said. "Throughout my childhood, my young adulthood, there was this sense of rudderlessness."

Colleen left her father's home when she was fourteen, a runaway. Her teen years were troubled, and she was in her midtwenties when she finally got hold of herself and finished college. "I always had a deep longing for a safe place to call home. When I became a mother, that's what I wanted for my kids. It means a house, but also more than a house. It means a neighborhood, too, a community they can have a stake in."

COLLEEN'S DOG HOUSE

When Colleen set out looking, she gave up on finding a home right away, certain she'd never locate or afford what she needed. But she kept being lured back by the possibility. Regularly, she'd remember the house she'd lived in before she married Rick, a little place up in the hills. It was a rental home, and yet Colleen had been wildly happy living there: "I could have stayed there for the rest of my life." If she could be so happy in a little rental, she reasoned, there may be plenty of other places where she could be happy, and that gave her hope.

All the Tao Gals have had an experience of settling for less—in their house-buying choices, careers, family structures—and found, to their everlasting surprise, that they could be happy under those circumstances. We've come to agree that people are the worst predictors of their own happiness, and have the worst track record in deciding what will make them happy. We've all had the man, the car, the living situation, the horse, the pet, the job that was supposed to bring us happiness—and didn't, or it didn't bring happiness in the form we anticipated.

In searching for a home, we found it was a good idea to separate our wants from our needs whenever possible.

"What did you really need?" Michelle asked Colleen. "And what could you do without?"

For Colleen, her kids were first and foremost in her mind. "Looks count for nothing," Colleen replied. "It doesn't matter to me if the house is a dog. Kids don't care at all about what the house looks like. I need a sidewalk and a neighborhood where the boys could play. I want them to be able to run up and down the block and be safe. And for me, I need to know I can manage it financially and the ceiling isn't going to fall down on my head."

When Colleen's future home presented itself, it *was* a dog, but she recognized it as what she needed, and grabbed it.

The good-size, three-bedroom, two-bathroom ranch-style home is shingled in dark wood, like an alpine cabin, and sits on a quiet street with an eclectic mix of Craftsman-, Cape Cod-, and Spanish-style homes. Colleen's backyard is large and long, with a freestanding garage in the far back. Inside, skylights, installed in the '70s, routinely leak. Other "renovations" were shoddily done, and the dim, Navajo white rooms have been battered after a decade of renters.

But this is a *Leave It to Beaver* neighborhood—wide streets with rolling front lawns and mature trees. Happily, there's also a lot of racial and economic diversity in the mix. The dad across the street takes care of people's pools; next door lives a rocket scientist who's married to a prosecutor. Throughout the year, kids ride their bikes up and down the sidewalk, neighbors stop by for a chat, and in the balmy Southern California nights crickets creak away like hundreds of unoiled hinges. Every year there's a Fourth of July parade and picnic. Kids from three parallel streets gather. A slow car with music and a flag starts the parade. "It's very hokey," Colleen says. Everyone walks their dog, which they dress up for the occasion, and the kids all ride bikes, also decorated. After the parade, there's a block party and barbecue that is held—as it has been for decades—right under the huge oak in Colleen's yard. "It's the coolest spot in the neighborhood during the summer," she says.

Colleen's present happy circumstance did not happen overnight. Moving out, dissolving a marriage, learning to be a single mom, adapting to a new environment, and letting her emotions even out, all while working long hours in her high-tension job, was a time fraught with insecurities and fear. Meeting weekly with the Tao Gals, Colleen says, saved her in more ways than one—by giving her a chance to vent, a place to cry, and the opportunity to see that her dreams of creating a safe and loving home for her boys and herself might yet be possible.

BERNADETTE, AND THE REAL HOUSE BLUES

I'm waking up at three A.M., sweating the real estate market. It's especially bad on Sunday nights, when, after reading the Real Estate section in the Sunday paper, I have to remind myself that the bubble can't last forever. The past few years have been the best ever for Southern California. When 2003 drew to a close and I thought we were at the height of an insane market, the median price of a home hit a record $326,000, up more than 19 percent since the previous year. At that time, fewer than 25 percent of those seeking a median-priced home were able to afford one. "The result was a win-win situation for homeowners and the economy, which greatly benefited from the year's record refinancing," the author of one article at that time gloated. "The average Southern California home increased in value by $54,174 in 2003," the article rhapsodized, "'earning' homeowners $4,514 each month."

That's great news—break out the champagne!—unless you're someone like me who isn't in on the deal. Since then, it's only gotten worse.

The median price of new and existing homes in Los Angeles County has now increased to $495,000 (as of May 2005), up from $394,000 a year earlier. The affordability index has continued to plummet as the prices rise. My husband John and I, along with our three kids, are in the 80-or-so percent who can't afford it.

We can't compete in that world. John and I have been saving like packrats for years and yet, if things keep going the way they've been going, we'll never catch up. All it takes to set me off now is for a For Sale sign to show up on a property in my neighborhood. Undoubtedly, the asking price will be at least $100,000 out of my price range and the house will be a fixer-upper (real estate speak for "slum"). I'd be willing to go for some sweat equity (real estate speak for "increasing the value of your home by virtue of your own unpaid labor"). I could learn to use a hammer and screwdriver—but today, you need a lot more money than I have even for a fixer. And the condos that come on the market, those lowly dwellings that I wouldn't have consented to a few years ago, have also rocketed out of my price range.

At cocktail parties, the conversation will invariably turn to the sky-high cost of property. "Can you believe it? Half a million for that dump!" Those of us who aren't homeowners feel our stomachs clench; we've really blown it this time.

For me, though, all this talk of rising home prices and fast-building equity is a queasy form of déjà vu. In 1990, my husband John and I bought at the peak of the real estate market hoping to reap financial rewards. Within months of moving in, however, the market tanked and John was laid off. We tried to make the untenable situation work, only to give up after eight years of struggle, walking away from our only investment with a major black eye—a foreclosure—on our record. After saving for many years, we have money in the bank again for a down payment; the black mark on our credit report will be coming off next year. But we can't quite shake that skittish fear in our bellies.

John, our three kids—Jarrod, fifteen; Neil, twelve; and Hope, nine—and I are currently living in a delightful rental house in Glendale, eight miles north of downtown Los Angeles. We like the neighborhood, and we like the 1910 Craftsman home, despite its many plumbing and roof-related woes and tiny bedrooms. We'd like to stay here—to buy it, even.

I remind myself that the skyrocketing prices we're seeing

now are signs of heady days. They won't last forever. I don't think the prices will come down to their former lows, but I do think the market is overheated at the moment and will regain some semblance of sanity in the next year or two—possibly when the present owners of our rental will be ready to sell (they've said as much). Certain industry watchers even agree that the market will adjust downward, and I tune out those who don't.

Inside my head, though, a little voice taunts: *What if you're wrong? Two years ago, you thought the market was overheated. Looking back on those prices, they now seem like bargain-basement deals compared to what's going on today. This might be your last chance.*

Sometimes, I buy into the hype, even when I know better. I start to scheme: Let's take that nest egg we've gathered so carefully since losing the house and let's buy something— anything!—to get into the market before the prices rise any further. A family of five could fit into a 900-square-foot condo, couldn't they? Maybe we could all fit in two bedrooms? So what if we're dozens of miles from the kids' schools, living in a neighborhood we don't care for, and the commute for John is far too long. We have to do something—now, now, now! Act, quick, before it's too late.

It's the same feeling I get when I'm driving on a winding mountain highway. I have no thoughts of committing suicide, but the urge to pull the car off the road sometimes tickles my brain. I could swerve the wheel, just like that, and all the problems of that particular day would be over. Flying off a cliff.

The thought of buying property right now, in this extreme market, feels like that. I could do it, just like that, but it would be financial suicide.

You think I'd be immune from the hype, but I'm not. I'm

still waking at three A.M. in a cold sweat, worried that, in decisions John and I made fourteen years ago, we've blown our family's financial well-being to smithereens.

As I write this, my daughter, Hope, is sitting on the living room floor. She had a big bedroom in our old house; on the walls was a mural hand-painted by a friend, Hope's name woven into a garland of flowers that surrounded her bed. She knows these details mostly from photographs but often says she wishes we still lived there. Her present bedroom in our rental is the size of a closet. In general, though, we're happy here. Today, she's building the outline of a house with Jenga blocks on our hardwood floor. She's laid the three-inch-long strips of wood on the floor as if to inscribe an architect's floor plan. "Here's the front door," she shows me, "and there's the kitchen and the living room. There's a bedroom there for me, a proper-sized one"—she nods at me knowingly at that phrase—"and here's one for the boys." She points.

"It's a great house," I tell her. "Can I live there with you?"

"Yeah. You and Dad can have that room," she looks up at me, smiling. "I just wish it were big enough to be a *real* house."

Funny how kids absorb our dreams.

I once read that freedom from fear is more important than freedom from want. Indeed, even more than I want a house, I'd like freedom from the *fear* of insecurity that is ruining my sleep and giving me stomachaches. I know that buying a house won't remove the fear, especially if I run out now and buy something, anything, just to shush that fear. (Having already bought and lost a house, I know that security is only temporary.) I have to persevere, wait for the market to cool off and trust that there'll be a place for us, even when, from today's perspective, it looks like we may be screwed.

Intuitively, I know I don't want to be in a crazy chase. I don't want to jeopardize my family's well-being in exchange for the security and prestige of owning house. This time around, I do crave a home to nourish our souls, not our ambitions.

I turn to the Tao Gals at the next meeting. Is this the right time to buy? Should I proceed or withdraw? How did you know the time was right to buy? What decided it for you?

Even with soaring prices, an unsteady income, a foreclosure on my record, and knots in my belly, they tell me, there is hope. Thus do friends show us what might be possible.

Tao Worksheet

Write a response to the following questions. As you write, try to tell a story. Illustrate your thoughts with specific examples. Be fearless. Tell the truth.

1. What were the prevailing ideas about home ownership in your family of origin? How have these influenced your choices?

2. From your personal life, whose story of successful home ownership can you take courage from? Tell that story and what it indicates about your own path.

3. From your personal life, whose story about real estate loss or difficulties can you learn from? Tell that story and see if you can find a moral for yourself in it.

4. Do you think that owning a home will provide happiness? How so?

5. Is expecting happiness from home ownership realistic?

6. Then, if not outright happiness, what benefits do you think home ownership might provide you with?

7. Are these expectations realistic?

8. Make a list of those people who might be willing to help you walk this path, should you decide that buying a house is what you're going to do. If you can rally the courage, call one of them now and read your responses to the above questions. Invite others to help you along this path.

CHAPTER THREE

MAKING THE DECISION TO BUY—OR NOT

Do you have the patience to wait
till your mud settles and the water is clear?
Can you remain unmoving
till the right action arises by itself?

T0 RENT 0R to buy, that is the question.

For generations, home ownership was a predictable step in the established social order, which went marriage, family, home ownership; or, marriage, home ownership, family. (One woman reports that nothing made her more desperate to have a child than when she and her husband bought a large home and suddenly found themselves with "rooms to fill.")

But times are changing. Many more people are single, and/or single parents. Women are frequently their own means of support. A breadwinning husband is not the only ticket to getting one's name on a deed. Women who once encountered resistance from real estate agents and lending institutions can now leap into home ownership without raising a single eyebrow along the way.

Yet given today's wild market, why bother? Why jump into that stew of rocketing home prices, seductive interest rates, and numbing property taxes?

The reasons are many. Rose feared eviction and wanted a forcible savings plan. Michelle was evicted and couldn't easily rent with her menagerie of pets. Colleen was divorcing. Bernadette's growing family was bursting out of her rental house. Gayle simply dreamed of owning her own home.

The six Tao Gals, when they first began meeting, counted only one homeowner in their midst—and she wasn't one of the three parents, either.

Now four of the six women own homes and one teeters on the verge, while one (a parent) remains firmly committed to renting. This chapter looks at the decisions of two other Tao Gals and the factors that made home ownership viable, necessary, or completely off-limits to each of them.

MARIE, THE LEVELHEADED DECISION

Marie, a forty-three-year-old vice president at a small investment firm, is easily the sweetest, most empathetic of the Tao Gals, and the girliest—she drives a Mercedes sports coup, wears her dresses skintight to set off her voluptuous figure, and her porcelain nails are an art show that changes every other week. She's also the numbers gal.

Marie has almost always had her fancy fingers in real estate. She answered phones for a real estate office in high school. For a dozen years, as a legal secretary for real estate attorneys, she routinely drafted purchase and sale agreements and shepherded sales through escrow. Later, she joined a public storage firm where she structured the company's real estate purchases. In her personal life, she and her husband bought a home soon after they married more than twenty years ago. Over time, they refinanced and remodeled—and that's when Marie took some well-informed but risky risks.

Among all the Tao Gals, Marie not only has the most financial expertise, but she also has the most conventional and stable history of home ownership. Thus, whenever one of the Tao Gals has a real estate or financial question, wants advice, needs a spreadsheet, or is simply freaking out, she turns to Marie, who invariably keeps a level head in such matters.

"To buy or not to buy—I'm going nuts, or driving myself nuts," Bernadette blurts out at a meeting, "It's such a crazy-making decision for me. Marie, how do you handle the emotions that come up in a real estate deal?"

Marie draws herself up in a most queenly manner. "Emotions," she says, "have no place in real estate transactions."

Then, settling back in her chair, she adds, "That's not to say I didn't have a full-bore anxiety attack after Dennis and I took out our first loan. Oh my god. I was lying in bed thinking that my heart was going to bang out of my chest. I was paralyzed with terror. I was twenty-four at the time, and a thirty-year loan seemed unimaginable. Here I'd married Dennis without a second thought, no worries, no panic, no sense of sealing my fate. But a thirty-year loan from a faceless institution? It felt like going to prison. Lock the door. Throw away the key."

Otherwise, she and her husband approached buying a home in the most rational, thought-out, step-by-step manner imaginable—the way we should all do it (and almost never can). Their decision to move from a rented town house to a home of their own was "absolutely money-driven." They wanted to stop renting, lose the landlord. They needed a tax break. They had the savings for a down payment, the incomes to pay a mortgage. Buying was simply the next indicated step.

Before they started looking, they sat down and figured out how much they could spend. They considered the amount they'd saved for a down payment. Marie and Dennis then asked themselves how much of their lifestyle they were willing to give up in order to pay a monthly mortgage. "The answer was nothing. Zero. We weren't willing to give up eating out, taking vacations, or going to the movies," says Marie. They calculated that they could pay a hundred or two more a month without altering their lifestyle, no more.

Between what they could put down and what they could pay monthly without pain, they established precisely which price range they could consider. They weren't going to tempt themselves by looking at more expensive properties that would compromise their lifestyle.

Next, they talked about where they wanted to live; there was plenty of inventory then, and a young couple pretty much had to limit their search parameters or be overwhelmed by choices. Marie and Dennis settled on La Crescenta, a pretty, somewhat rural sidekick to Glendale that has since become an increasingly exclusive area with strong schools, low crime rates, and unlit streets where the occasional coyote or deer roams. "It felt like a small town, only without the possibility of me running into anybody from high school," says Marie. They found a small, one-story, two-bedroom, one-bath house built in the late '20s or early '30s.

Because her own decision to buy was so practical and level-headed (except for that one fit of nighttime terror), and because she has seen and overseen so many different real estate deals, Marie is able to maintain a no-nonsense, slightly cool detachment in real estate matters. She tells the Tao Gals: "Do the numbers first."

"But the numbers always add up to bad news for me," Bernadette bursts out. "I may have enough for a 20 percent down payment, but the monthly payments on any mortgage would kill us with our three kids. We have music lessons, a math tutor, private school tuition, none of which I'm willing to forfeit. If this market continues, I'll never afford a home."

"Maybe you won't," Marie says softly. "But that will be okay. I'll tell you what, though . . ." she pauses. "I'd give back every square foot of house if that meant I could have had kids."

In the silence, the Tao Gals recall the heartbreaking failure to conceive and the couple's painful decision not to adopt.

"We don't always get what we want," Marie says quietly. "And our job is to live with it and make the best of it."

She takes a deep breath. "My advice to you, Bernadette, is first to open yourself up to the possibility of buying—don't count yourself out of the running too soon. Then, when you're ready, start the footwork: assess your finances, decide what you can afford, start looking in that price range. Remember, you're already in a good living situation, and no matter what happens, you're still okay. Don't get your heart set on any one thing, or in having things work out in a specific way. If one deal doesn't work, try again. Don't get hung up trying to force something. I've worked on deals that we tried to force and force and force and, if it wasn't going to happen, it just wasn't going to happen."

GAYLE, ON DECIDING NOT TO BUY

Gayle is a fifty-one-year-old single mother who works as a researcher for the *LA Times*. She cares deeply about many things—her close-knit family of four sisters and a brother, her job, her writing—but first and foremost, she cares about her twelve-year-old daughter, Sophie. Sophie's father died in a traffic accident when she was six months old and Gayle has shouldered both parental roles ever since.

Gayle and Sophie live in South Pasadena, an area lauded for its fabulous public schools. It's said that the price of condos and homes in South Pasadena is more than $100,000 higher than comparable properties just over the border in Pasadena or Alhambra. In fact, South Pasadena home prices are carefully calibrated to take into account the savings home owners incur by sending their children to public schools. That is, if you have only one child, it's probably cheaper to live elsewhere and pay for private school. With two or more young children, it is more cost-effective to buy in South Pasadena and send them to public school.

Gayle's apartment is older and full of character and color. Her development, known as Raymond Hill, is composed of four-unit buildings—two units on the bottom, two on the top, joined by a central staircase. Gayle's large front window has a vast view into the eastern part of Pasadena, with no close neighbor in sight. The floors are hardwood. The apartments are acoustically sound. You can hear birds calling, but not the neighbors. Each unit has a small private garden. The kitchens are small and efficient, the bathrooms done in pastel tiles that are all the rage again. In short, Gayle's home is like a 1910 Craftsman bungalow that happens to be attached to others— nothing like the soul-deadening postwar apartments you see all over LA.

But it's still an apartment, a rental. No long-term security. No pride of ownership. How does Gayle feel about that, especially now that the Tao Gals are buying real estate and talking about it so much? Does she feel left out, as Bernadette often does?

"I'd like a space of my own, and to express myself in my home, and have it be a reflection of who we are. And, God, I'd love to have a yard."

Sophie, she says, also wants them to have a house. "When she talks about it, I *do* feel angst. I encourage her to write about it and draw pictures of it. Hold it in her mind." Still, for Gayle, the idea is so far out there that she tries not to spend much time thinking about it.

Buying a home in Los Angeles has become so expensive that it's out of reach for Gayle and millions like her.

"I once tried to become a homeowner," she admits to the Tao Gals and relates a cautionary tale.

Gayle's mother had just died of Alzheimer's disease, and Gayle was grieving when an old family friend named Charlotte came forward with a proposal. "I'll make the down payment on a house, you and Sophie live there, you pay the mortgage, we'll fix up the place, sell it, divide the profit, and start again."

Gayle liked the idea of acquiring equity. One of her sisters had made a small fortune buying houses, living in them, selling at a profit, slowly moving up. Gayle saw the opportunity Charlotte offered as a way to get her own toe in the real estate pool. But there were certain realities to consider. She told Charlotte she could only pay a set amount every month: $600. She had a set salary and certain obligations—she had some loans to pay off, Sophie was in private school, and they were both seeing counselors. There was no wiggle room.

Charlotte still wanted to proceed. A modest, mutually satisfying house was found. Gayle and Sophie moved in.

Within a few months, property taxes came due. Charlotte asked Gayle to pay half of them. Gayle was flabbergasted, as this was the first mention of any additional costs. She simply didn't have the money. She reiterated that she could only afford $600 a month. Charlotte then started an IOU. When the house insurance came due, Gayle was again asked to pay half. Again, she couldn't and half of the insurance premium was added to her IOU. After that, whenever taxes and insurance were due or repairs were made, the IOU grew.

"Instead of gaining equity, I was going into debt to Charlotte!" Gayle says "Eventually, what I owed her would all but cancel out any share I had in the house. I thought, when I was renting, at least I wasn't going into debt."

Charlotte suggested that Gayle should take Sophie out of private school and that they both stop seeing counselors so Gayle could pay her share.

At that point, Gayle decided to withdraw from the deal. She walked away from what remained of her investment and the friendship—and what was probably her one and only brush with owning real estate in Southern California. "I learned a lot—about Charlotte and doing business with friends, and most of all about myself, and my priorities," Gayle says.

Gayle found an apartment in South Pasadena and was able then to take Sophie out of private school. Although she would never be able to afford to buy a house in that community, she could still enjoy the city's famous amenities. So, she made her choice: Get the school system; forgo the security. "The one part of the American dream that I buy into is that my daughter will have better chances, a better life, and make better choices than I did. Most of the decisions I make are about giving her the education and the tools she needs to get by in life. And I'd rather provide her with those tools now than leave her a house later. She'll have the tools to get her *own* house."

Gayle still sometimes thinks about moving to a place where

the schools are good, the air is clean, *and* the houses are actually affordable. "I get on the Internet," she says, "and house hunt."

She likes the looks of Canada and New Mexico, where she has a sister. Lately, she's been visiting Alabama Web sites and has found some good-looking homes for around $90,000.

"But what would I do there? You know, it used to be you could drive around north LA County and there were neighborhoods people just didn't consider moving into and you could get a really good deal on a great big, beat-up old house. That possibility was always there. But now, everything around here has been nabbed and gentrified; prices are high everywhere. It's fun to go online because you can still find big old messes that can be had for a song and remade with a little elbow grease."

For the present, it's enough for Gayle to know the possibility exists. "I keep checking to make sure there's still a place in the world where I could afford a house. Knowing that makes living in this apartment OK. I *do* have faith that I will have a house one day."

In the meantime, she and Sophie live in and enjoy the amenities of a lovely town where the high quality of the schools has otherwise driven the home prices into the stratosphere. In Gayle's case, not buying a home makes great sense.

Rent vs. Own

In the hottest real estate markets in the country, it has become far more expensive to buy a home than to rent. Still, some believe that the appreciation and tax benefits of owning still make it a worthwhile choice. Unfortunately, there's no easy way to figure out what the appreciation will be in the future. Keep in mind that some areas have seen amazing appreciation, with values doubling over the course of a few years. While that makes for a great investment for those who bought when prices were lower, it may mean that future appreciation may be less than what's occurred in the past. Historically, appreciation has hovered between 3 and 4 percent—essentially the cost-of-living adjustment. Fill in the anticipated rental and owning costs to compare below.

Monthly Rental Costs

Monthly rent   _____

Utilities   _____

Other costs, such as parking, cable TV, gardening or pool care if not included in rent, etc.   _____

Total monthly rental costs   _____

Monthly Owning Costs

Mortgage payment   _____

Property taxes ($1/12$ of annual tax bill)   _____

Insurance ($1/12$ of annual insurance bill) _____

Maintenance ($1 per $1,000 of the purchase price is good rule of thumb)   _____

Utilities   _____

Homeowner dues or co-op assessments   _____

Pest control   _____

Sewer   _____

Other costs, such as parking, cable TV, gardening, pool care, etc.   _____

Total monthly owning expenses _____

Monthly Owning Savings

Tax Savings Call your accountant for a
rundown, but generally, if you are in the
25% tax bracket, as most people are, you
can plan on saving about 25% of your
mortgage payment in taxes each month. _____

Appreciation To be safe, go with the
historical trend of 3% to 4% per year.
Thus, for this calculation, figure the annual
projected appreciation and divide by 12. _____

Total monthly owning savings _____

Subtract the monthly owning savings from owning costs. Then compare
to the monthly rental costs. Keep in mind the intangible of appreciation—
it could be much greater, or if the market tanks, you could lose money.

BERNADETTE, A STUDY IN INDECISION

I'm trying to get up the nerve to call my Realtor friend Sylvia,
who has just sent me a brochure announcing that she is now
selling real estate. "If you're ever in the market..." she'd
scrawled in the margin.

I've tried for some time to convince myself I'm not in the
market. It's the wrong time. It's the height of the market. I'd
be an idiot to buy now. Still, I'd like to know where I stand.
Having lost our last house, I don't know if I can qualify, if
I've become too timid even to find out, or if I really am
priced out.

Fear keeps me from phoning Sylvia, but is it healthy fear? Can I, should I, confront it?

Instead, I call my friend Thom, a real estate expert to feel him out.

"Tao and real estate," Thom says, pondering the subject matter of the book. "That's perfect! Why didn't someone come up with it before now?" The way Thom sees it, fewer people would be tied in real estate–related knots if they practiced a few Tao principles along the way.

"It's all about detachment," Thom says. "So many people go about it with a set agenda. 'I want this house.' If you can open yourself up to what might be, you'd be amazed at what happens. The best deals I've made have been the ones I haven't forced. I was in the right place at the right time and saw the opportunity for what it was."

Thom is what I'd consider a hard-core real estate investor, though he became one in a roundabout way. He bought his first property, a condo, back in 1992 and then watched the value of the property drop to below what he'd paid for it. He held on and eventually made his money back. When the condo regained its value, he realized that buying real estate for the long term was the way he wanted to go. But how was he going to come up with the chunk of change he'd need as a down payment to buy a second property, an investment property that he'd rent out?

He had a tidy sum of cash in his 401(k). If he could borrow that money from himself, he figured, he could start buying rental properties. Thom learned that he could borrow up to 50 percent of the value of his 401(k) to use as a down payment. That's what he did in 1997 and has never looked back. He now owns ten properties—five are single-family homes that he rents out, the other five are multi-unit rental buildings. He quit his job not long ago as a big-deal management consultant to concentrate more on his real estate investments.

I ask Thom to educate me in the best way to buy real estate. "If you qualify for a $400,000 mortgage, meaning you could buy a $500,000 home, buy a $400,000 house and pay off more and have more equity," he says. He's an investor at heart, so he says that the equity could then be turned into a down payment on yet another property.

"You won't hear any Realtor say this, except for me, but buy under your means. Live way beneath your means and build up equity. The way to build up equity is to pay more on your mortgage. That's a real easy way." Living beneath your means, he points out, doesn't necessarily mean buying in a bad neighborhood. "Pick a neighborhood that should be getting better and work to make it better." As an example, he cites friends who bought on a busy street and then worked to have speed bumps put in to slow the rush of traffic, thus improving the neighborhood.

"Look at the view, the streets, the other houses in the neighborhood. Are the other owners starting to fix them up? Say you want this dump of a house; it just hasn't gotten fixed up yet. Maybe you don't fix it up for five or ten years. That's OK. You live in the dumpy house for five years and you just bite the bullet. You don't get new plumbing. You use one shower at a time because if you turn on two you'll get nothing but cold water. That's OK. Don't analyze it too much. If you can pay for it, go for it."

But how do you find those neighborhoods that are going to improve? Are there real estate psychics to consult?

Thom laughs and says, "Look at where the gay guys are going. They look for architectural integrity, what's really there beneath all the baggage of the neighborhood. Where are the great houses? They don't look at the yards, they don't look at the chain-link fences. They say, 'What could I do to put my cosmetic touches on something and really bring it out?'"

He cautions that no matter how you look at it, in this market, buying is going to be more expensive than renting. Still, keep in mind that appreciation—particularly in California and other hot real estate markets—continues to grow. "California's not getting any cheaper. Over the next twenty years, it's not going to get any cheaper."

If I'm not sure how much I want to spend, he suggests I have a best case/worst case scenario in mind. If I can live with the worst case, go for it.

"And if the market goes down?" I ask.

"It doesn't matter. This is where your Tao principles come in. What matters is, can you make your payments?" As long as you can make your payments, you can stay there until the market recovers, which always happens.

Rumors have been circulating that the real estate market may be slowing down. Inventory has become a little more plentiful recently, and houses are taking a bit longer to sell. I wonder if Thom is actively investing right now.

"I'm actively looking. Contrary to what you might be hearing, now is not a time to wait. 'Wait' implies that you're not doing anything. I think that's what happens when the markets start to get soft, then everyone jumps in and says, 'I'm going to start looking.' By the time they get calibrated and prepared to buy, it's like, 'You know what? The good deals were way back there.'"

Always be actively looking, he advises. Keep in mind that the

reasons real estate exploded in the first place remain valid: demand outstripping supply. If the market softens, which he's not
sure it will, it's going to happen slowly.

"Consider the wild cards of the stock market and terrorist
attacks, which I think caused the nesting impulse in the first
place. People want a secure home. They put their money in
what they understand. The whole corporate-scandal issue—
who wants to put their money in the stock market? Put your
money in something you understand. Even though real estate's
inflated, if you buy in a good area and you get a good price, at
least it's pretty secure. It's going to be good long term, and you
still get great tax benefits."

I confess to Thom my addiction to the Web site
Realtor.com and he shakes his head.

The best way to look for real estate is to look for real estate,
Thom says. Don't just follow the databases—get out there and
drive. "Get a map. Go check it out. Look at the boundary
streets. What are the good parts of town? Where would you
want to be? Drive it. You find some neat stuff that way."

I meditate. I bug the Tao Gals with question after question. I think about Thom's words. Eventually, I see a bottom
line: I need to know if I am making an informed decision not
to buy at the moment, or is the market making that decision
for me?

It occurs to me that I can approach Sylvia, the real estate
agent, under the guise of writing this book. I'll ask all the questions I'd be otherwise too afraid to pose and say I'm just doing
research. Still, I'm nervous.

I pick up the phone and call Sylvia.

Tao Worksheet

1. Make a list of the reasons to buy a home. Make a list of the reasons to keep renting. What do you see?

2. What is standing in your way today that is keeping you from buying a home? What can you do about it?

3. The light guiding you homeward—where is it leading? Can you picture where you belong?

4. Think about neighborhoods. What's important to you about where you live?

5. Do you plan to be an active member of your community? If so, what kind of community? Envision a place for yourself. Are stores within walking distance? What about public transportation? Make a list of what you're looking for in a neighborhood and why.

6. What do you need, physically, in a house? Is beauty important? Do you want to do work on a fixer-upper, or do you need a house in move-in condition?

7. What about a fireplace, a garden, wood floors, aluminum window frames, curb appeal? What are the most important features to you? What can you live without?

CHAPTER FOUR

A WORD ABOUT REALTORS

Knowing others is intelligence;
knowing yourself is true wisdom.
Mastering others is strength;
mastering yourself is true power.

MICHELLE, ON DOING THE FAMOUS BAD THING

IF YOU CALL about a house, you will talk to a real estate agent. If you wander into an open house, you will talk to a real estate agent. If you talk to someone who has a For Sale sign in their front yard, they will most likely tell you to call their real estate agent. In other words, the moment you start house hunting, your education about real estate agents will begin.

Before I had a relationship with any one Realtor, the Tao Gals offered pointers. "Anybody got a good Realtor?" I said.

"It's pronounced *reel*-tour," said Rose. "Not reel-ahh-turr. Two syllables, not three."

"And besides that," Bernadette chimed in, "you probably mean 'real estate agent' because Realtors are only those real estate agents who belong to a national organization."

"Oh. Okay, Reel-a-turr, Real-tour, real estate agent. Anybody know a good one?"

"I'm not convinced there's any such a thing," said Marie.

Beginning to house hunt, I met some real estate agents who were helpful, some who were pushy, and many who were a combination thereof. When I phoned about a house, some quickly gave me information over the phone, some first took down all kinds of information from me, then told me about the place. Some also sent me e-mail listings and offered to drive me around. One very successful agent I knew from church said that she would work with me only if I signed exclusively with her. "I'll work hard for you," she said, "but not if you're going to give your business to someone else later on." Fine, except I wanted to hunt in neighborhoods and areas she didn't know well, or at all.

When I first started looking, I'd meet real estate agents at a property or open house and they would make a play to become my agent. Sometimes, I agreed to look at houses with them. Often, the strangest thing would happen. I would tell the agent what I wanted and my price range. I would tell them the absolute top of my price range, beyond which I was completely unwilling to go. Then, the first house they would show me would be $20,000 or more over what I said I was willing to pay.

True, I was looking near the bottom of the market. True, their commission from any sale to me would be low. But it was also true, I only had so much money.

I wanted—no, needed—a real estate agent who listened to me.

I was astonished how few real estate agents heard *any* of the simple things I said. "Two bedrooms. Older. Yard important. No aluminum-sash windows. Fireplace, wood floors desired but not absolutely necessary. Beauty of some sort—in yard or house—a must."

Many of my friends reported similar problems.

My friend Hannah and her husband were looking for a bigger

home with a lot of land. They were willing to do a lot of fixing up. They wanted a house with fairly good bones and a great piece of property—neighborhood, curb appeal, and condition were all secondary concerns for them. They'd also be happy, they said, with a loft-type industrial space. They hired a real estate agent recommended to them by a friend.

"She kept showing us these really middle-class, conventional properties," Hannah complained. "She looked at us and thought, 'oh, young yuppie family.' She'd go on and on about copper pipes and crown molding and built-in Sub-Zeros. She didn't hear a word we said." In the three months they tried working with her, several terrific raffish, oddball properties had sold for a song—properties their agent didn't even show them. "We'd find out about these great properties we never even heard about and just feel sick."

My old friend Michele bought her gorgeous Spanish home only by defying her real estate agent. "I told our agent that we didn't want to see *anything* postwar—nothing built after 1946. And she was constantly showing us these hideous houses built in the '50s and '60s and even '70s. After a while, we'd refuse to get out of the car." One day, when Michele and her husband were out driving around, they saw a house for sale—just from the street—that they really liked. "Our real estate agent called about it and told us there was already an offer in on it. She wouldn't even meet us there to look at it. We met with the seller's agent and made a backup offer. And guess what? We got the house."

Michele's agent didn't want to be bothered writing a backup offer. On the other hand, some real estate agents love to write offers, the more the merrier.

When I was barely beginning to look for a house, I met a

real estate agent at a party; she was self-possessed, businesslike, and knew one desirable area of the city very well. I liked her; she seemed no-nonsense and very smart. She took my number and promised to call when houses in my price range came up. And so she did. But her calls did not so much announce the possibility of home as they did the occasion of a frenzy.

"There's a gorgeous little house up in the Franklin Hills," she'd say. "Great view, hardwood floors, fireplace, perfect for you. It goes on the market tomorrow, so go see it first thing. Eight A.M., if you can. Move fast. There are already nine offers."

Nine offers!

And the listing price was already $30,000 beyond what I could pay!

I don't know about anyone else, but the mention of multiple offers immediately puts me off—and knocks me out of the running. Multiple offers must bring out the fangs (and checkbooks) of some buyers, but they automatically discourage me. If so many other people want a house so badly, let them have it. I didn't have the money to compete. I was house shopping, not playing the heartbreak lottery.

When I finally decided to buy the ugly house on the huge lot, I did the famous bad thing. I went with the Realtor who also represented the seller of the house. Using a seller's agent, I knew, was not a recommended procedure. The agent is in the impossible position of representing two potentially colliding interests. Real estate agents, however, like this double-duty arrangement because they get all of the commission and potentially double their earnings on a sale.

Real estate agents get paid by commission. Typically, a 6 percent commission is computed from the selling price of the house. The seller's agent determines how that commission is divided. Some sellers' agents split the commission fifty-fifty with buyers' agents, some take 60 percent, and give the buying agents 40 percent. Other agents make other arrangements. If a house is $400,000, the full commission will be $24,000, a tidy sum, so it's easy to see why a real estate agent might want the whole banana and not just half.

But what happens when the buyer and seller have a disagreement, or even enter into a raging, seemingly insoluble conflict during the course of the sale (which is what happened to me)? In such circumstances a double-duty real estate agent needs to be as wise and impartial as Solomon, and of course, mine was not. If he had been that wise, he most likely would not have been a real estate agent at all, but a federal court judge.

Perhaps this was my cosmic payback for not bringing Raoul in on the deal. When I called and told him I was buying the house in Altadena with another agent, he was actually very sweet. "I knew you were going to do that," he said.

"You did?"

"You talked about that house a lot," he said.

"I did?"

"You mentioned it every time I saw you."

"I did?"

"Big trees, huge yard, ugly house, but fixable? Behind your old friend—that one?"

He really did listen to me!

"I'm sorry. I really appreciate the time and trouble you took with me."

"Don't worry," he said. "In this business, you win some and you lose some."

Nasty business, this. No wonder real estate agents have an edge.

BERNADETTE, ROSE, AND WRONG EXPECTATIONS

"I'm doing some research on real estate agents," I mention, nonchalantly, at a Tao meeting. I know if I say outright that I'm thinking of entering the market, I'll be prematurely inundated with suggestions. "So . . ." I turn to Rose. "Uh, how did you find your agent?"

"Are you finally going to make a move?" Rose asks, growing eager on my behalf. The other Gals, who have been visiting with each other, stop their conversations to tune in.

"Just doing research for the book," I reply, certain my face is blushing. I'm a lousy liar.

"OK, for research purposes only . . ." Rose winks. "The agent I used was someone I knew from a twelve-step program. I liked her as a person. She was a little crazy and seemed like fun." Rose raises her eyebrows and shoulders, as if to say, "What do you expect—was I supposed to *search* for an agent?"

The Tao Gals nod in recognition. None of them went about finding an agent in a straightforward, organized fashion, either—which would mean getting recommendations, asking for referrals, checking out reputations. And they were *all* sorry they hadn't.

"What I really wanted from my real estate agent was a teacher," Rose continues. "Someone to shepherd me through the process, explain what was going on, calm my fears. Someone to tell me I was making not only a good decision, but the best decision." Rose laughs all of a sudden. "Having those expectations was probably wrong of me."

Meanwhile, Rose was not in any hurry. "I wanted to know as

much as possible about the entire process." Knowledge, Rose hoped, would provide a degree of comfort, and she'd scrounge for any comfort she could get, even if it meant tormenting her agent with endless questions and a long, drawn-out search.

Rose asked her agent to tell her about loan qualifying. What's the best kind of mortgage to get? How do you calculate the property taxes? Does this plumbing look good to you? What about the roof: how do you know if it's sturdy? Do those rain gutters need to be replaced? How do I know if this house has 'good bones'?

"My real estate agent became very irritable with me."

About halfway through the process of looking for a house, the agent lost patience with Rose—with the houses she wanted to look at, with the details Rose wanted to know about the houses, and with Rose's frequent admission of fear.

"I kept admitting, 'Yes, I'm really terrified about taking this step. Help me to feel less afraid by explaining some of this stuff to me: At this price, what is that going to mean monthly? Tell me the five most important things I should be looking for: The roof? The foundation?'"

The more Rose asked for reassurance, the more unwilling her agent became to fulfill this assigned teacher role. Instead of calming Rose's fears, she began to play on them. In no time, she was bullying Rose into making a decision.

(Which is saying something. Rose is the least likely person to be bullied, what with her commanding physical presence and strong personality. If buying real estate can turn someone like Rose faint of heart, imagine what it does to the rest of us!)

"This house is perfect for you," the agent would say. "Don't you love this house? Isn't this okay? Let's do this one, quick. Let's hurry."

The more the agent pushed Rose to make a decision, the more agitated Rose became and the less she knew what she wanted to do.

"You have to hurry," her agent kept telling her. "The prices are leaping. Interest rates will start going up. You need to do this now!"

Whether the agent was right or not—prices *were* leaping and interest rates, for a moment anyway, *were* rising—wasn't the point. "There was this crescendo of anxiety about getting it done and getting it over with," Rose says. Though she bristled under the treatment, Rose didn't look for another agent, as perhaps she should have. "Maybe the agent *did* have my best interests in mind," she'd think, though gut instinct told her to ditch the bitch.

Though determined to buy a house, Rose had hoped to take her time. That was not to be. Eventually, she succumbed to the crescendo of anxiety and bought a house—a house for which she felt no more or less passion than many of the other houses she'd seen. A house that would be serviceable, would do the job she needed, but toward which she felt little magnetism. She's not sure if her decision was a result of the agent's escalating pressure, or if she was finally just ready to make the move. Once she made the decision, however, she would not budge, even if it meant ignoring her friends' advice to look further.

She came to the Tao meeting the night she made the offer. The Tao Gals were all wanting to high-five her and celebrate the fact that she'd taken this momentous step, but Rose wanted nothing to do with the festivities. She was in mortal terror. Throughout the evening, Rose sat on the couch quietly, participated minimally in the group. It was just too much. She was terrified to check her voice mail messages—afraid that her offer might have been rejected and equally afraid that her offer may have been accepted. She was scared senseless of what she might have gotten herself into.

The Tao Gals urged her to check her messages. They waited while she dialed, listened, hung up the phone.

Offer accepted!

The Gals clapped and cheered, but Rose was in a state of shock. "I have no idea what I've done," she said.

For months the Tao Gals periodically checked in with her, to see how she was feeling about her big purchase. Each time, Rose repeated that she didn't feel well-enough schooled in the process and wished she'd insisted on a real estate agent who would have worked with her more, someone who wouldn't have fanned her anxieties, who could have directed her to resources that would've educated her.

In fact, she traces her ongoing reservations about home ownership to having too many unanswered questions at the time of her purchase. "Sure, the value of my house has gone up dramatically since I bought it, and from an investment point of view, it's been a good thing. But maybe," she says with a tinge of sadness in her voice, "I should have waited until I knew more."

The Lingo

Buying real estate is hard enough on its own, but then there's all that esoteric lingo you have to learn: *points* and *closing costs, title searches* and *liens.* Why can't these things be explained in simple English? It's not as if a potential homeowner doesn't have enough on her mind!

Likewise, the term *Realtor.* You see a sign for a real estate agent, or have one recommended by a friend, and you make a call. Do you really care if the agent is also a Realtor (a real estate agent who is a member of the National Association of Realtors, a nonprofit professional association that holds members to a strict code of ethics)? What really matters is that any real estate agent—Realtor or not—is licensed by his or her state to sell real estate. The business practices of all real estate agents are overseen by the state's Department of Real Estate. Realtors, however, are also monitored by their local boards, which arbitrate complaints from the public and board members and provide discipline when needed. This oversight is meant to keep Realtors accountable to the consumers they serve.

Realtor, real estate agent—whichever term is used, such a person should represent your interests in the process of buying or selling real estate, making sure that a purchase this large is well informed and properly executed. That said, you actually *do not* need a real estate agent to buy or sell a property. If you find a house you want and decide to execute an agreement with the seller (who is likewise not represented by an agent), you can create a purchase agreement on your own, though it is wise to have a real estate attorney or a real estate agent look over the contract.

Most people choose to work with real estate agents because, typically, agents know what they're doing in a realm in which most of us are rank amateurs. The work of buying and selling real estate has a steep learning curve, and some agents have invaluable connections and esoteric knowledge gleaned from experience that can speed up a process, or finesse the unexpected surprises kicked up in a title search or home inspection. Just as you could learn to fix your own car if you wanted to, you could sell or buy your own house. But it also would be more expedient to turn your car over to a mechanic who has lots of experience. It will cost you more money, perhaps, but you'll probably save a lot on time, heartache, and frustration. Besides, when such vast sums of money are involved, it's good to have an advocate who knows the ropes.

MARIE, A DIY GAL

"At least you gals didn't have to type up your own offer," Marie says one night when the conversation moves her way. "Let me tell you about *my* experience. The whole terrible thing."

Twenty years after Marie purchased her home, her disillusionment with real estate agents hasn't lost its sting. When she and Dennis were making an offer on what would become their home, she knew from her various real estate–related jobs what she wanted included in the paperwork. "I wanted to be sure that we had the right to review the entire title record and copies of the underlying documents," she says, ticking off items on her pearl-polished, fuchsia-tipped fingernails. "In those days—the '80s—you actually had to specify that you wanted copies of all the items of record." (Items of record are those documents that reveal everything about the property—liens, easements, surveys, etc.)

"I wanted to ask the buyers to help finance our down payment. But the agent argued strenuously against it, refused to put it in."

Marie's real estate agent, it seems, wasn't sure how to present even the changes she'd approved. She'd keep stopping, trying to decide how to phrase things and where to put certain stipulations. Finally, Marie had had enough.

"Move aside," Marie said to the agent, who was stalled over the typewriter. Marie settled herself into the agent's chair and typed up the offer herself, putting it exactly the way she wanted it. Among other things, Marie added the request that the agent had argued against.

Marie asked in the written offer for the sellers to take back a second mortgage on the property to help make up a portion of the down payment she and Dennis lacked. This meant, essentially, that the sellers gave them a loan for part of the down payment, a loan to be paid back at market interest rates. The real estate agent kept telling Marie and Dennis that the sellers would never agree to such an offer.

"They want all cash," the agent repeated. "Plus, if you're going to do that, you'll have to pay more."

"I doubt it," Marie said, typing away. "Let's just try it this way and see what they say."

The offer was accepted exactly as Marie had written it.

"It worked for them," Marie says of the sellers. They were going into retirement and wanted security down the road. Having a second mortgage with Marie and Dennis meant they'd have ongoing income. Marie had been looking beyond the immediate deal into how certain details might work for both sides of the contract. The agent hadn't been able to see beyond the standard deal, hadn't dared to take a chance lest the deal fall through.

Marie now has a list of attributes she looks for in an agent:

They're in the business for the long haul—not out to make a quick killing. They have a long record, many sales, many happy customers.

They're knowledgeable about the market, proactive about putting you in the right property. They're mindful of your criteria and your stated objectives. They're not dragging you around to things you don't want to see.

Their associates respect them. They have a good reputation in their professional community. When you walk into an open house, the other real estate agents there don't eye them with skepticism or dislike. You can tell.

They hook you up with the right lender, the right escrow company. They have an appraisal company that works expediently and professionally. They have a home inspection team that works expediently and professionally. They have a termite guy. They've got a whole group of referrals—good, reliable referrals.

Good agents are out there. If you don't find them, make a second call, a third. "Be as ruthless as they are," Marie says.

How Agents Get Paid

Real estate agents make their money from a commission on the property being sold. The commissions are figured into the asking price of the home and the real estate agents—both the buyer's agent, representing the person purchasing the home, and the seller's agent, representing the person selling the home—will be paid out of the proceeds of the home's sale. The seller, in other words, pays for both agents. If you're a buyer, the services are essentially free to you.

Typically, a total of 6 percent of the purchase price goes out in commissions. On a $500,000 house, that means $30,000. Usually, half goes to the seller's agent—$15,000. That agent's brokerage will take a share, from as little as $1,500 to as much as $7,000, depending on the agent's agreement with the brokerage firm. The other $15,000 will go to the buyer's agent and his/her brokerage firm.

In today's hot market, though, these commissions are negotiable and many homes—particularly expensive ones—sell with lower commissions.

COLLEEN, A TALE OF TWO AGENTS

"Just don't hire an agent who happens to be your friend," pipes up Colleen, the single mother of two and district attorney. "At least, if you want to keep her as your friend."

When Colleen was looking for homes, she explains, she decided she didn't want to move out of Altadena and began looking for places with an agent who happened to be her friend. "Not such a good idea," she says.

There were several houses she made offers on with this friend. "With another agent, I could have gotten one of those houses." With a market this tight, the strategies and aggressiveness and relationships of the agent were critical. It was truly a seller's market, so the buyer's agent really had to go above and beyond business as usual to get the house.

"My friend had me make *at-asking-price* offers at a time when every house generated a stack of over-asking-price offers the minute it went on the market. My offers were just disregarded. The agent didn't pitch me as a potential buyer. She didn't tell me how to best go after a house."

Colleen admits she made a common error. She didn't go shopping for an agent. She went for the easy, available friend and worked with her for about six months, going out every available weeknight and weekend, making offers, and still not landing a house. Meanwhile, she was still living in Rick's. It was a frustrating, tear-inducing, and anger-inciting process. She bid on houses, one after another, and her offers were all ignored.

The market was hot and just getting hotter. "At that point, I was still making offers in the $300,000 range," she says and the Tao Gals take pause. Now, *that* amount sounds ludicrously low.

But at the time, Colleen says, it was a cold, rude shock.

"It was like, oh my God, $300,000! The houses I was looking at were like the first little place I'd owned in Atwater. I was making offers on these houses at $320,000 telling myself, 'It's a transitional house. Never mind that it's a questionable neighborhood, and there are no sidewalks. Never mind the issues with the foundation, the roof, and that there's nothing nice about the house—nothing!'"

Colleen made more offers that didn't wash. "I started to think about renting again. This was all just too much." Then, she stumbled on a different real estate agent.

A friend whom Colleen had gotten to know through a mothers' network at work had just recently bought a house in an Altadena neighborhood—exactly the kind of neighborhood Colleen had been looking for. The house shared a driveway with the rental next door. When Colleen visited her friend, she noticed the house across the driveway. She liked it. "It was very funky and wood-cabin-y looking. And I said, 'Now there's my house.' It had all these little hippy things hanging in the window. Little stained-glass things, prisms, crystals."

A couple months later, her friend called. "You know," the friend said, "my real estate agent told me that the house across the driveway might be coming up for sale. Is that something you'd be interested in?"

Colleen made an appointment to meet her friend's agent at the property. The agent's name was Dorothy. She let Colleen into the house.

Colleen loathed it.

"I loved the way it looked from the curb, but when you crossed the threshold, it felt like you were going into a cave." After living in Rick's house, with the high ceilings, all the air and light, this dim, close, battered space would never do.

"No," she told Dorothy. "I cannot live in this house."

Still, she took the tour. The house was relatively large—

2,000 square feet—and on a nice-size lot, though it seemed small to Colleen at the time. The two-car, detached garage was falling apart. The house had been hard-used by renters for fifteen years.

Dorothy told Colleen sotto voce that the house was not officially on the market. But the seller's agent—and presumably the seller—would just as soon sell it fast. Colleen could snap it up.

Colleen said, "Thank you, but, no." But she began to appreciate Dorothy. She liked that Dorothy was jumping the gun on this house; this was how people finessed their way into homes in this market frenzy. Side deals. Little advantages. Colleen had heard with envy many stories of agents performing such tricks—but her friend-agent never had. Now someone was offering her an extra advantage.

Dorothy showed Colleen other homes and made a point of getting to know her. "I liked her," says Colleen. "I liked that she was smart and sly and working for me."

And how did Colleen's original agent, the friend, take this defection?

Colleen was upfront with her friend and told her about the rental house. "If I decide to get that house, it's with someone else," she told her. "You understand?" Yes, she said she understood. She even put it in writing.

But obviously she didn't understand.

"We haven't been friends since," Colleen reports.

That house, the rental Colleen loathed—yes, the horrible dark cave across the driveway from her friend—never did reach the market. No one else even saw it. Dorothy "kind of massaged" Colleen into thinking it was a good house to buy. The seller's agent was still willing to make an easy, no-energy sale. The house came as-is.

"It was \$435K!" Colleen still wails at the price. "I could not afford it. The \$300K house was more my price range. This was way, way out of the league. But my dad liked the house, and the good neighborhood, and ponied up with the down. We'll just see how long I can hold on to it." She shrugs.

"But if it weren't for Dorothy," she adds, "The boys and I would probably be living in a motel."

BERNADETTE, CERTAIN QUESTIONS ARE POSED
The morning after hearing the Tao Gals' stories, I sit down to wait for Sylvia, the real estate agent I've arranged to interview—and am secretly thinking of working with. I fret. I worry that I won't be able to discern if Sylvia might be the right agent for me. I want someone who can help me with my fears and yet offer solid, pragmatic advice. My sense is to stay put for now, to put off buying until the market cools a bit—will Sylvia confirm that impulse? Or will she get me all worked up about what I should be doing this very minute? And if so, will I know if she's acting in my best interests or if I should find someone else?

Sixteen years ago, when John and I were newlyweds and first looking to buy, we hired my father's real estate agent. She did an OK job for us, driving us around, showing us what was available. What I wished we'd had, in hindsight, was someone to advise us on what we were getting into, how to maximize our down payment, how to buy as much house in as good a community as we could afford. Rather, she followed us around, willy-nilly, as we vacillated between a small cheap house in a good area and a larger but more rundown house in a worse area. We were afraid to get ourselves into too much debt, and were much more timid than we should have been.

Eventually, we found the first piece of property we bought by ourselves. (The house we lost was our second purchase.) It wasn't the house we'd been out looking for every Saturday and Sunday for weeks, but a condo. It wasn't in the areas we'd initially wanted, but a bit farther out. How could our real estate agent have known we'd settle for a condo that far away? We didn't know until we were worn down by our search for a house-house. But that's one of the things working with a real estate agent will do for you: show you your real options and help you over the hump if you're going to have to settle for less.

It fell into place like serendipity. One weekend, on the way home from water-skiing with friends, we saw an Open House sign and stopped on a lark. We'd never really considered a condo before, but the complex was well designed, with interesting architecture. The unit was spacious and airy, lots of light. There were two items that clinched the deal: a fireplace with a walnut mantel, for which I'd pined for years, and a huge wraparound wood patio that made the place seem as if it had its own yard. There was even a small patch of soil at one end of the patio, a perfect spot for a few tomato plants or roses. Plus, the condo would cost us less than we'd originally planned on paying. (Those were the days!) We liked the idea of not being financially squeezed. We had no children at the time and didn't need a full-size house.

We called our real estate agent that night and told her what we'd seen. She wrote up our offer the next day and it was accepted. We could finally relax. She hadn't helped us find that exact place, but all the driving around she did with us helped us recognize the right place when we happened upon it.

Two years later, when we sold that condo to move to a "real" house (the debacle house), we hired the same agent again to sell the condo. I suppose she did whatever real estate agents were supposed to do, but we had no offers, not even a bite, for far too long. Were we asking too much? Were we not being aggressive enough? If she advertised the condo, we didn't see the ads. She planned no open houses and I remember no caravan of real estate agents coming through. As far as I can tell, she just took the listing and added it to the computer database of listings and waited for a buyer to materialize.

At first, we didn't mind. The house we were purchasing was in a new-home development and wouldn't even be finished until May. We'd put the condo up for sale in December and figured we'd have loads of time. But the weeks kept slipping away and no one came to look—and this was in the early 1990s, when LA real estate was peaking in a big way. Real estate agents were raking in massive commissions on expensive properties. Sellers like John and me, with our puny little condo were low, it seems, on the priority list.

We grew desperate—we didn't want to lose the new house because the condo didn't sell—and we started hosting our own open houses on Sundays. An open house, we reasoned, was how we'd found the place originally, after all. We borrowed signs from our real estate agent (who was too busy with other houses to host an open house for us) and posted them around the neighborhood. We stayed home Sunday after Sunday for months, welcoming lookie-loos into our home, quite a few of them neighbors, just coming by for a glimpse and to figure out what their places might be worth.

When we were beginning to think we'd have to give up our new house, the right couple came through the door. They saw the very things we had—the huge wooden patio, the little garden, the fireplace with the mantel—and made a decent offer. Our real estate agent did little more in the transaction than fill out the forms and collect a check. Escrow went through without a hitch. To this day, I'm not sure if the agent should have done more. What are reasonable expectations? That's one thing I want to ask Sylvia when I meet with her this morning.

Of course, Sylvia doesn't know I'm actually shopping for a real estate agent. I'm meeting her in the name of book research.

I doubt I'm her target client. I have a down payment saved up, but as a freelance writer, my income is strictly feast or famine. John has a real job, but we'll need both our incomes to qualify for anything. Plus, even when we figure out what we could qualify for, it's still below the median in the greater Los Angeles area by more than $50,000. What would that buy us—a small condo in a community with poor schools?

Sylvia comes to my house—the charming, if small, Craftsman rental with hardwood floors and great character in the heart of Glendale. We settle on the couch. She's probably in her midforties, with dark hair and huge, lively eyes. She speaks very quickly and with a slight accent, the result of living in South America for twenty years before she returned, as a newly single mother, to the United States five years ago. "Until then, I had never worked a day in my life outside of the home," she says. Her mother, however, had been a successful real estate agent for two decades, and Sylvia decided to follow in her footsteps, took courses, passed her test. She's been an agent for three years now—new, but committed.

I feed her journalist's questions, hoping that if I act as if I'm just researching the subject in an objective way, she'll inadvertently answer the real question filling my mind, a question I'm far too afraid to ask directly: Is there any hope that I might become a homeowner again?

What is her overwhelming philosophy of selling? I ask.

"I always try to act as if I were buying a home myself. I put myself in the buyer's place. So first I sit with them and listen, find out exactly what they want."

Most potential buyers who approach Sylvia haven't gone to a lender and found out, officially, how much they are qualified to spend—they're not prequalified. Therefore, after the initial interview and before they look at a single house, she has them obtain a prequalification letter. "They don't have to disclose their financial details to me—those are between the client and the lender. I only need to know what the client can get approved for. Once that's established, I can start to search for properties they can afford. I won't show them houses until they have the letter. A lot of people think they can afford, say, $500K. So you go out, show them a $500K property, and they fall in love. Then they get an approval letter from a bank and they only qualify for $400K. They're crushed! You show them stuff in the $400K range and they still have that darling $500K place in their minds. It's very disappointing."

What if, like some of the Tao Girls, they don't know about lenders, or where to turn for a prequal letter?

"I can happily turn them on to somebody. Most real estate agents can refer them to a lender. A prequal letter is free. They're under no obligation to stick with that lender in obtaining a loan."

In addition to helping the buyer keep her expectations realistic, Sylvia adds, the prequal letter adds clout in the making of an offer. In fact, some sellers' agents won't consider an offer that isn't backed up with a loan approval.

When Sylvia starts working with potential buyers, she asks a lot of questions, takes notes. "They tell me what they want in a home. And it's my job to be realistic with them." The main thing that buyers, particularly first-time buyers, need to keep in mind, Sylvia says, is that they're never going to find the perfect home. "A first home is not going to be your dream home. That's just reality."

To help buyers find a compromise between what they dream of buying and what's available to them, Sylvia suggests that her clients make a pro-and-con list for a possible property. "It makes them see a little more reality—so, the bathroom's little, but what the heck?! The place is beautiful."

If the pros outweigh the cons, Sylvia says, *buy the property*. Don't wait around. "The biggest mistake I see first-time home buyers make is not making a decision, God love them. They wait three months, four months. That place you saw on Pacific was darling. Your mind keeps going back to that little town-home that was so cute. Four months later, you want to go back and see it, but it's gone."

You can wait yourself right out of the market, she says. She saw it with one young man shopping for a condo. "He was a sweetheart. He had $280K to play with. A year and a half ago, we looked for three or four weekends. We found a darling one right here on Piedmont, everything that he wanted. He got frightened. I couldn't make him buy it. Three days later, the place was gone." Sylvia and the young man continued to look intermittently, and the market continued to skyrocket. A year went by and the young man's purchasing power shrank. "There's nothing he can buy in this area now," Sylvia says. "I can tell my clients these things, but I can't force them into anything."

I now move to a list of questions based on the Tao Gals' experiences. For Rose, I ask Sylvia just how long a buyer can expect a real estate agent to work with her before the agent throws in the towel? How much hand-holding is acceptable, and at what point are buyers considered simply too needy?

"You know, honey, I prefer to give it about a month." Clearly, as in the case of the terrified male condo-shopper, she will make exceptions.

And another concern of Rose's: Is it appropriate to ask the real estate agent's advice about the roof, the plumbing, the electricity, etc.?

"We're not contractors," Sylvia says, "And that's why there are inspectors." She reminds me that buyers in California legally have seventeen days to walk away from a deal and not jeopardize their deposit. An inspection is scheduled during this time. If the home inspector says a $300K house is only worth $250K, that there's damage and leakage and what-all, then the buyer can walk without losing a cent. "For a real estate agent to say, 'Oh, the roofing's fine,' or 'The foundation's fine,'" Sylvia adds, "well, we don't know about that."

Michelle had mentioned having a real estate agent ask her to sign an exclusive agreement. The request freaked Michelle out and she didn't sign it. What should a person know about these agreements?

Such an agreement is designed to protect the agent, Sylvia answers. "A lot of times, you spend months of your time showing a buyer places. She likes this one but she's not sure. Then she walks in, on her own, to an open house. She loves it and signs a contract with the seller's real estate agent right there and then. Three months of work—poof!—down the drain!"

Will a real estate agent work hard for someone who doesn't sign that kind of agreement?

"The real estate agent should be working hard, period."

What about real estate agents who insist on showing clients properties that aren't in their price range? One of Michelle's big gripes.

If that happens, Sylvia says, being careful not to slam her fellow agents, you're working with the wrong real estate agent. Some people do qualify for more than they feel comfortable spending, and some agents may try to convince them to spend more. Sylvia herself prefers not to push clients. "You can be qualified for a million dollars, but if you only want to spend $400K—fine. My job is to show you $400K properties."

And what about the fact that real estate agents always have an escrow company and loan agent waiting in the wings: Is that ethical? Do they receive a kickback?

"Kickbacks are illegal." Sylvia herself, as a matter of course, suggests names of loan brokers and escrow companies to her clients because they're companies that have done a good job for her previous clients and they work well with her Realty firm. "For example, we're affiliated with First Southwestern Escrow; they're right upstairs, so it's perfect, very convenient. I tell my clients that we're affiliated with this company, but it's always up to the client. The client gets final say on who will be the loan agent, who will coordinate escrow—everything."

Finally, I ask my own pet question: Will the market remain so frantic much longer? For those of us who have waited, hoping for reality to reassert itself and a sane market to regain its foothold, are we screwed?

"You know what, honey," Sylvia says, seeing right through my pretense of objectivity, "no one has a crystal ball. I really can't say."

The one thing she *does* know is that Southern California is an extremely desirable place. And like other desirable places throughout the country, the real estate market reflects that desirability. There are just too many people who want to live in these areas for the market to soften in a significant way.

At least right now, she goes on to say, with whispers of a slowdown in the air, more inventory is showing up on the market. But prices so far are staying fairly high. "The larger inventory is good for the buyer, but prices are still good for the seller."

And what about the adage of "location, location, location"? I'm living in a great location, I say, but only because I'm renting. Would it be smarter to move to a less-desirable location and buy? Or lower my expectations and buy a condo in this great area?

Sylvia won't provide the simple answer I hunger for. "It all comes down to what you want and your comfort level. How do you feel about renting? What about the tax benefits of owning a home? You're always taking the chance that a couple years from now, the cost of buying may be even more expensive."

Like I needed to be reminded of that.

And home ownership, she points out, is one of the best investments you'll make in your life.

I want to yell, *It doesn't always work out for the best!*, but I hold my tongue. "So, to sum up," I say instead, "how should a person pick a real estate agent?"

"It's a personal thing. You should feel comfortable and confident with the person. There has to be trust and respect. It's a gut feeling. If the person seems professional to you, forthright, you feel they're going to be very straight with you, honest with you, that's all good. If not, keep looking."

And what about Sylvia herself—does the shoemaker wear her own shoes? Has Sylvia sold herself a home?

"Not yet!" Her eyes flash and, funny as this may seem, her "houselessness" all at once puts me at ease. She understands, then, the hunger to own and the frustration of being priced out. She has three sons and shares the need for enough space, for good schools.

"I have a written goal: two years from now I want to purchase something. It will still be a little tight, but I'll have more breathing room. I'm going to be scared, but I'm going to do it."

On that note, my confidence begins to rise enough to float my dream idea past her. The house I'm renting is part of a larger property—four units in all, on a busy urban corner. I've already told the owner we might be interested in buying this place. He's thinking he'll sell it in a year or two. Would such a purchase be possible? I have a foreclosure on my record, though it should be coming off next year, seven years after having lost the house.

Sylvia's big bright eyes open even wider: "That would be great!" Her enthusiasm is infectious.

"Do you have any idea," I venture, "as to what the market price might be?" In truth, I'm terrified to know the answer, afraid that such knowledge will slam shut the door to my dream once and for all. I know we could afford a place costing around $400,000. But the three rental units in the back would generate income of around $3,200 a month. Between our income and that rental income, it might be possible to buy this place . . . as long as it doesn't cost a million bucks.

If I can provide her with the names of the owners, Sylvia says, she can do a title search and come up with a figure. My hand shakes as I write my landlord's name. I don't want the little flame of a dream I've protected so carefully to die, but I also want, and need, a reality check.

The rest of the afternoon I'm slammed around by emotions, hoping one minute that I might be able to buy the place, and certain, the next, that I'd be in over my head.

Sylvia calls later that evening. I startle at the sound of her voice and steel myself. If the market value is too much, I know I'll plummet into depression and give up. But the number's not too bad: $700,000. Conceivably, the purchase might work. John and I know nothing about being landlords, how to devise a contract, or fix a broken garbage disposal, but we could learn.

I never thought that $700,000 would sound reasonable.

Yet somehow, that gives me hope.

Tao Worksheet

1. What is the "inner" work you need to do before you commit to looking—and to finding a real estate agent? Are you sorted out emotionally on the idea of purchasing real estate? If not, what's standing in your way?

2. What "outer" work do you need to do? Make a list of people who've bought homes that you could call for a real estate agent referral. Who do you know who has had a good experi-

ence with a Realtor? Call that friend and make notes on what she suggests you do.

3. Write about how it makes you feel to work with someone who's trying to sell you something?

4. How can you keep your own objectives in the forefront of your mind when an agent pressures you to make a quick decision?

5. Describe the personality traits of the real estate agent you think would be right for you.

CHAPTER FIVE

WHERE THE MONEY COMES FROM

If you look to others for fulfillment,
you will never truly be fulfilled.
If your happiness depends on money,
you will never be happy with yourself.

FOR BERNADETTE—INDEED for all potential buyers—there comes a time you have to get into the money mess. Without a clear idea of your financial capability, no Realtor, no seller, will take you seriously. Thus, this is the first (*of two!*) chapters about money. So swallow hard, and keep reading. Here, we'll explore the early financial steps you have to take when you're serious about buying—or even looking for—a house. You'll need to know what kind of down payment you have. You'll need to learn your credit score. You'll need to know how much you can prequalify to borrow. In other words, you'll need to know—and be able to document—what you can afford to buy. Here's how we did it.

Assessing Your Assets

When you're going through the loan-approval process, you're going to want to show proof of the assets you possess. Fill in the blanks below and be prepared to back up your numbers with documents.

What You Own	Cash Value
LIQUID ASSETS	
Cash	_____
Checking accounts	
Acct #	_____
Acct #	_____
Acct #	_____
Savings accounts	
Acct #	_____
Acct #	_____
Acct #	_____
Money market accounts	
Acct #	_____
Acct #	_____
Acct #	_____
Life insurance policy	_____
Other liquid assets	_____
TOTAL LIQUID ASSETS	_____

INVESTMENTS

Stocks _____

CDs _____

Mutual funds _____

Real estate investments _____

Retirement accounts _____

Other investments _____

TOTAL INVESTMENTS _____

PERSONAL ASSETS

Car(s) _____

Motorcycle _____

Boat _____

Jewelry _____

Antiques _____

Rare artwork _____

Other personal assets _____

TOTAL PERSONAL ASSETS _____

ADD TOTAL LIQUID ASSETS, _____

TOTAL INVESTMENTS, AND _____

TOTAL PERSONAL ASSETS _____

TOTAL ASSETS = _____

MICHELLE IN HER UNDERPANTS

Getting a prequalification letter is no big deal. If revealing your true, complete financial state is like getting naked, getting a prequal letter is like stripping to your slip, a little revealing, but the major bulges and stretch marks are still well draped.

My therapist once said that her clients would far rather talk about sex than money.

In the process of buying a home, there's no choice. You talk about money.

Raoul, the real estate agent who took me looking for houses, told me I needed a prequalification letter when we set out to see the first house he showed me. The prequal was a way that he and any buyer we approached could see that I was serious about buying, and not merely curious and wasting everyone's time. (Now, most agents preferred a preapproval letter, which entails a more in-depth financial assessment.) Raoul said the broker who shared his office could probably provide me with a prequal letter, but I wanted to find a broker on my own. (At that point, I didn't understand or trust the connections agents established with brokers, inspectors, mortgage companies.) So my friend Michele sent me to her broker for my prequal letter—and hopefully my loan as well. "Jack's a bit of a philosopher," she said. "But we've gotten some good loans from him."

So I phoned and answered a few questions: how much rent I was paying, what I had in my savings accounts, my credit card balances. I needed to be qualified for about $200,000.

"No problem," he said. "When can you come get the letter?"

We talked some more about loans. I told him, as Marie instructed me to, that I would probably need a no-documentation loan. (Because of my freelance status, my tax returns showed only intermittent promise.)

"No problem," he said. "We're looking at, oh, a 6.5 percent loan."

I couldn't believe it. A great rate at that time. And for me, a first-time buyer.

I went a few hours later; I found Jack's office upstairs from a Soup Plantation cafeteria. I waited in a swank, hushed anteroom with his secretary, then was called into his office. It had a lovely view and high-grade office furniture. But Jack himself seemed to be exactly the kind of jock/fraternity type I'd avoided in high school, college, and life: good looking, clean-cut, smirking.

He handed me a prequalification letter saying, "To Whom It May Concern," that I could afford a loan for $245,000. "Wow. That's a lot more than I need."

"Oh, you might want to borrow more," he said. "Why put all your cash into a down payment? I'm a great believer in having cash on hand. Life is for living right now! Why tie up all your money in your assets? No! Seize the day! Don't scramble! Cash on hand is the only way to go!"

Oh, he *was* a philosopher.

"Thanks for the letter," I said. "Hopefully, I'll be seeing you again soon."

"Don't worry. We'll get the right loan for you," he said. "I'm a mortgage banker, not a mortgage broker. Do you know what the difference is?"

"No."

"I have the money to loan. I'm a banker. A broker shops for loans. I make loans. You won't have to pay those extra fees because you'll be dealing with me directly."

Ah, so that's why he could offer me such a good rate!

TALKING WITH THE PROS

The Tao Gals learned that it's a good idea to have, at the minimum, a letter of prequalification from a loan broker or lending institution, stating that you're prequalified for a mortgage of a certain amount. Such a letter can often be obtained with just a casual phone conversation; you won't have to prove you have the cash for the down payment and a credit report won't necessarily be run. Better yet is a preapproval letter, in which a lender gathers all the background financial details—verifying income, cash on hand, and credit scores—and gives you a green light on a loan. Especially in a hot market, these items can make a difference to sellers. Think about it from the seller's standpoint: If you receive two offers on your house, one from a person with a loan in the bag and the other from a person who'll need five days or so to arrange financing, who are you going to go with? No one likes to see a property fall out of escrow, and this financial documentation can help demonstrate that the prospect of your offer falling through is slim.

In order to become prequalified or preapproved, you'll need to determine a few things. First, do you have a down payment? Though there are loans available that don't require a down payment, you'll get a better interest rate on a loan with a hefty down payment, and with at least 20 percent down you won't have to pay private mortgage insurance.

Bernadette and John gathered their current down payment by saving for a number of years and cashing out stock options he had with his company. Michelle's down payment materialized from an earlier inheritance and was supplemented when she sold her second novel. Marie and Dennis had saved up, and had been given some money by Marie's grandmother. They were also able to get the seller to "take back a second mortgage" on the property, enough to make up for part of the down payment they lacked (i.e., they borrowed money from the sellers). Colleen had her father purchase the property with his own down payment and then bought the house from him after the divorce was final. Rose had saved a down payment, but needed to borrow extra money from family to cover the costs of repairs her house required. When she went to her father, however, the money came at great emotional cost.

HITTING UP DAD

When Colleen decided to take the plunge and buy, she had no cash available to her. "There's always my dad," she'd said to the Tao Gals. "I hate to ask him for anything."

"Yes, yes," the Tao Gals had said, at once empathetic and impatient. They tend to have minds like traps and don't forget many details. One detail in particular occurred to all of them at once. "But didn't you tell us recently that your dad just bought your brother a whole *building*?"

"Yes, but . . ."

"No 'yes-buts' allowed," the Tao Girls declared. "He should buy you a building too. He's lucky you only want a house! Figure out the best way to approach him. Then do what you have to and get out of the way, let go of the results . . ."

Thus strong-armed, Colleen went to her father. "Look," she said. "I'm going to be renting for at least the next year until this settlement happens with Rick. I'd rather rent from you. I'd rather pay you than pay some stranger." The stock market had been doing poorly and her father wasn't making the return on his investments that he'd have liked. With what was happening with the LA real estate market, Colleen's proposition made financial sense: an investment for him, and a break for her.

He agreed to make the down payment, put his name and credit report on the line, and she'd make the mortgage payments. Once the divorce was final and she'd received whatever settlement monies the court decreed, she'd repay the down payment and take him off the mortgage. It all went off without a hitch.

ROSE ASKS FOR HELP

Emboldened by Colleen's experience, Rose considered similar strategies.

"It's way more expensive than you think it's going to be," Rose tells the Gals about her experience of buying. "That's what I'd always heard. It takes a lot of money to make it the way you want it. Even the simple stuff. And I consider insulation and floors to be simple stuff."

In making the decision to buy, Rose figured that if she could handle the down payment, maybe her parents would help her with the other stuff—repairs, upgrades, etc. As it turned out, she was wise to have thought ahead. Her house required much more fixing up than she had anticipated.

"I had to tear out all the walls and put in insulation and floors. I needed $20,000 more than I had. I had heard the same old thing: buyers should beg, borrow, or steal the cash, do whatever you have to do to get in." In her case, "whatever you have to do" meant going, hat in hand, to her parents.

Prior to making that move, Rose spoke with many of her women friends—Colleen included—about the prospect of asking her family for help and had slowly come to believe that her father might actually want to help her. "I had been told that a lot of parents enjoy helping their children buy their first home." Not only do they not mind it, she'd heard, but they often enjoy it and want to help, are happy to help. After all, Colleen had gotten into her house with help from her father—a father from whom she was somewhat estranged. If Colleen's father would do that, why not Rose's?

"This has been the story of my life: asking other people what's normal. And then finding out that 'normal' doesn't apply to me," Rose adds as an aside, laughing sardonically. She screwed up all her courage, and with more than a little trepidation, approached her father.

"I'm thinking of buying a house," Rose said to her father, "and I need some help."

At that, her father went into a rage.

"What are you thinking, at this age?" he asked, sputtering with anger. "You should have the nest egg! You should have the down payment! I can't believe you're asking this from us!"

Rose didn't understand her father's reaction. He had the money. It wouldn't have been a financial hardship for her parents to help her. But there he was, spitting nails.

"He was completely enraged. He was red in the face, he got sweaty, he got huffy-puffy. He was *furious*."

Rose stayed calm, up to a point.

"You know, I've been talking to my friends about this for a couple of years," she told him. "Everybody says this is a good time to buy, and it's the smart thing to do, that I'm making the right choices. I come here and I feel not good enough and not smart enough."

The air went silent, then crackled at the edges. Her father looked right at her.

"That's because you are *not* good enough and you are *not* smart enough!" he said.

Rose's first thought was "Oh wow. That's the sense I've always gotten from my parents." Here she was, an Olympian who's inspired athletes the world over, who has survived cancer, and who has given generously of her time and talent to help other aspiring athletes and cancer patients, and her father thought she wasn't . . . well . . . good enough.

In a way, his words were a vindication: Rose had always intuited his opinion—and tried to convince herself it wasn't true. Sure, she thought, maybe her parents and siblings weren't into the sport she'd chosen, but really, on some level, they must have admired her accomplishments.

"And now he finally verbalized how they really felt." In that moment, Rose realized she wasn't now, nor had she ever been, the daughter her father wanted, and this kicked up a tremendous amount of shame for Rose. "Shame about my lack of success, financial success, because my father made me feel like I should have been able to do this by myself by now."

At the moment her father erupted in a rage, Rose realized that she didn't feel safe or happy in her parents' company. "It didn't make me want to *not* take his money. In fact, it kind of made me want to take his money even more. Like, give me the money *and* I'm never going to talk to you again."

He did write a check and she took it. After several mutually silent months, she did speak to him again. But the damage to their relationship has still not been resolved and their interactions remain frosty. "I wish this hadn't happened to me, but it did. I wish I were somebody who didn't react this way. It was horrible." She shakes her head then buries her face in her hands. "So then I was angry and hurt—I mean *really* angry and *really* hurt." She looks up at the Gals, her face displaying the pain. "And in the process of shopping for a house. At that point, I was just determined I was going to do it."

Part of her father lives for decorating, Rose tells the Gals, going to his kids' houses, decorating, buying them furniture, rugs, and stuff. "Part of my anger and hurt over the whole thing has manifested in not letting him do that for me. I don't invite him over. I don't talk to him about the house. I didn't talk to him about any part of the process of buying it. Basically, I just took his money and went and did the rest of it on my own."

Whenever Rose has had her family over to her place (which is almost never and only at their insistence), the shame comes flooding back. Her father doesn't seem to think much of the house she bought. He hasn't voiced that thought directly, but she can tell. It's not the kind of neighborhood she'd been raised to admire, not the kind of neighborhood that would do her folks proud. But it's home to her. Her family has trouble embracing her housing choice just as they've always had trouble embracing many of her life choices. She is who she is. Yet that person doesn't seem to please her family.

Who would have thought that buying a house could unearth such subterranean and heartrending family emotions? Yet, we found that time and again: Buying a house is more than a simple transaction, even for the Tao Gals who didn't ask family members for help. It brings up questions of worthiness—are we good enough yet for our parents to approve of us and our lives? No one seemed to escape this issue.

Even if Rose decides to fix the relationship with her father—which she still isn't sure she wants to do—she thinks she still may regret having taken the money. "A lot of this probably wouldn't have happened—well, none of this would have happened—if I hadn't taken the money, if I hadn't asked for it," she says.

"I know my father loves me, and I also knows he's a rageaholic as well as an alcoholic. He still thinks I should have been able to do this on my own. I don't think they're mutually exclusive sentiments."

Rose walked through the anger and pain to buy her house and fix it up, but the emotional ache of coming face to face with how her father saw her was nearly devastating. For the Gals with rocky family relationships, asking for help—or simply not measuring up—can be a painful journey.

BERNADETTE AND THE SCARY LOAN BROKER

After speaking with the real estate agent and digesting Marie's suggestion that I take stock of my financial situation, I make an appointment with a loan broker. I could ask John to talk to the people at his job (he works for a mortgage company), but he's not thrilled with the idea. "Why are you bothering?" he asked me. "It's a terrible time to buy." More important, though, he was hesitant to let his employer know we have a foreclosure on our record. When he'd been hired thirteen years earlier, the company did an extensive background check on him, including a credit report. They may not care that he's since had a foreclosure, but why take the chance?

I'm not quite ready to take this step, I tell the Tao Gals on Tuesday night, but if I do so under the mantle of "research for the book," I can get all my questions answered without having to put myself on the line. We're just talking theoretically, after all. What I would need to consider *if* I wanted to buy a house. Which, of course, I'm desperate to do, but I'm not going to let that cat out of the bag.

Whenever I think about asking the crucial questions— how much of a mortgage might I qualify for, will a lender approve me?—a vise grips my chest. What if no one will lend to me because of my foreclosure? I've heard that it's always possible to get a loan, even with crappy credit, but that you'll pay through the nose in interest for loans that aren't traditional. With house prices being what they are, I can't afford a pricey loan on top of things. I'm certain that I'll be the one person who still won't qualify.

My palms are actually sweating as I dial the number Sylvia gave me. But Shirley is perky! Real upbeat. I tell her I'm thinking of buying this property, rentals and all, and that I have a lot of questions about how the whole thing works, especially with the rental units. She tells me not to worry, she'll go over everything with me, so we arrange a time to meet. She tells me to bring two years of tax returns and the last six months of bank statements.

Before we hang up, I need to tell Shirley about my history. I take a deep breath and say, "Oh, you probably need to know that there's a foreclosure on my record!" I just let the information sink in for a moment. "But it's been six and a half years," I add, "and by the time we're ready to buy, it will be more than seven years and it should be dropped from our record!" I am just as perky as she is!

But Shirley says, "No, no, the rule has been changed; foreclosures now stay on your record for ten years." She can't say when or how exactly the rule has been changed—but she insists that foreclosures take ten years to vanish.

I am speechless. Here, for nearly seven years, I've been shut out of the hottest real estate market in history. I've bided my time, knowing that I would get a second chance—granted, in my forties, but still. How can they change the rules midstream? How is this fair?

Only Marie's advice at a Tao Gals meeting keeps me from

losing my sanity. "I'd double-check her facts if I were you," Marie says. "She may not know what she's talking about."

"Oh." I tuck Marie's advice away before I meet Shirley face-to-face.

SHIRLEY IS A middle-age woman, impeccably dressed. Everything about her seems polished—her hair, the Chanel necklace glinting in the afternoon sun, her pin-striped suit. I'm in a pair of linen capris and a T-shirt—a nice T-shirt, but still, I feel woefully underdressed. Are you supposed to dress like a banker to get a loan?

Shirley pulls out a prequalification worksheet to go through with me. She makes a box in ink around the section titled "Lender Guidelines."

"This is what we need to pay attention to," she says.

There are five items within her box: credit scores, employment, debt-to-income ratio, appraisal, and cash available.

"This"—she circles "credit scores"—"is the most important. You're given a credit score that's calculated by taking the reports of various credit agencies into account. The magic number is 700. If you have a score of 700 or more, you're golden. You could buy a house with no down payment and borrow up to a million dollars without having to verify all your income. That is the number we're looking for."

I write down 700 and wonder how far short I'll fall. When I get home, I decide, I'll go to the Web site of the agency Rose told me about—Equifax—and order a copy of my score, so at least I'll know what it is and will have found out in the privacy of my own home without impeccably dressed Shirley looking at me. Before I can finish this mental plan, though, Shirley asks to see my tax returns.

"The information on the first sheet is what I'll need to run your scores," she tells me.

I gape at her open-mouthed. Now? She wants to get the scores *now*? I fumble with the stack of papers I've brought.

"We'd discussed that on the phone," she reminds me. "That when you were here today, we'd get your scores and see where you stand."

I mumble an assent I don't really feel, but console myself that once this is over, I can walk out of here and never see perfect-looking Shirley again. I give her the first page of the tax return and wait in the stultifying conference room with its lame, wood-looking Formica tabletop while she sends the information to who knows where. I wish I were anywhere on the planet but here.

"It's still printing," she says, coming into the room waving a piece of paper, "but the scores are good." As the details of my credit report spew out of her printer in another room, she puts the paper on the table and circles two numbers in red.

"These are the ones we care about, the FICO scores."

(*FICO*, I will learn later, is an acronym for Fair Isaac Corporation, which constructs credit scores to make it easy for lenders to weigh the risk involved in lending money to a potential borrower. Though there are other companies that offer credit scores, FICO scores are most commonly used in mortgage loan transactions. To come up with a number on you, Fair Isaac crunches numbers from your credit report to determine the chances that you may one day default on your mortgage. A higher score means you are less risky to a lender, and thus, the lender may decide to give you a larger loan or a more favorable interest rate. The opposite, of course, is also true: a low score may mean a higher interest rate and a smaller loan amount, or, being denied a loan altogether.)

"Your husband comes in at 736," she says, showing me the numbers in black and white. "And *you*," she says, winking at me, "are even higher: 811."

I'm stunned. What about the foreclosure? What about the debt I'm still paying off with society?

"When they compute the scores," she tells me, "they take into account how long it's been since that happened, and how well you've paid your debts since then. Being on time is important. Paying things off. Being a good credit risk in all areas."

I'm stunned and tickled, on top of the world. Fair Isaac says I'm OK. Better than OK. *I'm golden!* I can hardly wait until dinnertime, when I'll crow my high score to my husband.

(That evening, when I proudly present him with the proof of my superiority, John will look over the scores and note that the broker circled the wrong number for me. My *real* FICO score, he'll point out, is 739. "Still," I can't help but reply, "it's three points higher than yours!" Amazing the pettiness such a market brings to the fore.)

Shirley hands me the complete credit report, seven pages of detailed data on me and John. Every charge card. Every address. I scan for the black spot. There it is, on the bottom of the third page. *Derogatory Accounts: Foreclosure*. Fair Isaac didn't overlook it and yet still thinks I'm golden. I could kiss him! I decide that Fair Isaac has earned his kindly name and should be designated as the patron saint for lost credit causes.

I'm still in a state of giddy shock, but Shirley gets back to business, filling in the prequalification worksheet. She takes me through the remaining four items. You need to have at least a two-year employment record, she tells me.

"No problem there," I say.

On the next item, the debt-to-income ratio, there are two numbers listed: 33/38. She explains, "The mortgage you want cannot exceed 33 percent of your gross income. Keep in mind that's *gross*," she says, "not net."

I nod, trying to take it all in.

"The second number, 38, is when you take into consideration all your debt—housing, credit cards, student loans, car payments—as a percentage of your total gross income. When it's all put together, you cannot exceed 38 percent."

"I think we're OK there too," I say. I've worked up a sheet detailing my own erratic income, as well as my husband's stable salary. Opposite those numbers, I've listed our debts, including the car that will be paid off in a few months. (*That*, she tells me, won't even count. If there's fewer than ten months to pay on it, the lender won't take it into consideration.) There's my small-ish student loan from graduate school and a paltry balance on a Visa card.

"You could pay that off that credit card if you wanted to, couldn't you?" she asks.

"Yeah."

"Then you're fine, here."

We move on to the appraisal. The house must be worth what it's being sold for and the appraisal must confirm that amount. Fine by me.

Finally, we're at the last item on her lender guidelines list, "cash available." I pull out another sheet where I've figured out what's in our savings account, what John's 401(k) is worth, the value of my SEP-IRA and the kids' college accounts, as well as the unexercised stock options John has with his employer. I knew I'd feel badly about the foreclosure, so I'd pulled together every number I could find. At least, I want to show her, I've been good about saving toward this purchase. She looks over the data.

"I don't need to see anything else," she tell me. "Based on your scores and the cash you have available, I have no doubt you could qualify to buy this property."

"THIS IS WHERE it gets weird," I tell the Tao Gals that night. All along, I thought I'd be tickled pink if I could buy the place we're renting. As soon as Shirley tells me I'm in the clear, I start getting bigger ideas. Maybe I could buy a condo in an area with good schools. Could I buy a real house without the rental hassles and repairs, a place with a backyard? How much of a mortgage would I qualify for, without the rental units' income?

A surge of adrenaline hits me: I have money in the bank, a credit rating that's golden, and the need to do something big. It's intoxicating, being let out of the foreclosure prison. Get out of my way, all you naysayers, I'm ready to buy.

"Say we decide to look in the Montrose neighborhood," I say to Shirley, thinking of the strong schools in that area. "What other options do we have?"

"How much do you want to spend a month?" Shirley asks.

"Two thousand dollars."

Shirley laughs. "You can't buy anything for that," she says, sounding just like the narrator from the cereal commercial: "Silly wabbit, Trix are for kids." Still, she works out scenarios that vary from $1,956 a month up to $2,500 a month, an amount she continues to tell me we can afford. Depending on what we want to pay, she says we could buy up to a half-million-dollar home. I don't quite believe her.

"Besides," she points out, "look at the tax savings." She reviews our tax returns again. "John's withholdings last year were more than $4,000 and you paid additional taxes on top of that. You'd have to check with your accountant, but I bet you'd get to keep a lot of that with a mortgage to deduct."

The adrenaline gives out as I think about those hefty monthly payments—in some cases, twice what we're paying for rent.

I tell the Tao Gals how, ever since the meeting, I've been calculating all the numbers Shirley didn't count. The parochial school tuition. The private music lessons for three kids. The math tutor. "Sure, if I wanted to give all that up, I could afford a $500,000 house," I tell the Gals. "But do I want to give it up?"

Again, Marie is the voice of reason. "This is all good news. Quit being such an Eeyore! And if you move to Montrose," she goes on, "you won't have to pay for parochial school. If you've saved up that much money for a down payment over the last few years, you're obviously earning more than you need to live on. Add in the savings you'll get in income taxes, and you may be fine. Check with your accountant," Marie advises. "And if the numbers add up, get looking."

The next morning, I call my tax preparer. Will the tax savings be as significant as the mortgage broker claimed?

"It depends on your income level," she says. Typically a person will save about 20 percent on her income tax when she buys a house. "You already receive a $9,000 deduction as a married couple. You'd get to write off about $20,000 worth of interest as well as property taxes, of, let's say, $5,000." I can hear her punching keys on a calculator in the background.

In all, she tells me, John and I would save about $5,000 a year in income taxes. Yes, we'd still have to pay about the same amount—or more—in property taxes, but it would be a good deal. And if we decided to buy the property we're living in, with rental units and all, there would be even more tax advantages for us.

While I'm at it, I also look into the foreclosure information Shirley gave me and learn that Marie is right there too. The rule, as best as I can tell, remains at seven years, though Shirley keeps insisting it's ten years. I learn immediately not to trust everything a loan broker tells me—and to listen to Marie.

Shirley was very helpful—and perky, but I decide to look for a loan broker I can trust. Not one who gives me the wrong information, and then insists she's right.

AND A WOMAN'S OPINION . . .

Before I'm ready to move forward, I want more advice. I call Christine, a financial adviser whose son is in my son's seventh grade class. When you're in the flow of the Tao, I remind myself, the answers will come if you open yourself up to them.

Unlike Thom, my real estate friend, Christine doesn't see home ownership as the holy grail. Sure, it's a good thing if you can do it, but women especially need to be aware of what they're getting themselves into.

"Women generally have a much stronger emotional attachment to their house than men do," Christine tells me. "And that attachment can play out into financial areas in ways that are not always to the woman's benefit." As an example, she brings up the case of divorce. Often, when a couple splits up, particularly if there are children involved, the woman's priority will be to keep the family house no matter what. And that, she says, is often the worst financial decision possible.

"All assets are then tied up in this thing that costs money

every month just to keep it. Sure, a house may appreciate, but you cannot get at that money that quickly." Many who have made this decision end up being house-rich but cash-poor, a situation that can be incredibly uncomfortable.

As a general rule, Christine says that you should plan on having your mortgage paid off by the time you hit retirement. "That's a rule of thumb, unless you're loaded with money, which most people aren't."

Whether or not real estate is a good investment for a woman, Christine says, depends on the woman and her circumstances. Many people may think of buying a house as a way to get a great tax deduction. And yes, compared to renting, which isn't tax-deductible, home ownership offers a significant tax savings. But you're also taking on a larger obligation. "In the long run, for most people, it is wise to buy their home. Keep in mind that while you have the mortgage deduction, you usually end up putting more out—more than if you were renting—because you have taxes, maintenance, insurance, all kinds of other things that people don't always calculate," Christine says.

Another factor to consider—especially if you're a single woman who's not very handy, or you're part of a couple who're not into home-improvement details—is that if something breaks, you have to fix it. "If you don't know how to fix it, you have to pay to have someone fix it. We're in a generation right now where we grew up with our dads doing a lot of the stuff, so we didn't generally learn how to fix and repair a lot of things," Christine tells me. For people who want to take on the added expense of the mortgage, insurance, etc., as well as the repair burden of a house, that's fine. "But it's not right for everybody."

The whole key with finances, Christine tells me, is to have

things structured so you're not waking up in the middle of the night, worried. If everyone around you is telling you, "you have to buy a home, you have to buy a home, you have to buy a home," and if home ownership is not right for you, then don't listen to them. We're taught about the American dream and how everything is tied up with home ownership. In some cases, it might be best to move those ideas aside. While it's generally better to own your home, you have to be careful how you go about it.

"If it's stretching you more than you're comfortable to make your monthly payment, then you're buying too much house. Don't kill yourself for it. Now, there's a difference between 'it's a stretch at first' versus 'it's a *real* stretch.'" The debt a household carries, she reminds me, has a powerful effect on how everyone in the household lives.

"Get out of debt first, before buying a home. One of the things lenders will look at when you purchase a home is your ratio of debt to income, even during the whole process. A lot of lenders will check when you initially apply and they'll check again a few weeks later when you're ready to close. If, in the meantime, you got this house thing going on and you went out and charged up a bedroom set—whoa—it's different now. You might not qualify."

Women, particularly younger women, sometimes have the Prince Charming idea in the back of their minds, Christine says. They run up their credit cards. "'I'll have great clothes and I'll have a great lifestyle and when I get married, then I'll be responsible.' Well, news flash: It's time for everyone to be responsible now."

If you can't afford the house you want, buy smaller. "Adjust back down. Think of how our grandparents did it. They bought something smaller and then they moved up. Just because all your friends have a bigger something or better something, doesn't mean you have to. They're paying their bills, you're paying your bills. You need to do what's right for you."

And with today's hot market? Is it a good time to buy?

"There's a certain amount of logic and illogic that goes along with real estate, just like the stock market. Look at the tech crash a few years ago: People were thinking, 'Oh, it's going up, I have to get some now, I have to get some now!'" Christine equates that thinking to a more prosaic commodity—shoes. If Nordstrom has a sale on shoes, would you say to yourself, "I'm not going to buy those shoes now because the price is low"? And then, later, "Oh look, they're raising the price: I have to buy them now!" Christine laughs. "When you put it into something tangible like that, you think, well, that's nuts. 'I'm going to buy the shoes tomorrow because they're going to be up 10 percent!'"

The market, Christine believes, is ripe for a correction. "What's happened over the last couple years is that, as prices kept going up, many times over, faster than wages, we also saw all these new mortgage programs come out—no money down, 3 percent interest, interest only." For a few people, these programs make sense, but for most people, they don't. The basics of home ownership are kind of boring: You get a mortgage. You try to get a fixed rate because we don't know what interest rates are going to do in the future. With all these new mortgage programs, she thinks many may be headed for the rocky shores of foreclosure as interest rates rise and people find they can't pay what they owe.

Say you got into a house that was really kind of a stretch, but you were able to afford it with an adjustable-rate mortgage. You bought with 3 percent down, so you pretty much owe what the house is worth. As interest rates go up, your mortgage payment per month may go up by, say, $300. Maybe you can do it, maybe you can't.

But then, what if someone loses a job? In many places, they'll find another job. But it may not pay as much. Let's say it pays $20,000 less a year. Then how do you do it?

Whatever goes up, she tells me, will come down. "People say real estate is always a good investment, that real estate always goes up. Well, those of us who lived through the downturn know better." (Christine sold her house on the beach a few years ago after owing more than it was worth for nearly a decade. Now she's waiting for the market to regain its sanity before she buys again.) If you look at the market over a fifty-year time period, a seventy-five-year time period, it *does* always goes up. "But there are those years in between where it doesn't and you need to have a way to make it through those years."

I digest all this information and call the financial institution that holds our savings accounts. Forget Shirley. If I can qualify with our financial institution, a very upstanding firm, I'll be able to qualify for a loan with just about anyone. When I find the right property, *then* I can select the exact lender, but this will let me know where I stand. I give the young man on the phone all the data he requests—account numbers, social security numbers, etc.—and wait, listening to Muzak, while he runs a credit report on John and me and crunches the numbers. Within five minutes, he's able to provide me with a mortgage amount that will allow me to buy a $500,000 home. If there are rental units too, I can go quite a bit higher. The preapproval letter, stating that my accounts and credit records have been checked and approved, will be faxed to me this afternoon. Maybe I can buy this house, after all.

Tao Worksheet

1. Write about your relationship with money. How does it make you feel? How do you respond to a lack of money? How comfortable are you sticking with a budget?

2. Banks and lenders can be seen as authority figures. They have the power to say yes or no to your dream. Write about how you interact with authority figures. What do you need to know about yourself to walk through the prequalification process with ease?

3. Borrowing from family can be a dicey thing. Write about the support you might like to receive from family members. Is this a reasonable expectation? How can you go about asking for this help while staying detached? That way, whether they say yes or no, you won't be crushed.

4. No one has a crystal ball that will tell what the real estate market will do. What if you buy a house tomorrow and its value goes down next month. Can you get comfortable with that? What if it takes years before you can recoup your investment: what do you need to do to be ready, just in case?

5. Buying a house is not a risk-free proposition. Consider all the other areas of life that are rife with risk: your health, the possibility of an accident, the ordeal of raising children, your job security. Think about how you live every day with these areas of potential insecurity.

6. How can you apply this to your real estate dealings?

CHAPTER SIX

SEEK AND YE SHALL FIND

True perfection seems imperfect,
yet it is perfectly itself.
True fullness seems empty,
yet it is fully present.

MICHELLE, ON LOOKING

B ERNADETTE CALLS ME on the phone. "I think I'm going to buy a house!" she announces. "*This* house!"

"Really?" I say. "Maybe you want to look around as well."

"Maybe, but you know, we could break through the back wall and give the kids more room, and rent the other units and pay our mortgage that way!," she says.

The more excited she gets, the more my heart sinks. She's in love. She's in love with her current residence. And the best advice I received when house hunting was this: Don't fall in love with a house.

I myself fell in love with a house once, a house that I didn't even really like—just like I've fallen in love with a man or two against my better judgment.

This was not even a house I was looking to buy. It was a rental house. I saw it and decided its fenced yard and two bedrooms would work well for me. In a matter of days, I became desperate, obsessed, a different person because of that house.

My life stopped. I was consumed with waiting to hear if I could rent it. After a few wan efforts, I stopped looking at other properties. Almost overnight, I'd become a jittery, excited, anxious stir-fry of nerves. For a week that felt like a year, I was beside myself.

It was exactly like falling in love with a bad boyfriend. Will he call? Does he like me? Am I in? What can I do to influence events?

An acquaintance had told me about the house, a private little cottage set far back from the street. A fenced yard for the dog—and no objections from the landlord to my having one, either. The landlord even said he'd make a $50 reduction in the rent since I was a single person, not a family. "Okay, I'll take it," I said.

"I'm not done fixing it up," he said. "A couple of other people have looked at it too. But I'll get back to you in a few days."

I waited by the phone for a number of days, a week. Then, I made the phone call. "I am sincerely interested," I said.

But he still hadn't decided on whom to rent it to, me or somebody else. "I'll get back to you in a few days," he said. He did not sound very enthusiastic.

What was the matter with me? I had good references! I wasn't a late rent payer! My dog was little! Why couldn't I make the cut?

I couldn't think of anything else but the little house. My life was in suspense. Never mind that I didn't have to move. Never mind that I was under no time pressure to leave my present digs Suddenly, my entire well-being hung on a house I didn't even know existed until two weeks ago.

See? Just like falling in love, in the worst way.

When the landlord finally called to say he'd rent to me, all those big feelings departed as suddenly as they'd arrived. Quickly, I found I had to talk myself into renting the place, given its bleak neighborhood, the absence of any beauty, interior or exterior, the slapdash repairs and paint job. Once it was mine, I had second thoughts. But I said yes.

Reader, I moved into that house.

When I was house hunting to buy, I didn't want to fall in love like that again. How could I stop myself before I did? I wondered. What had triggered that fever of irrationality and obsession?

Obsession comes with trying to control the uncontrollable. In the case of the rental, my obsession was triggered by the landlord's indifference. I'd showed him my blemish-free credit, my glowing references, the balance in my checking and savings accounts, and made general professions of sincerity, but he remained curiously unmoved. (Much later, he admitted that he wasn't keen to rent to a writer. The previous tenant had been a writer who had lost his job, then his marriage, and finally hadn't paid rent for six months, ignoring eviction notices and refusing to answer the phone or the door.)

In my younger years, I was always a patsy for the guy who didn't care enough. Rather than dumping the creep to look for the guy who did care enough, I devoted myself to trying to get the creep to care more. This landlord's indifference set off that familiar reaction. Rather than push on to find a more-welcoming and eager landlord, I dug in with Mr. Indifferent.

I vowed, then, to be wary of any huge upsurge of that ole, desperate, lovin'-you feeling.

Also, when I settled my affections on that one little rental,

I'd spent exactly one day looking at apartments. One day! One day, and I was a goner. One day, and I was obsessed with the first real possibility to come along.

This time, I vowed, I was going to look a lot longer, at least long enough to give myself options.

When I fell in love with the rental, my sudden, desperate yearning was also fueled by unacknowledged insecurities and other dim, shadowy feelings. I was moving to a more centrally located city neighborhood, which, however modest, nevertheless was a more expensive area than my present home. Part of me whispered that I didn't deserve it. Part of me heckled that I was biting off more than I could chew. Thus, when I found that little rental house, I was afraid the landlord would somehow see through me, see that I wasn't good enough, reliable enough, and otherwise undeserving of the place. I was putting far too much emotional baggage on a financial transaction.

I vowed to try to remain at least semiconscious during my house hunt, and not let myself be crushed by ongoing lifelong virulent neuroses.

Another error I made in letting that rental become the sole object of my focus, was to act out of low expectations. Because I had such low hopes, I didn't believe another such rental existed, anywhere.

I vowed not to encourage my usual sense of deprivation, that for once, even in a tight housing market, there would be multiple solutions to my housing problem. I wanted options, this time, a variety of future dwellings. I would try on houses the way I sometimes tried on a variety of clothes—to see the multiple possibilities.

"Well, Bernadette," I tell her, "when I set out to find my house, I had one rule. No falling in love with a house."

Secondly, I tell Bernadette, I tried hard to be conscious of all the queasy neurotic feelings that came up while looking—the feeling that I couldn't have a home, couldn't afford one, that my money for some reason wasn't as good as somebody else's, my freelance income not as substantial as a full-timer's.

When I did get it bad for a particular house, I appealed to the Tao for its wisdom about letting go. Do your work, then step back. To me, that meant show up at the open house, keep any appointments, fill out loan applications, make an offer, do whatever footwork I needed to do, then move on, keep looking, and let go of the results.

Because, to tell the truth, as all-consuming and powerful as house love can be, I neither like it nor trust it. Falling in love with a house may be a signal that "this is it, this is the house I need to live in." More likely, it's an alluring property that sets off all my half-conscious hopes and dreams and projections and anxieties. That's not to say hopes and dreams and anxieties shouldn't get stirred up during the house hunting process—they will. But having them swallow you up is pure misery, and unnecessary if you can manage to keep your head.

I tell Bernadette about a friend who has been hunting for a dream house for the three years I've known her. She has fallen truly, madly, deeply in love with two properties, both of which "got away." One property obsessed her and occupied all her thoughts for two months while the owners irresponsibly and unfairly equivocated over offers. "All her love, all her devotion, all those hours of circular obsessive thinking did not get her the house, Bernadette," I say sternly. "It just made her miserable!"

It's foolish to fall in love when multiple bids are in play, foolish to let love make you pay far more than a house is worth (a little more is fine). Still, the heart has to be consulted, just as neuroses must be frankly examined, hopes and dreams must be aired and well known—lest all these different elements of ourselves make themselves known by ferociously attaching you to an unworthy object, or even a worthy one.

Of course, it's hard to keep the heart open and unattached when the market has been so insane, unpredictable, and uncontrollable in the past few years. The market is like a hundred bad boyfriends, triggering all our issues of deprivation, just desserts, ambition, security, and insecurity. I've seen intelligent, educated people frantic, crazy-obsessed, and sobbing over *dumps*! It's tricky enough to keep your head in a wild housing market, but it's imperative to keep hold of your passions, because they can make a stressful-enough procedure into a living hell.

To paraphrase what a friend's mother used to say about men. Don't worry honey. Houses are like trolleys. Miss one and another will come along soon.

Patience. And detachment.

Do your work, then let go.

What Do You Need/Want in a Neighborhood?

What kind of neighborhood do you want to live in: suburban, urban, exurban?

How many bedrooms do you need?

Is a garage an absolute necessity?

What is the commuting distance between the neighborhoods you're considering and your work? Is there public transportation? What would a typical rush-hour commute be like?

If you are a parent, are you planning on using public schools? If so, which neighborhood gives you access to the school(s) you like?

Is it important to you to have recreation options nearby? Parks?

What about arts options? Do you need/want a neighborhood with theaters, music venues, museums, libraries?

Have you looked into crime rates in the neighborhoods you are interested in? Are you willing to move into a less-desirable neighborhood in order to afford a bigger or nicer home?

Does age and ethnic diversity appeal to you? How do your proposed neighborhoods stack up on that?

If you have kids, is the neighborhood kid-friendly?

Do you need/want to have services like grocery stores, hospitals, shopping malls, etc. nearby?

Do you need/want to live close to family?

BERNADETTE: YES, BUT

I had gone looking before! I'm not just fixated on buying my own rental home. Last summer, Gayle from the Tao group offered an idea that might perk me up out of my real-estate–focused depression. "There are these homes," she told me, "owned by the California Department of Transportation. They're cool, older homes; some are Craftsman. From what I hear, Caltrans has its hands full with the homes and may be willing to sell. It would be a good place to go look."

Gayle sent me *LA Times* articles about the properties to read. It seems that in the 1950s, Caltrans bought dozens of homes spanning from Alhambra to Pasadena to make way for an extension of the 710 Long Beach freeway. "At the time they were purchased," a *Times* reporter wrote in one of the articles, "construction of the extension seemed imminent. But since then, lawsuits, lobbying and legislation by some of the cities that would be affected by the freeway have managed to block its completion. Caltrans, as a result, has spent the last 30 years as a reluctant landlord to homes in Pasadena, South Pasadena and El Sereno."

Caltrans owns some 600 homes in the area and the prospect that the freeway extension will ever be built is all but dead. Many of the homes, in fact, are vacant.

"Let's just go have a look," Gayle suggested. "Who knows? Caltrans may decide to get rid of them in a rush and it could be the break you're waiting for."

I was skeptical, but Gayle knew I had a weakness for Craftsman homes and love that part of the city. When you're utterly without hope, any spark looks good.

We met on a cool Friday morning and drove to an area where a number of the homes are located—along a stretch of Pasadena Avenue, right where the 110 freeway ceases to exist, spilling over onto a broad avenue that takes its place. To the right, there's a park with huge old-growth trees and earth-toned play equipment. The park was small, but well maintained and added a welcoming mood; there's a family feel to the area. "I could live here" was the thought that kept running through my head. "I would *like* to live here."

All along the left side of the street, homes taken straight out of my dreamscape lined the road. Wooden homes with big front porches, Craftsman detail, largish front lawns. Surely, it's too good to be true. I was afraid to believe, lest I be disappointed. I looked for the flaws.

"It's a really busy street," I pointed out, but Gayle gestured to the little side streets flanking Pasadena Avenue. "There are Caltrans homes on those little streets too. Just wait." We parked and got out to explore.

You could tell the vacant Caltrans houses by the faded flyers taped to doors and windows, warning off trespassers. One or two of the homes had For Rent signs posted, but the signs were so unobtrusive as to be nearly invisible. You had to know what you're looking for, it seemed, to find these places.

But find them, we did. Scores of homes. More than I could have imagined. According to a *Times* article, some forty-five homes were vacant along the proposed freeway route. Some were small and hideous and unkempt—post–WWII, flat-roofed, ugly things with dirty windows on the busiest of streets, front lawns landscaped in what looked to be hay, and rotted-out window frames. But more often, we found charming houses a bit down at their heels, but with fabulous potential. Some were Craftsman, one or two story, with wood-shingled, angled roofs. Some were Spanish-style stucco with tile roofs. Still others were would-be mansions awaiting a Prince Charming owner who would love them and see their diamond-in-the-rough qualities.

"I will love you," I called out to the mute homes. "I will fix you up."

My mind ran with possibilities. If Caltrans had this many homes, surely it would make a few deals to unload them. Most were in disrepair. I'd read that many of the homes had been a source of controversy for Caltrans. The houses that hadn't been rehabbed were eyesores about which the homeowners in the area regularly complained. And those that had been re-habbed had only brought ridicule upon the agency. "A mid-1990s rehab of 39 of the 92 historic homes nearly exhausted the $19.4 million Caltrans received for renovating them, according to a state audit. And many residents of the rehabbed homes have complained, both privately and in public forums, about faulty work and ongoing, unresolved maintenance issues," said the *LA Times*.

We stumbled upon one huge house that was open as workers stripped plaster from the dining room walls and repainted the living room.

"Can we have a look around?" we asked.

The workers nodded us in.

Gayle and I, both priced out of the market, felt like we were sneaking into the palace garden, gaining surreptitious access to a place—a thing, a dream—that had been denied us.

The house was massive, straight out of a 1920s Hollywood set. A red-tiled entryway led to a fabulous spiral staircase, down which I pictured ladies in organdy dresses descending. Upstairs, there were more bedrooms than I could count. "Let's buy this place," Gayle said, "and all the Tao Gals can live here." The house could easily have accommodated all of us and our respective broods.

"Is this *another* bedroom?" I asked Gayle, opening still another door as we wandered through the labyrinthine upstairs.

"I think it's a closet," she said, though it's bigger than my daughter's bedroom.

Downstairs was equally stunning. There were two full kitchens, both lined with mahogany cabinets and some kind of marble countertops. From off the large living room with its gigantic fireplace—I could have walked inside the fireplace hardly bending my head—arched French doors led to a courtyard with a desiccated fountain. "Imagine the parties you could have," I said.

Yet both Gayle and I knew the house was far out of our price range, even if we were to go into it together. But something happened inside of us. We, who had felt utterly disenfranchised from home-buying prospects when the day began, were now having fun, dreaming of what might be possible. Given the right set of circumstances, who knows . . .

We left the mansion and continued exploring the neighborhood. There was one house that seemed just about right. It sat on the corner of busy Pasadena Avenue and equally busy Columbia, a route used by many commuters since the freeway extension was never completed. The house was quite modest and thus, we figured, couldn't be too terribly expensive. Workers were toiling there too, and they let us in to walk around. There were three small bedrooms. A basic living and dining room. One bathroom. A tiny, token backyard. Nothing to be overly excited about, except the prospect that the American dream might still be alive. In spite of all the talk about unaffordable real estate, maybe this house would do it. I could live here.

The house was blue with white shutters, the paint faded and peeling. Like all these Caltrans houses, it needed some TLC. Since the workers were actively doing something to it, I figured, it might be available for rent soon.

From what I had heard, talking to people who have rented other Caltrans houses in the area and those employees working for Caltrans itself, if and when the homes came up for sale, those people who'd been renting them would have the first option to buy. Renting this house and hoping to one day buy it might be our chance, I thought.

For once, I was excited about the possibilities. When I got home, I called Caltrans and asked about the homes: Was there some way I could buy one of the not-yet-rehabbed homes and fix it up myself? Could I take one of them off its hands?

"No," the woman who answered the phone told me, "but

you can look at our list of what's for rent and try to position yourself that way."

I asked to speak to her supervisor, anyone with pull. The answer remained the same.

"No, you can't buy the house."

"No, you can't rent the ones we're not ready to rent."

"I don't care how many are vacant: No. Look at the list: That's what you can rent."

Out of the reported forty-five homes that were vacant, maybe eight showed up on the list at any given moment, all with high rents. These were not meant to be affordable housing, the Caltrans Web site points out, and anyone wishing to rent must document earnings at least four times the rental cost. Those income requirements were even more stringent than what's required to qualify for a mortgage. I called and called and waited and waited and months later, after looking at the situation from just about every angle, I finally gave up.

It's been a year and a half since Gayle and I went through those homes. I can't drive down Pasadena Avenue without wishing I might someday be allowed to live there. I know Michelle's right when she counsels me not to fall in love with a house, and I haven't. But I have fallen in love with a neighborhood, one that won't have me. The inventory of houses available in that neighborhood is pretty much nonexistent and as long as Caltrans holds on to those homes it owns, not much is likely to change.

The big house we'd seen being replastered, the one with the fabulous red-tile entry? I image great celebrity-studded parties happening there. But they're not. The house is still vacant. I've never even seen it on the For Rent list. My little blue one with white shutters? Also vacant. Just about every house we'd seen that day remains vacant a year and a half later. Only a handful at a time show up on the Caltrans For Rent Web site.

"For people who have that kind of money," Gayle commented about the income requirements, "they might as well buy, especially with equity building so fast." So the houses remain vacant. And the little spark of hope that flared that day in Gayle and me gets buried again.

It all seems so unfair sometimes, and yet I feel like a crybaby when I dwell on it. I drive through the neighborhood by my kids' school; I'd happily live there. But in the past three years, the prices have doubled. Back when the home prices were more affordable, I didn't have the down payment. Now that I have the down payment, it's priced far beyond my reach.

And beyond most people's reach, I have to remind myself. According to the California Association of Realtors, the median price of a home in Los Angeles County in May 2005 was $459,000—and that amount, believe me, is not going to buy you much if you want a good school district. The minimum income needed to purchase such a property is more than $100,000. Only 17 percent of the population has that income, thus, the remaining 83 percent of us can only stand at the candy store window and look in.

BERNADETTE MEETS HER GURU AGAIN

After talking to Michelle, I meet Thom again, the real estate guru, for breakfast at a local deli. He's offered to come look at my rental house and see if it is a good investment—or an irrational whim I should just get over. Walking back to the house, still a block away, I point it out.

"The white one, there, on the right corner."

"Needs a new roof," he says, and my heart lurches.

I don't know how he can tell that from this distance, but he's right. I've known for some time it'll need a new roof. We get closer and walk the perimeter of the property. There's no question it's a neat neighborhood—a bit funky, but nice enough. Schools are not great, however. Thom looks around, calculating.

"That back area is probably not permitted," he points to the unit the owners live in, the back quadrant of the house. "Are there cooking facilities back there? It may not be legal. You could use that in negotiations, see if you can get the price lower."

We walk up the front steps. "The porch needs to be replaced. The wood is rotten."

Casing the house, Thom agrees that the place has great character. "Still, it's a white elephant," he says. "Lovely, but it's going to take a lot of work."

The electrical wiring is ancient. If you run the microwave at the same time you make toast, you'll blow a fuse. The plumbing, all original, is feeble. A well-used plunger sits next to the toilet.

Before making an offer on it, he counsels me to get an inspection. "You could probably use the results of the inspection to negotiate a lower price."

In the meantime, he tells me, don't wait around for the owners to be ready to sell. "Don't be myopic. Get out there and see what else is available. You can only see what's happening— really happening—in the real estate market by driving the neighborhoods, checking out the listings, seeing what's there."

He gives me a plan of attack for the day: Go to Realtor.com. Find some interesting listings. Drive the neighborhoods. See for myself.

First I look online for South Pasadena, where Gayle lives. Schools there are great. We could save on private school tuition if we moved there and then could possibly spend close to the top of our budget on a house. The commute for my high schooler, Jarrod, would be a cinch. If I could find a nice townhome there (I know a house is out of the question), one with some character, three bedrooms, and maybe hardwood floors, that might be a good compromise. I search at Realtor.com. The only things showing up in my price range in South Pasadena are empty lots. There isn't a single townhome for sale in that city for half a million or less. This is going to be harder than I thought.

OK, I'll be flexible. I'll regroup. South Pas is out. If I want to buy the most property, I need to spend near my limit. To do that, I need to be in an area with good schools. The La Crescenta–Montrose area, where my younger kids currently attend parochial school, is the next choice. The community's OK. Very white-bread and removed from city life. Not that much for kids to do locally. Still, Crescenta Valley High School rates very well. It has a good music department and great sports—important considerations for my seventh grader. I go back to Realtor.com and make a list of properties found there. Though there are a number of condos in my price range, a house-house would be my preference. When I find four that I might be able to afford, I begin to feel hopeful. The good news from the mortgage broker has emboldened me. Why not a real house in an area with good schools? Who says it can't be done?

By the time I get back from looking, though, I say it can't be done. I'm utterly bereft. The first house I passed was a tiny, tiny box on a busy corner. Ugly. I didn't even stop to look closer—there's no way we'd fit in it. Next I found a house that might be doable, though I felt skeptical. It was boxy, stucco, in need of a good deal of repair. Why would I change the problems of the house I'm currently living in, I wondered, for these myriad unknown problems and pay twice as much?

Then there was a kind-of cute house on a peaceful street. The other houses around it were nice enough. The yard was overgrown and the place needed a facelift. Then I noticed that there was no For Sale sign on the front. It must have sold or has been taken off the market. When I got back and checked with Sylvia, my hunch was confirmed. I was too late.

I visited the final house on my list and wanted to cry. The front yard looked down upon the 210 freeway, humming with afternoon traffic. I suppose I could live with that. From the outside, it was clear that the house was a fixer-upper, but there was some charm potential, I told myself. It looked like it might be big enough, about 1,200 square feet. I snapped a few photos and thought it over. I could hire a contractor or two to help clean it up. It might work. I was about to drive away when two men in their twenties pulled up and got out of their cars.

"Are you a Realtor?" they asked me.

"No. I was just looking."

The house was going to be auctioned off, they explained. One of the young men was interested in buying it and had brought along his buddy for advice. The potential buyer walked to the front door. "It's open, you know," he gestured for me to follow. "But it's going to need a lot of work."

We entered the house and it was far worse than I could have dreamed. Windows were rotted out of their frames. Plaster was peeling in giant sheets from the ceiling and walls. We walked through the property with our T-shirts covering our noses and mouths against the stench and dust. The walls were stained brown from leakage. The potential buyer's buddy pointed to proof of termites.

He must have been a contractor, the buddy, because he began to list all that would need to be done to make the place habitable. Walls torn down. Even supporting beams might need to be replaced. All new plumbing. All new electricity. Just replacing the windows alone, he told his friend, would cost $50,000 to $60,000. He shook his head. "You're looking at $150K to $200K in repairs alone."

That's on top of the $439,000 asking price. His words of warning were my cue to say good-bye. I was not cut out for this kind of thing.

"Are you going to bid on it?" the potential buyer asked me as I ducked out the door.

"No," I told him. "This is more than I can do."

I drove home emotionally stunned. For the first time in years, I'd allowed myself to think I might be able to buy after all. This experience, though, had knocked the wind out of me.

The rest of the day passed in an anesthetized haze. Why did I have all this cash in the bank, I wondered? Just think of the trips I might have taken. All the times I'd scrimped when I could have indulged. And for what?

OF COURSE, I immediately tell the Tao group about my latest real estate incursion and the defeat I'm feeling.

"And this was what," Marie asks me, "your first day looking? And you didn't even go with someone?"

"Yeah."

Colleen tells me about Dorothy, the Realtor who sold her her house. "She knows what's coming on the market. She'll help you find what you need. Just because you didn't find it doesn't mean it isn't out there." Colleen writes down Dorothy's information.

I feel guilty taking the number, thinking of Sylvia. But then again, I'm pretty sure I'm never going to speak to another real estate agent as long as I live.

"This is the one area in life where experience really pays," Colleen tells me. "You have to go with someone who knows the market." Colleen recaps her experience of looking for homes with her first realtor, who was a friend. "If I'd stuck with her, I never would have bought. I felt as dejected as you do, as if it would never work out. It's amazing the difference a good, experienced Realtor will make."

"I'll take the number," I say, "but clearly, this isn't the right time to buy."

"And you're deciding that based on one outing?" Marie is incredulous. "This is the time to take contrary action," she counsels. "Even though it feels like the wrong thing to do, call Colleen's agent, or let your own agent take you out. Find out what's really there before you decide it can't be done."

When I get home, I tell John about the day I've had.

"I thought we'd decided to wait the market out a bit more," he says, confused by my sudden interest in buying, and my equally sudden complete misery.

"After the credit report boon, and learning that we might be able to buy this house," I tell him, "I got my hopes up. And now . . ." I start to cry.

I've surmounted what I thought was the impossible—the foreclosure on my record—only to realize there are still many more impossible boulders littering the path. This feels like just too much work. Maybe I'll stay here and rent forever.

LOOKING FOR A house is never a fun thing, unless you've got oodles of cash and live in an area where housing is affordable. For many of us, the process brings with it shame and despondency. How is it our friends can afford a nice place, and even if we pull together every dime we've ever had, we can only afford a dump? And when prices are soaring and the pressure's on to make a quick decision before everything is out of reach, the process can be downright hideous. None of the people we interviewed said they'd liked the experience, but it must be gotten through to get to the other side. Just buckle your seat belt, they say. Flow with the Tao and trust that the right place will show up when the timing's right. Our job is to prepare ourselves to recognize opportunity when it appears.

Tao Worksheet

Think about your own home-searching process. Can you make a simple list? What's your criteria? How can you leave your heart open to opportunity and yet not fall in love?

1. Would you rather live as well as you can and not save, or live more modestly and save? Write about these two issues and how you feel about them. Your choices will become clearer if you're candid about what's important to you.

2. Write about the lifestyle options you feel you need to hold on to, and which you can let go of. Are you willing to move to a less-than-desirable neighborhood if you'll get a decent return on your money? Or would you rather earn less on the investment and live the way you want to live? Write about these priorities in your life.

3. How do you feel about the choices between townhomes, apartments, condominiums, and houses? Write about all forms of housing and how you might fit into them.

4. Remember what Sylvia said: No one buys their dream house the first time around. What can you settle for, knowing you can trade up later? Imagine the ways you might be happy, even if it seems, at first, like settling.

5. Write about the place you imagine yourself living. It won't be perfect, but it could meet your needs and you might be happy there. Can you envision it? Write it out and share this vision with those who support you.

6. Make a time line of how long you'll look. Don't pressure yourself to make a decision prematurely, but don't plan to keep looking until you find the perfect place, because it may never materialize and you'll get sick of the project. Can you allow yourself six months? Three? A year? Give yourself a deadline to make a decision, even if that decision is to decide not to buy now and to reassess your options. Not making a decision is the same thing as making one not to buy.

7. Write about what the process of seeking for real estate does to you emotionally. Do you feel unworthy? A loser? Is that a fair assessment? What are the roots of those feelings?

8. Can you trust that you'll find the right place when the timing is right? Have you seen the trust pay off for other people? What would it take for you to trust that idea?

CHAPTER SEVEN

STORIES OUR REALTORS TELL

When they think that they know the answers,
people are difficult to guide.
When they know that they don't know,
people can find their own way.

WHAT'S THE BEST way to go about buying a house? The worst? The Tao Gals asked around for names of the top Realtors in the area and then met with three of them one by one to gather their pearls of wisdom. What stories, we asked, can you tell us that will shed light on women buying real estate?

James (Jamie) Foreman is a Realtor with Sotheby's International Realty in Los Angeles. He's been working in real estate, both in New York and Los Angeles, for nearly twenty-two years. Many of his clients are big names in the entertainment industry.

THINK ABOUT YOUR SELF-IMAGE. Where and how do you need to live to be the person you think you're meant to be? I'm not sure if the self-image question has more impact for women than men, but it has come up several times with the women clients I've worked with. In many cases, it's surprised me because I would have thought such successful people would be confident and settled on their own self-image. I think it may have surprised the buyers as well.

I worked with one woman, a film director-actor-writer, who was very successful. Her first film had won a prize at Sundance and she was moving to LA. She went out to buy a house and the whole question of self-image became a big deal. She had never thought she'd buy a house on her own—with no husband or family. The prospect of doing so got under her skin. She still lives in the house she bought with me—now with her husband and son. The house is worth three or four times what she paid for it and the experience worked out well, but that self-image thing was a tough hurdle to get over. Who would she be if she bought this house on her own? She had to grapple with that.

There's another instance where self-image played a big role. A friend of my wife, who's a big-name writer in New York, spent several years looking for an apartment. It wasn't her first apartment. She'd had a place in the Village and sold it for a good price. Now she was living in a hotel, trying to find a new place. She lived in that hotel for more than a year as she was looking to buy on the Upper West Side. She'd find very nice apartments, and each time she did, she'd bring her husbands— a progression of exs—to see the apartment. Invariably, one of them would tell her not to buy it. She kept bringing over people who would tell her not to do it.

I knew she couldn't stay in the hotel for the rest of her life. Finally, we found a penthouse on the Upper West Side. It was a beautiful apartment. There were no more reasons she could come up with to not buy the apartment. Still, she didn't buy it.

I told her, "Sit down. First settle on an image of who you

will be in the place you buy, and then pick the apartment." What I didn't know at the time was that she was thinking about becoming a mother. She'd been trying to adopt and didn't know if she'd need an apartment that could accommodate a child or not. Her future lifestyle was completely amorphous. Amazingly, once the child question was settled—she conceived—she was able to make a decision quickly.

WORKING WITH WOMEN IS NO DIFFERENT, I'VE FOUND, THAN WORKING WITH MEN. Women are generally no more or less knowledgeable when it comes to buying real estate. Other than people who continually buy houses, no one's particularly knowledgeable in this field. That's important to remember, and to surround yourself with people who *do* know.

THE BEST THING YOU CAN DO IS KNOW WHAT YOU'RE GETTING INTO WITH THE MARKET. See ten houses, twenty houses, know what's worth what. You'll miss some deals, sure, but you'll have a good idea of the going rate. When you know what it is you want and are certain it has a relative value, move as quickly and clearly as you can. But always, make sure you have someone protecting you, like a good real estate agent.

THE BIGGEST MISTAKE I SEE PEOPLE MAKE IS NOT UNDERSTANDING WHAT COSTS WHAT. Buying a house is not going to happen if you don't understand all the costs involved and are not prepared to go forward.

REMEMBER, THERE ARE PSYCHOLOGICAL ASPECTS TO BUYING AND SELLING A HOME. On that life list you've seen—the one that tells the top-ten stressful experiences?—buying a home and moving is at the top. It's a big stressor. And though I recommend that you stay emotionally detached from the process, it's hard to do. I had a boss in New York who'd worked in real estate for ages. She was buying an apartment for her son and came back exasperated from looking one day. "I am behaving like every insane buyer I've worked with in my entire career!" she lamented. It's hard to stay out of the process emotionally, even for the pros. But it's important to try.

DO WHAT YOU CAN TO LEARN THE MARKET. Make choices and then go after what you want as hard as you can. And remember, if you don't get this one, there will always be another.

Realtor Checklist

Interview and compare at least three real estate agents before going forward. Below are some questions you might want to ask. Be certain you feel comfortable with the person you choose. This is an important relationship in your journey toward home ownership.

Question	Agent A	Agent B	Agent C
What geographic areas do you specialize in?			
Do you work primarily with first-time buyers, or those moving up?			
Typically, what is the price range of the houses you've helped your buyers obtain?			

Question	Agent A	Agent B	Agent C
How long have you been in the business?			
Do you have an assistant, or will I be working solely with you?			
How many homes have you sold this year in the specific area I'm interested in?			
How long have you been with your brokerage?			
Do you require an exclusive agreement to represent buyers?			

Jeanette Costabile is a Realtor with Coldwell Banker. Though she's only been in the business for six years, she's established a huge clientele via word of mouth and has become much more successful than she'd dreamed. She's seen prices rise and rise and rise, and yet has been able to get her buyers into what they need. The Tao Gals asked her about the blunders she's seen first-time home buyers make, as well as the clever strategies she's also witnessed.

THE BIGGEST MISTAKE I SEE FIRST-TIME HOME BUYERS MAKE IS TRYING TO DO THE HOMEWORK ON THEIR OWN. They don't understand that they can get a buyer's agent for free. Ultimately, the seller is going to end up paying the buyer's agent a commission, but sometimes the buyers don't realize that. A lot of first-time buyers will ask me, "For all of this work, what do we owe you?" You don't owe me anything. I'm going to work hard for you, I'm going to negotiate the price of the property for you, and make sure you have all your inspections and disclosures. It's for free. The seller will pay for me. Some people think they'll save money, taking themselves from open house to open house, scrolling through listings on the Internet. Really, they're not saving a dime. That commission will be paid, whether you use a buyer's agent or not. If you don't use the agent, then the listing agent will get the money. You won't save anything.

And while it's true that the house will cost a bit more than if there were no real estate commissions involved, it's the smart way to go. Say you're approached by an owner who is selling without an agent. It could be that the property's been for sale before with a real estate agent and there are some major disclosure issues with it. Now, the seller does not want to disclose those issues to the new buyer. "Let's just open up escrow and you can pay me what I would get minus the commission." That could be a big mistake. Keep in mind that the commissions encompass insurance—a liability insurance in case anything should go wrong with the property. Say you move in and the foundation falls apart. With a real estate brokered deal, you're covered for, I believe, three years.

California really protects its buyers. We have countless disclosures: the Megan's Law disclosure, the mold disclosure, the zone disclosure, which gets into property details like liquefaction, earthquake fault lines. As Realtors in California, we have to give buyers all those disclosures before we can move ahead with a sale. If you do the deal without a Realtor, how will you be sure everything's been disclosed?

ANOTHER NO-NO IS TRUSTING SOMEONE YOU DON'T REALLY KNOW AND HAVEN'T CHECKED OUT TO NEGOTI-ATE A DEAL FOR YOU. I had a couple I was working with. All of a sudden, I received a phone call from the wife. They'd been at dinner and a real estate agent at another table had overheard that they were looking for a property. The agent swooped in on top of them. They went out with the agent that evening and bought a house. They didn't call me. Within a week, the wife was in tears on the phone. The agent had sold them a house right behind a gas station. They hadn't fully noticed it and didn't think much about it at the time they made the offer. But really, you can never take away the fact that it's a gas station, right behind your property! Appreciation is going to be diffi-cult. Being near commercial property is fine, but if it's a gas station, power lines, things that are health issues, it's a differ-ent thing. When you want to sell, you're going to eliminate 50 to 60 percent of the buyers because of that. The couple was not able to get out of the deal and I wasn't able to discuss it with them at that point because I had lost my agency relation-ship with them. It's unethical for one agent to talk to another agent's client and guide them. They made the mistake of breaking the relationship with me. I never would have put them into that property.

ONE OF THE BIGGEST MISTAKES I'VE SEEN IS BUYERS WHO ARE WAITING AND WAITING. I don't really see the prices coming down much. They've come down a little now, but it's still a supply and demand thing. Whenever you have supply as tight as it is and demand as strong as it is, it's going to keep prices up. It's very competitive out there right now. But haste can also make waste: You run right into something and buy the first property you see—it might not be the right decision too.

USUALLY, I SAY NEVER WAIVE YOUR RIGHT TO AN INSPEC-TION. BUT . . . I had a single woman who bought a house with me within the last six months. We knew there were going to be eight offers on this property, but this woman had to have this house and she had the funds to do it. She's very smart. Before we wrote the offer, we went to the lender and made sure the house would appraise, and that she'd qualify for the loan. Then, we could write up an offer that removed the appraisal and loan contingencies. Also, we made an appointment to go back and see the house with a "friend" of hers. While she wandered around for an hour and a half or so, deciding if it was really her dream house, the man she had brought did a mini-inspection on the property. The listing agent and the seller didn't know that the gentleman was actually an inspector. He checked the water heater, the plumbing, the foundation, the electrical sys-tems, the attic—he checked all the major components that could pose a problem. At the end, she felt quite comfortable removing her inspection contingency. With so few contingen-cies on her offer, the house was hers.

WHEN I PRESENT AN OFFER, I INCLUDE A LETTER AND PHOTOGRAPHS. I like to find out as much as I can about the sellers—do they like dogs, do they like children, do they have plants, do they travel? Then I incorporate some of what they're interested in into the letter, depending on the buyer, showing similarities and interests held in common. This helps develop rapport between the two parties and often ensures that my client will then get the house.

WHATEVER YOU DO, STAY OUT OF MULTIPLE-OFFER SIT-
UATIONS. Unless you can stay emotionally detached from the
house and you have an agent working for you who will make
sure you don't pay too much, run in the opposite direction. You
might end up with an agent who's been working with you for a
while and is ready to get you into escrow, even if you will have
to pay too much. That's the wrong person to get into a
multiple-offer situation with. You need someone who'll hold
you to your budget, who'll tell you to let go of that one. There
will be another house. If you don't have that someone working
for you, stay clear. It's too easy to get swept away.

SHOP BETWEEN OCTOBER AND FEBRUARY. A lot of people
are tucked away for the holidays during those months. Things
are very slow. You can take your time making a decision. When
spring and summer roll around, everyone's thinking of schools
and trying to get their kids situated before September. It's the
hardest, most competitive time to buy.

BUY IN AN UP-AND-COMING NEIGHBORHOOD. Go to the
local coffee shops, the grocery store. Check out the smattering
of different types of individuals living there. Look at the auto-
mobiles. You can see the couples and the younger single
women and businesswomen coming into the area who are going to develop it and make it creative, nicer.

Schools, too, are something that people want to look for, but
they're not always a sure thing. Remember, schools can change,
and when it comes time to sell the place, potential buyers may
not be adamantly looking for school districts. Why spend $500 a
square foot when you can get something for $200 a square foot?
Ultimately, it's about where are you going to be happiest living.

SHOP AROUND AND COMPARE. At every stage of the process, comparing is what the smart people do. When choosing a Realtor, when deciding on a lender, choose at least three that you'll check out. Don't go with a friend because she's a friend. Compare her to the others. This is a big purchase. The smart buyers interview, ask the questions, and are honest and upfront.

CHOOSE A REALTOR WHO WORKS FULL TIME. That professional will get information daily and know what's going on—right now—in the market. Someone who's not full time will not have the same connections and access. If your agent isn't returning your phone calls, hire someone else. The first question you should ask a real estate agent is "why did you get into this?" Listen carefully to the answer. Also ask: What qualifies you to help me? How long have you been doing this?

Tracy King works in Eagle Rock, a small older suburb of Los Angeles sidelined thirty years ago when a freeway took traffic off its main drag. When Tracy moved there almost twenty years ago, Eagle Rock did not look like the next hip place to live. Along its two big commercial streets, for example, there were seventy-four car-related businesses—gas stations, body shops, mechanics. As a Realtor, however, Tracy discovered a wealth of lovely character homes— Craftsman, mission revival, midcentury modern—all of which had been quietly sitting there, many untouched by remodel fever. As they came on the market, she set about finding owners for them.

She also began publishing a regular newsletter about her adventures in the real estate trade in and around Eagle Rock. She writes about the art walks, garden tours, and architectural tours. (She also recently published a list of Eagle Rock restaurants, with capsule reviews, that will no doubt be magnetted to every refrigerator in town.) She also lists every house she's bought or sold for people, the addresses and the prices, and she always includes a short, frank essay on the market, and often one of her "rants." "I'm a preservationist!" she declares proudly. "I believe that older homes that have character and style should be preserved. I campaign about not stuccoing your wood frame house. And I truly believe that the way to make money on your house is to preserve it and restore it in the style it was originally intended to be and you will add value that way."

Seven years ago, she remarked in her newsletter that Eagle Rock needed some kind of coffeehouse scene, and a woman named Tricia Swork took her seriously. Swork Coffee House, in fact, started the whole rebirth of downtown Eagle Rock; now, there's an assortment of very cool places to sit, drink coffee, grab a sandwich, and rub shoulders with the ever-gentrifying townsfolk. Tracy King knows her neighborhoods, street by street, and her architecture, and her job—and she freely shares what she knows with the public. If a person wants to buy in Eagle Rock or nearby suburbs (Pasadena, Highland Park, Glendale), King may or may not be the right Realtor for them (it's a personal thing, after all) but reading her newsletters and Web site is a must.

CHOOSE AN AGENT YOU KNOW SOMETHING ABOUT. A recommendation is very helpful, especially from someone who's worked with that agent. A lot of people come to me through the Internet. They see my Web Site . . . they lurk on the Web Site for a while, and then maybe they come to an open house and introduce themselves. My newsletter has brought me tons of business. I've done best with people who have been referred to me by people I've worked with.

DON'T HIRE THE LISTING AGENT! The biggest mistake I see is clients hiring the listing agent of the house they want to buy. Because the market is so competitive and moving so fast, buyers get kind of desperate. They're looking for a bargain, they're looking for some kind of an "in" on a place. They think that if they go directly to the listing agent, they'll get a better deal, which is usually not true. Most likely they won't be well represented.

A lot of Realtors believe they can represent both sides. It's not a legal issue, and it's not even an ethical issue, so long as it's disclosed. To me, it's an emotional issue—it's a squeeze being in the middle—and a trust issue. So I generally won't represent a buyer on my own listing. I might refer them to somebody, and even accept a referral fee. I'd rather represent one person at a time, and I think everybody feels a lot better about it.

YOU HAVE A RIGHT TO EXPECT CERTAIN THINGS FROM A REALTOR. A customer should expect loyalty, trustworthiness, and a certain amount of accessibility. There are people who believe they should be able to call at one o'clock in the morning and I don't believe in *that*! But I try to be accessible to my clients during normal business hours. They should also expect that their Realtor knows the neighborhood, and the general area.

REAL ESTATE AGENTS CAN'T SEE THROUGH WALLS, BUT A GOOD ONE CAN TEACH YOU MOST OF WHAT YOU NEED TO KNOW ABOUT BUYING A HOUSE. A real estate agent really is a teacher and much of what they have to teach is what's within their area of expertise. A real estate agent hopefully has the expertise to know if a house is in fairly good shape or not, but he or she doesn't know about things like roofs or electricity. What I do know is to tell the buyer, "this is something you won't know about until you've got an inspection, and know what your options are."

Preparation is a lot of what a good Realtor should be doing. Preparing the buyer for what's coming next, what can happen, and what they can realistically do or not do about it.

SOMETIMES YOU JUST HAVE TO BE INDEPENDENT, AND LISTEN TO YOURSELF—AND YOUR AGENT! I worked with a first-time buyer in the fall who was referred to me by a client. She was a schoolteacher, a single woman, and all she could afford was $350K, which is *nothing* in this area. But there happened to be a little lull in the market. So we went out and looked at three or four houses, then one came on the market in Eagle Rock right in between the two schools where she worked. It really wasn't a bad house, actually kinda cute; another single woman had bought it and fixed it up a little. They were asking $355K. So we went in with an offer of $355,500 and we *got* it! In the course of the inspections, we found out that the house wasn't nearly as well put together as it appeared on the surface. There were some sagging ceiling joists, and a funky bit of foundation in the back. These were things that would be no fun to fix. But you could live with them for a while until you got the money together. The owner had lived with them for years. And so my client had to make a choice.

There was no way we were going to get anything done about the problems. The seller was not going to help much. My client basically had to decide if she really wanted to buy a house or not. She wasn't going to find anything better for that money—just something different, and most certainly she wouldn't find anything as well situated. Well, everybody else—her parents, her friends—was saying, "You shouldn't do it!" Or, "Make them fix it!" Of course, all your friends know everything and your own Realtor knows nothing!

I was just very straight with her. I said, "This is the way it is. Really, your option is to accept it with this deal or move on. I'm with you whichever way you want to go." I also reminded her that there hadn't been anything in Eagle Rock that sold for under $400K in months! I said, "You know it's an ideal location for you and it's not a bad little house even though it needs more work than you thought. And that's the way it is."

She said, "There's no question in my mind. I'm buying this house. I don't care what my parents say. Or what my friends say. I know if I don't do this now, I may never do it."

I said, "You go, girl!" And you know, she bought it and she never looked back. She had a great attitude. I'm very proud of her.

DON'T UNDERESTIMATE YOUR AGENT. My *best* advice to first-time buyers—which of course they won't believe—is find a Realtor you can trust and that you can believe *and don't listen to anybody else!* Because all your friends have all this advice, and most likely they're wrong. Even if they're relating their own experience because they think it applies to you, it usually doesn't. No two situations are ever the same. The safest thing for anybody to tell you is *no,* don't do it!

THE RIGHT TIME TO BUY IS WHENEVER YOU'RE READY TO BUY. I think that people who try to outthink the market are actually afraid of buying and that's an excuse. We've had this rising market for going on eight years now and every year people say that it's over, it's a bubble, and now it's going to burst and prices are going to go down. I know people who have sold their home and moved into rentals. They were going to wait until the prices went down and make a killing in real estate, and now they can't afford to buy a house because they've dipped into their equity, prices have risen, and they're stuck. Trying to outsmart the market is folly; it just is.

EVERY BUYER IS A LITTLE BIT AFRAID. Buying a home is *always* scary. I've bought and sold several homes in my life and every time, it's scary. Is it the right decision? What am I doing? In 2000, when my husband and I were making an offer on the house that we're in—and we had been in our previous house for seventeen years, so obviously we were not impulsive—I woke up at four A.M. and I said, "What are we doing? It's so much money. There's no storage"—the house had been designed by a kind of socialist-type architect who believed that people shouldn't own a lot of stuff, so he didn't put in a lot of closets. I thought, "How can we even think of doing this?"

And then, I thought, "Who says we have to have a garage and attic, and maybe it *will* be spiritually cleansing to get rid of some of this junk that we have packed away."

And then, I thought how I'd be leaving my lovely old Craftsman, which may have had lots of storage but was close to a very busy street—and that had always been irritating. If we got the new house, we'd be moving three blocks up the street to a place with a huge, 14,000-square-foot lot, views, and a lot of style. So it didn't have any storage! So what?

Fear is such a big thing. You really have to get through the fear. It's a big deal buying a house. Of course you're scared, but the people who can move through their fear are the ones who are going to be okay. To move through it, you have to talk to someone—preferably your Realtor—a lot. The more questions you ask, the more I can educate you, the more you know what to expect.

KEEP WITHIN YOUR MEANS AND BE FLEXIBLE. So long as you don't get in totally over your head, you hardly can go wrong—that is, so long as you have the good fundamentals: you're working with someone who's explaining everything to you, you understand what you're getting into, and you can deal with things not working out exactly the way you planned. You need to be flexible and independent.

REMEMBER THAT NOTHING'S PERFECT. There's a kind of fear-based perfectionism that infects people buying a home. People who've lived all their lives in imperfect homes—homes with a roof leak, or an unaddressed foundation problem, or crumbling back steps—may suddenly want everything in their prospective home to be perfect, done, just so. They don't want other people's problems. They want everything the inspector finds to be fixed—preferably at no extra cost to them. Some people come up with long lists during escrow of what would make a certain house acceptable—that's really the fear talking. In certain price ranges, you may well have to buy a problem or two along with the house. Really, that can happen in any price range. I mean, it's okay for the house you love and want to be a million-dollar fixer-upper.

IT'S TIME TO CHANGE YOUR AGENT WHEN IT BECOMES APPARENT THAT THEY'RE NOT HEARING WHAT YOU'RE SAYING. Or you're not hearing what they're saying. It can go both ways. You should feel like you're understanding each other and can communicate with each other. If that's not going on, you need to say something—talk about it—and then maybe think of doing something else.

ARE YOU REALLY, REALLY, REALLY READY TO BUY? One of the biggest mistakes buyers make is in thinking they're ready to buy when they're not. Once, I had somebody so mad at me they filed a grievance against me. They claimed I didn't write up their offer. I didn't refuse to write the offer, I just kept saying, "We need to talk about this some more, because you're not going to get this house unless you step up to the plate and make more than a full-price offer." The man said, "I will never pay more than full price for anything!" And this in a boiling hot market! He wouldn't come up, and during the time I was trying to talk him into it, the house sold for $50K more than asking price to someone else. Somehow, I was to blame.

Another time, a couple called me on the carpet claiming that I represented them and someone else on a property at the same time. But that is not what happened. They made an lowball offer and it was rejected. Then, someone else I worked with made a much higher offer that was accepted. This was a situation not of my making. The angry couple kept making these lowball, very unrealistic offers in a very hot market, and not surprisingly, they didn't land a sale. People like this are just not ready. It's not anybody's fault. I had to tell them, maybe this is not your time, or our deal.

A NIGHTMARE CLIENT IS . . . SOMEONE WHO IS VERY DEMANDING AND THEN DOESN'T DO WHAT THEY SAY THEY WANT TO DO—GET OUT THERE AND BUY A HOUSE. Those are the worst.

Tao Worksheet

1. What stories have you heard from family and friends about Realtor mishaps? Write them here and see what you can learn from these experiences.

2. What stories have you heard about stellar Realtors and their methods? Write them down and decide what might be most important for you as you search out a Realtor to represent you.

3. Do you have concerns about not being a good enough or big enough buyer to warrant a Realtor's efforts? Perhaps your budget is small and you worry you'd be wasting that professional's time. Write about those concerns here and realize that Realtors are in business to serve *you*. If you're not a big enough client, a Realtor can choose not to take your business. But if a Realtor agrees to represent you, that person is working as *your* agent and doing *your* bidding. Write about how this makes you feel.

4. What are your prejudices for and against working with a Realtor? What are your concerns? Your hopes and expectations? Are these realistic?

CHAPTER EIGHT

WHERE THE MONEY GOES— THE MORTGAGE CHAPTER

Chase after money and security
and your heart will never unclench.
Care about people's approval
and you will be their prisoner.

T HIS IS THE second (*and last!*) chapter about money. This chapter is about what to do when you've actually found the property you want to buy. Bernadette's not there yet—still hasn't found a house—but say that you are. You've already been prequalified for a loan, and your offer has been accepted. Now, you've got to take that prequalification or preapproval to a bank (or broker) and actually purchase a mortgage. Welcome to the world of paperwork. If you haven't been preapproved, now is the time when you may have to cough up those bank statements, rent checks, pay stubs. If you are preapproved, or once you get approval, you'll have to decide precisely how and how much you're going to pay for that property—will you pay over fifteen, twenty, thirty, or forty years? Will your interest rate be fixed, or will it start out low for the first few years, then rise in accordance with the prime rate?

With luck, getting the right mortgage for your new home

will be fairly straightforward. A kind and canny banker or broker—someone willing to explain things, and to give you a number of options—makes a big difference. The necessary financial scrutiny and decision making is never fun, but once you've jumped through the necessary hoops, you'll be—ahem—home free.

MICHELLE: THE PROBLEM WITH JACK

Once I'd made an offer on a house and had it accepted, I had five days to secure a loan. I called Jack, the loan guy, back. "No problem, come on in. I'm sure we'll get you a good loan for around 7 percent."

Seven percent! That was higher than what he said the first time around. This time he wanted paperwork—tax returns, rent checks, bank statements. Feeling nauseous and exactly like I was going to have to take off my clothes for exactly the kind of man I least liked, I gathered the paperwork and set off to see the philosophical mortgage banker.

A new woman was working in the office, Yvette. "I'm just starting out with Jack," she said. "But I've worked for a mortgage broker for years." She ushered me into his tony chambers.

"I'm a little nervous," I told Jack. "I've never done this before.

"I have," he said. "Trust me. There's nothing to worry about."

Yvette sat in on our conference. Jack looked at my papers. "Oh, you'll need a no-doc loan," he said.

"I know," I said. "I told you that the first time we talked."

He typed numbers into his computer. Frowned. Typed in some more numbers. "Ah, here we go, a 30-year fixed-rate no-doc loan. Oh, and an excellent rate: 7.5 percent!"

I was stunned. This was higher than all the loans I'd seen advertised in the paper. And a full point higher than what he first offered me over the phone. And then, he began rattling off fees—his fees, he said, were lower than anybody else's. But I was hearing five hundred here, three hundred there. I tried to take notes. My fingers were buzzing.

When he finished reeling off the numbers, I said in a really small voice, "You told me a few weeks ago that you could loan me money at 6.5 percent."

"Yes, but rates have gone up," he said. "And you'll need a no-doc loan."

I didn't know which argument to make first, so I took them in order. "But rates are going down!"

"Federal interest rates, not mortgage rates," he said. "The two have little if anything to do with each other."

Oh. Was that true? Who knew? How disappointing!

At the risk of sounding even more stupid, I said, "Also, I've said my loan would be a no-doc loan all along."

"I only know what I'm seeing here today. This is the first time I've seen your paperwork." The disdain in his voice was unmistakable. "No-doc loans cost more, that's all."

For once in my life, I didn't doubt myself. I'd been instructed by Marie to ask for a no-doc loan from the get-go. She warned it would add a quarter to a half point to my rate. This was adding a point!

"You're not going to get a better rate anywhere else," he said. "Of course, you're free to try. Though I can't guarantee this rate will hold." The bluster, the sneering self-confidence! No wonder I had stayed away from such financial types. He was exactly as I'd feared they would be.

"Okay," I said, "I just need some time to think about this."

"I'll have Yvette shop around, see if she can find you a better rate," he said. "But I already know she can't."

I thought he was a mortgage *banker*. I didn't think he shopped for loans. But I didn't say anything more. Clearly, I knew nothing.

I left, feeling slimed. I'd had the feeling that his first quote was too good to be true, but it wasn't so far off from the numbers I'd seen in the papers. Frankly, the numbers didn't scare me as much as Jack did. How quickly the disdain slipped into his voice—as soon as I questioned a single thing.

My accountant had his office nearby. I stopped in unannounced, but he welcomed me.

"I see ads for all these low-interest loans, but this guy's much higher," I said.

"Have you gone to your bank? Try your bank," he said. "Banks often have the best rates."

What a novel idea. From his office I went directly to my bank. The bank manager called the mortgage department (which was several miles away) and together, we left a message: he said I was a good candidate, and I left my phone number.

Then, feeling freaked out and incredibly ignorant about everything, I went home to stew. In the middle of my stewing, my father called.

"I'm in mortgage hell," I told him.

"I'm coming down tomorrow to help you," he said. "We'll get you a good mortgage."

This seemed unusually generous of him. But I said, okay. I suspected he would want me to borrow the money from him. He'd probably give me a low rate, but I didn't want to take money, even on loan, from him. I wanted a clean transaction with an impersonal lending institution. The impersonality was worth paying for, I felt. After all, this was the man who said single women were bad risks. This was the man who'd refused to help my sister and me with down payments (or anything else) with the money he'd inherited from my mother. But if he could help me in other ways, he was welcome to try.

After talking to my dad, I called Bernadette and stewed to her. She made her now-famous, brilliant suggestion.

"You should talk to my husband," she said. "He's worked for a mortgage company for years. He knows about these things. He'll be home later tonight."

I talked to John—as would Rose and Colleen when they set out to buy houses. A conversation with John became one of the Tao Gal's real estate rites of passage. In these conversations (recapped below), John explained fees, rates, and how to go about looking for loans.

For me, personally, John relieved much anxiety by telling me an insider's secret: Although there are all kinds of mortgages, and they are not the same, when you've determined what you want (in my case, a 30-year fixed-rate loan from a bank), most of the mortgages you have to choose between will end up costing more or less about the same—some institutions make their money from the fees, some from points. To see where the costs are in any mortgage, he also said I needed to get something called a Good Faith Estimate, which lists fees and closing costs, so there will be no hideous surprises during escrow—or later. A Good Faith Estimate was de rigueur, he said. Anybody, he promised, is happy to give you one.

I called Jack the next day and said, "Can you please fax me a Good Faith Estimate for the loan?"

"What do you need that for?"

"So I can see what things cost and how it compares with other mortgages."

"I don't do business that way," he said. "I'm giving you a great deal. I'm not here to provide you with free information just so you can use it to shop around."

"But I'll need to see what I'll be paying."

"I told you yesterday," he said.

"I didn't get it all down," I said. "Also, I need the figures so I can have a sense of what the closing costs will be."

"I already gave you a sense of that. It's all guesswork at this point anyway," he said. "I don't know what your escrow costs will be. I don't do business that way."

But John had said that a Good Faith Estimate was a simple, routine courtesy. A courtesy.

I might be ignorant, I thought, but Jack . . . Jack was a *slimeball*.

A few hours later, Yvette, playing good cop to Jack's bad cop, called and assured me she'd find me a loan and send me a Good Faith Estimate. "That's okay," I said. "I've decided not to do business with you and Jack."

But now I had to do business with somebody else.

The bank got back to me not long after my conversation with Yvette. The banker was a woman named Debbie. She asked me to come over at seven that night—she worked from three P.M. until midnight.

I arrived at her office with my package of paperwork. She greeted me warmly. She already had in mind a great loan for me, she said, a loan designed for people who had banked with the institution for a number of years. It required a $50,000 down payment and a credit rating of 680. It was a 30-year loan but an adjustable-rate mortgage, which meant that only the first five years were at a fixed rate, 6.75 to 6.85 percent with my no-doc requirement. After that, the interest could go up depending on the prime rate—but it could never, even given the worst-case scenario, exceed 12 percent. There would also be the usual bank fees.

"Interest rates are going down," she added. "This will get you started, and you can refinance whenever you like—there's no penalty for an early pay-off."

Thanks to my conversation with John, this all made sense. Sounds good, I said.

She ran a credit check. My score was three points lower than the loan required. "They still might approve it. I'm still going to try," Debbie said. She went through my bank statements. I had just gotten an infusion of cash, another installment on my novel advance. "You make more than $10,000 a month!" she cried. "We love clients like you."

"Not every month!" I said. "Not even most months! In fact, hardly ever!"

"We only care about the last three months," she said.

Everything else sounded fine. The three points shy of the required credit score were the only cause for suspense.

Best of all, Debbie gave me a Good Faith Estimate without my having to ask for one.

The next day, as I waited to hear if my bank loan had been approved, my father showed up. "I think I got a loan," I said. "I'm just waiting to hear. But in case I don't get it, I'm still shopping for other options."

"Let's see what you have," he said.

I handed him the Good Faith Estimate. He frowned. "Very high interest rate," he said. "I only charge 6 percent."

"It's a good rate for a bank," I said dumbly.

"And what's this 'generation fee'?"

"What it costs to generate the loan."

"And these other fees? You shouldn't have to pay these."

"What they don't get in points, they get in interest," I said with new authority. "Really, all basic mortgages cost about the same. They just juggle the numbers around."

"Bullshit," said my father. "I never charge any fees or points."

"Well, if I refuse to pay fees, I won't get the loans."

"You shouldn't buy anything on credit anyway."

"You mean, I should keep renting?"

"If you can't afford to buy, yes."

"I've paid $92,000 to live in this Atwater slum over the last nine years," I said. "I could've had some of that in equity."

"But paying interest is also just throwing money away," he said, waving the Good Faith Estimate. "I've never paid interest in my life," he said smugly. "I've just earned it."

It's true. My father, a carpenter in his youth, bought an inexpensive lot in his neighborhood, then years later built his own house himself from scratch, adding rooms as he could afford them. He built his second house—to accommodate his young family—with a generous gift from his father-in-law. He bought a small mountain lot in the Sierras with savings, then built a vacation cabin on it, again with a generous gift from my mother's father. The rise in property values over the decades eventually made him a fairly well-off man. He bought property and built his third home—for retirement—with cash earned from selling his second home, which had quadrupled in value. He never needed a loan!

It was also true that my father has been pathologically frugal as a result of growing up during the Depression. He saved fanatically, begrudged every penny the family required. He liked to sit down and figure out how much money it cost to raise two children. "You'll end up costing me over a million dollars," he once announced. Because of his frugality, I assumed we were poor people—the neighborhood we lived in, the clothes my sister and I wore—until I was applying to college and requested financial aid. My parents had to fill out what was then called the Parent Confidential Statement—and only then did I discover I was ineligible for any scholarship based on need.

"Are you saying I shouldn't buy a house?" I asked him.

"Not if you can't afford one."

I remembered Debbie exulting in my bank statements the night before.

"So you're saying I shouldn't buy a house unless I can afford the whole price up front."

"I'm saying it's never smart to pay interest."

I felt suddenly as if I were trying to have a rational conversation on LSD (not that I've ever taken LSD). Then, I exploded!

"I can't believe how unsupportive you're being. I'm in my late forties. I'm not married. I want a home of my own. And you're telling me I shouldn't have one because I don't have a quarter-million dollars in cash? Everybody has mortgages. All of America has mortgages—except you. You had rich in-laws. You weren't smart; you were just lucky!" I was on the verge of tears. "You said you came down to help me. But you are just being judgmental and unreasonable and mean."

For the briefest moment, he looked abashed. "I just don't want you to be taken advantage of," he said. "People see a single woman like you, they tack on all kinds of fees and assessments. My bank will give you a much better deal. They won't try any of these shenanigans if I'm overseeing the deal." He flicked the Good Faith Estimate. "I guarantee I can do better than *this!*"

"Okay, okay. I'm open to that," I said, mustering my good manners. "I'd appreciate anything you can do."

We made some small talk, ate some lunch, and he left.

He never did call me with the details of a better mortgage. His bank didn't phone me, either. I still wonder what the purpose of his visit was. One thing is for sure: It made me all the more confident and happy that I had decided not to involve him in the financing of my home. I was thrilled to be doing it myself and considered it a privilege to pay interest in exchange for no emotional ties.

Around nine that night, when I least expected any news, I got a call from Debbie. "Your loan has been approved," she said. "Congratulations!"

Checklist of Loan Approval Documents

Before your loan is approved, you'll need to have certain documents on hand. Each person listed as a borrower on the mortgage will need to provide these documents. It's good to start gathering them early. If you're doing a no-doc loan, like Michelle did, you'll only need to provide the specific documents the lender asks for—usually much less than what's listed here.

____ List of your addresses for the past seven years.

____ Copies of W2 forms for the past two years.

____ Copies of your tax returns for the past two years.

____ Proof of income (usually pay stubs) for the past month.

_____ Three months' worth of bank statements for every account, IRA, stock account, Keogh plan or 401(k). Bring copies of your most recent statements to validate any other assets you have.

_____ If you are using gift funds as part of your down payment or closing costs, you must provide proof that the funds came from a gift and that the person who gave you the money had that money to give. The giver will also have to fill out a "gift letter" (see chapter 2 sidebar for an example).

_____ If you have made a large deposit into your bank account in the past three months, you'll need to explain where the funds came from and offer proof. Likewise, if you opened a new bank account in the past six months, be prepared to show where the funds came from.

_____ Account numbers for all your credit cards and loans.

_____ Documentation for additional income, such as child support or alimony.

_____ If you are divorced, complete copies of all divorce decrees.

_____ If you are self-employed, copies of the last two years' tax returns and profit-and-loss statements.

ABOUT MORTGAGE COSTS

Though you may have seen ads for loans with no fees attached, or no out-of-pocket costs to the borrower, be aware that there are fees associated with *all* mortgage loans. What it comes down to is where, how, and when you'll pay those fees. In fact, some loans billed as having no out-of-pocket costs may end up costing more in the long run.

All mortgage loans that are secured by real estate will have certain costs associated with them. These costs include a fee for the title insurance, escrow fees, appraisal and recording fees. In all such loan transactions, these services are paid for by the borrower. If you obtain a loan for which you're not asked to pay these fees up front, know that the fees are still there— they're just covered by a higher interest rate or worked into the loan somehow. In such cases, the actual cost to the borrower may be quite a bit more over the life of the loan than if those fees were paid at the time the loan was generated.

Once you've selected your mortgage and made an application, a loan broker or officer should provide you with a Good Faith Estimate of Closing Costs. Among these costs may be the following items:

- loan origination fee
- loan discount points
- application fee/processing and underwriting fee
- document preparation fee
- appraisal fee
- credit report fee
- mortgage insurance (if you put down less than 20 percent)
- tax service
- flood check fee
- closing/escrow/attorney fee
- abstract or title search
- title insurance
- homeowners/hazard insurance
- city/county/state tax/stamp recording fees
- property survey fee
- inspection fees

As a general rule, closing costs will usually total about 2 to 3 percent of the purchase price. On a house that costs $500,000, then, your closing costs will probably be between $10,000 and $15,000.

Ask your loan agent for an explanation of what each fee includes (sometimes several items may be put into one category) and make sure you get clarification for any of the fees you do not understand.

Under the Real Estate Settlement Procedures Act, the borrower must receive a Good Faith Estimate of Closing Costs at the time of application or within three days of application. This estimate will list each of these expected costs either as a specific amount or a range of fees. If you're working with a broker who fails to give you such a document, ask for it. If, as in Michelle's case, the broker demurs, go somewhere else. Something is fishy.

INTEREST RATES AND POINTS

The interest rate is the cost of borrowing money expressed as a percentage rate. This rate changes regularly due to market conditions. An annual percentage rate (APR) is the cost of credit expressed as a yearly rate and includes the interest rate plus points, broker fees, and other credit charges you may incur—the interest amount you will actually pay. When comparing loans, ask lenders to quote you both the interest rate and the APR to make comparisons easier.

Points are fees paid to the lender or broker and are often linked to the interest rates. A point represents 1 percent of your loan amount. If your loan is $400,000, one point is $4,000. Points are often the price you pay for various stipulations in your loan: for example, a no-documentation loan may cost a quarter of a point to a full point. A borrower can pay for points when the loan is made or can "roll" them into the overall loan and pay for them over time. Typically, if you pay more points up front, you'll get a lower interest rate. Fewer or no points will result in a higher interest rate. Again, it comes down to much the same thing: you can pay me now or you can pay me later, but you will have to pay me. Ask the loan agent to quote you the points in dollars rather than percentage points so that you'll know how much, exactly, you'll have to pay.

TYPES OF LOANS

Though many different types of mortgage loans are offered, they will all cost you something. How much they will cost over the life of the loan is a gamble you take. We'll use the scenario above ($500,000 purchase price, loan amount of $400,000, representing 80 percent financing over 30 years) to give you estimated payments.

If you go with a FIXED-RATE MORTGAGE, you're betting that interest rates will rise over the time you hold the mortgage. Initially, you'll be paying more for the money you borrow than if you went with an adjustable-rate mortgage, but if your assumption that rates will rise is correct, you may end up paying less when those rates *do* rise. This kind of loan is best suited to the borrower who plans to stay in the property a long time and would rather not have to worry about what the payments will be. For our hypothetical scenario, your monthly mortgage payment (principal and interest) would be $2,430, based on an interest rate of 6.125 percent, an annual percentage rate of 6.238 percent, with 1 point.

On the other hand, if you go with an ADJUSTABLE-RATE

MORTGAGE, you're betting that the rates won't rise—or won't rise that much—over the time you have the loan. You'll pay less in interest initially and be able to qualify for a larger loan than you would with a fixed-rate mortgage, and if your calculation is correct, you'll save money over the long run. The initial monthly payments, for our hypothetical scenario, would be $1,881 for a loan that adjusts once a year, with a rate of 3.875 percent, an APR of 6.101 percent, and half a point. If you're wrong, though, you may end up paying quite a bit more each month than you planned to. However, if you only stay a few years in the property, you'll probably be just fine. First, though, be sure your budget can withstand the shock of higher monthly payments if you decide to go with an adjustable-rate mortgage. What would your payment be if rates went up 1 percent, 2 percent? Could you pay that?

Another type of adjustable-rate mortgage that has become popular is the INTEREST-ONLY LOAN. Typically, when you take out a mortgage, the idea is that the money you owe will be amortized over the life of the loan. Though most of your monthly payment will go toward paying the interest at first, a little bit will go toward paying down the principal you owe. The longer you hold the loan, the more the balance between interest and principal shifts, until, near the end of the loan, most of your payment goes toward the principal and very little toward interest. (Those who want to shorten the term of their loan without refinancing can simply pay extra each month, an amount that will go directly to paying down the principal and reducing the amount you owe. Check to see if there's a prepayment penalty.)

With an interest-only loan, you'll get a low interest rate and qualify for a larger mortgage than with other types of loans, and you'll only have to pay the interest on that loan each month for the initial few years of the loan, say three or five years. The initial interest-only payment for a $400,000 loan is $1,833 a month on a loan that's fixed as an interest-only for five years with an interest rate of 5.5 percent, an APR of 5.763 percent, with 1 point. After the five years are up, the loan becomes an adjustable-rate mortgage at the then-current interest rates. The good news is that you have the option to pay more each month, thus paying down the principal in the same way you would with a fully amortizing loan. If you have a bad month, you don't have to pay the extra amount that month, just the interest payment. This gives you flexibility, but it can also hurt you if you're not diligent about paying the extra amount. The reality is that the loan will never get paid off if all you send in is interest payments. Yes, the property may appreciate and be worth much more than you paid for it, but you won't have paid off any of the principal. It's like paying the minimum on your credit card—it's going to take forever to pay that sucker off. With our $400,000 loan, after five years of making interest-only payments, you'll still owe $400,000 on the house.

Once the initial interest-only period comes to an end, your loan payment will then jump, not only because the principal is now being added in, but also because you have to make up for the five years you didn't pay for the principal; you will now have a shorter time period—25 years—to pay off the balance than with a traditional 30-year loan. For our hypothetical house, assuming interest rates stay exactly where they are, the monthly payment, excluding taxes and insurance, would leap from $1,833 to $2,456. Again, this is assuming interest rates don't rise, and most economists think it's highly unlikely that rates won't go up.

Make sure you can afford the higher figure when loan officers waive this tempting offer before you. (It would be wise to tack on extra interest when calculating the figure, just in case.)

Weigh these factors and know yourself. If the loan broker pushes an interest-only loan so you can qualify for a bigger loan, and you know you're the kind of person who's never going to pay extra each month if you don't have to, or you will be squeezed dramatically when the interest-only period comes to an end, maybe consider a different type of loan. It's up to you to know what's best for yourself. Mortgage lenders will always try to talk you into bigger loans because their compensation is determined by the size of the loan; ditto your real estate agent. Know what you can realistically pay and resist temptation!

If you expect your income to go up in the coming years, you might want to go with an interest-only or adjustable-rate mortgage, knowing that when the rates rise or the loan becomes fully amortizing, you'll be okay with the higher payments. On the other hand, if your income is fixed and likely to stay that way, and you plan on being in the property a long time, the fixed-rate may be the best for you.

DOWN PAYMENTS AND PRIVATE MORTGAGE INSURANCE
Many lenders offer mortgage programs with low down payments—some, even, with nothing down. Note, however: If you take out a mortgage with less than 20 percent of the purchase price as your down payment, most lenders will require you to get private mortgage insurance (PMI), which protects the lender if you default on your payments. The cost of PMI may be an important consideration because PMI payments can significantly add to your monthly expenses, and they aren't tax deductible.

If you take out a loan for 95 percent of the purchase price (you put down, in other words, a 5 percent down payment), the PMI cost will be calculated at .78 percent per year of the initial loan amount, and then paid as part of your mortgage on a monthly basis. Thus, on a $400,000 loan on a property for which you put down 5 percent ($20,000), you will typically have PMI payments of around $260 a month—not a small amount.

The greater your down payment, and thus, your financial stake in the property, the lower the PMI payment: 90 percent financing will run you a little more than half a percent a year of the initial mortgage amount; 85 percent financing will be closer to a third of a percent. Thus, a loan of $400,000 on a property for which you put down 10 percent ($40,000) will typically have PMI payments of around $170 a month—still not a small amount when every dime counts.

Keep in mind, though, that lending practices have become looser and it's often possible to skirt the PMI requirement by taking out a second mortgage from a different financial institution to make up a 20 percent down payment. You'll pay a slightly higher interest rate, but you might be able to get out of the PMI requirement altogether.

HOMEOWNERS INSURANCE

Before you can close escrow on the property, you'll have to prove that you have homeowners (or fire) insurance on the place. Depending on where you live, sometimes flood or earthquake insurance also may be required. Get quotes early and arrange for the insurance as soon as possible *and make sure the escrow company has a copy of the insurance policy.* When Bernadette was set to close on the house she and John bought, and subsequently lost, there was a glitch with the insurance. Though she had arranged for it early on, the escrow company didn't have— or couldn't find—any proof of insurance. The day before the house closed, she had to drive hundreds of miles, shuttling between the insurance agent's office, the mortgage lender's location, and the escrow company—none of which were within easy range of the other—to make sure all the details were in place. A major headache at that stage, one that could have been avoided.

AND THEN, OF COURSE, THERE ARE *TAXES*

In all this talk of interest, points, and fees, don't forget, when considering the costs of homeownership, to factor in property taxes. The property tax rate will vary from state to state, but taxes on your new home will be a substantial bite of your budget. In today's hot and high-priced market, taxes cost much more than PMI—although they are tax deductible!

In California, for example, where the rates are famously low (!), at around 1.2 percent, property taxes on a $500,000 home will run about $6,000 a year—or $500 a month! You can "impound" the taxes (along with your homeowners insurance) so that you pay for them in monthly installments combined with your mortgage. That way, you're not looking at the big rude payments that come due, with unswerving regularity, once or twice a year—but you are looking at a bigger (if more realistic) mortgage payment. There are no cost benefits to impounding, but some people like the convenience and efficiency of lumping taxes and insurance in with the mortgage, streamlining their paperwork.

Many people, though, prefer not to use impound accounts because, if the lender fails to make the tax or insurance payment, the homeowner may be the one footing the penalty bill. Also, many homeowners would rather invest that money themselves and make some kind of return, rather than having it sit in an impound account. If your income comes in large payments—like Michelle's—this may be a better choice than impounds.

DON'T FORGET THE RESERVES

When you qualify for a loan, the lender is going to want to be certain you haven't spent every dime you had on buying the house, leaving you vulnerable to default on payments right off the bat. To this end, the lender will typically want to see that you have six months' worth of mortgage payments sitting in the bank upon the close of escrow. If your taxes, insurance, and PMI payments are impounded, you'll need to have six months of the full payment (including these items) at your fingertips. Make sure you factor reserves in when you figure how much you're going to use as a down payment.

KEEP YOUR CHIN UP

This money stuff can be tiresome, but if you deal with it directly, it will empower you to own your own home, to live the way you want to live, to take the reins of your financial life. Don't let money—the fear of financial matters or the fear of money-related paperwork—be an obstacle to your dreams. Put one foot in front of the other and you'll get through this stage in no time.

Talking to John: A Recap of John's Mortgage Tutorial

- A mortgage loan is a product. You may be able to save quite a bit of money by shopping around for the best deal on that product. Call more than one lender. Ask about rates and fees. All mortgages are not alike and learning about this process can pay off handsomely.

- Know that there are different places to shop for a mortgage loan. Banks, mortgage companies, and credit unions, for example, are typical lenders. There are also loan brokers, people who arrange the transaction with a lending institution for you.

- Traditionally, credit unions, then banks, have offered the lowest-priced loans, but demand the cleanest credit records. As the loan market has become more competitive, it is possible to find good loans through mortgage companies and brokers.

- Brokers typically have access to several different lenders, so they may be able to offer you a wider selection of loan products and terms from which you can choose. A broker's fees, which may take the form of points paid at closing, or a higher interest rate, must also be factored in. Ask brokers how their compensation is arranged so you can compare apples to apples (and avoid rude surprises).

- The Internet now offers a wide range of loan-buying options, and can often beat your bank's rates—at least at first glance. Educate yourself about loans before shopping alone on the Internet for mortgages.

Tao Worksheet

1. How do high-finance issues make you feel? Do you tend to go too far out on a limb, financially, and get yourself in trou-

ble? Or are you too conservative with money, holding on tight when you could let go? How can you balance your trust in the process with this knowledge about yourself?

2. Decide how much cash you can realistically come up with for a down payment. Can you make it over the 20 percent hurdle and save yourself the PMI payments? Do you have friends or family members who might like to help? If you can't come up with the 20 percent, be sure you calculate what your PMI payment will be and ascertain that you can afford it.

3. How much can you realistically spend each month on housing? Keep in mind the sacrifices you'll have to make. Can you give up ordering pizzas on the weekend? How much are you willing to change your lifestyle to afford this purchase? How much would you *have* to change to afford it? Are you calculating the costs of repairs?

4. What kind of loan is best for you? Do you plan on staying in your home a long time and that your income will stay the same? Or, is this just a quick step on the way to something else?

5. Are you the kind of person who will make extra payments if you get an interest-only loan? Know this about yourself before choosing what's best. Look at the long term.

6. What can you do to ensure your mortgage is paid off by the time you retire? See if there's a way you can do it. Write up a plan for yourself.

7. Do you have a friend who's savvy with loans and these kind of financial dealings? If so, ask the friend to help you in the

process. Rely on those who know. Write down the names of those who might help and call them today.

8. Have you talked with your tax person? Get advice from the experts. Don't let a mortgage broker advise you on taxes, or allow a real estate agent to talk you into higher payments than you can make. Write a plan for yourself, detailing who you'll contact before you make your loan decision. Stick to this plan.

9. If you're moving into a townhome, condo, or planned neighborhood that has homeowner association dues, be sure you add them in before you decide what you can afford. If the real estate agent hasn't yet told you about these fees, call now.

10. Remember, it's good to stretch yourself financially to get as much home as possible, but you don't want to be waking up every night at three A.M. wondering how in the world you're going to make this month's payments. Don't stretch yourself to the point of panic. Where is the line between what you can afford and what is really undoable? Write down the number here.

CHAPTER NINE

A GUIDED TOUR OF ESCROW HELL

> . . . [T]he Master takes action
> by letting things take their course.
> He remains as calm
> at the end as at the beginning.

MARIE, THE TAO Gals invaluable real estate hawk, knows more about the escrow period, the time between when you offer to buy the house and the closing, the completion of the sale, than all of us combined. The Gals look to her for advice and wisdom.

The first rule of escrow, according to Marie, is in two parts: One, something unexpected *always* comes up. And, two, almost everything that comes up is easily resolvable—*if* you keep your cool.

A good escrow agent can make the difference between buyer's bliss and escrow hell. Typically, Marie recommends, it's a good idea to use the escrow company associated with your own real estate agent's company. Be aware, though, if you're the buyer, you may be pressured into using the seller's choice of an escrow company. If your real estate agent believes that the seller's escrow company may be difficult to work with, you may want to negotiate that choice in your offer. If your lender, who has also had a lot of experience with escrow companies, says a company (a buyer's or seller's) is difficult, again, you may wish to negotiate the choice. The buyer can chose the escrow company. But the best time to discuss the choice of the escrow company is *before* you make an offer.

"It is best to build your escrow choice into the first offer because frequently it will not become an issue if you include it first," Marie says.

Escrow companies are regulated by the Department of Real Estate and most are reputable. "However," Marie says, "you want to watch out for companies that are 'captive' escrows—those that are run as a separate arm of the real estate or loan broker's office." Such long-established allegiances may involve illegal kickbacks and may make the playing field uneven. Escrow is a time when you truly want someone impartial and fair working for you.

How long escrow will last is usually established in the purchase contract. Typically, escrow can be established for fifteen, thirty, forty-five, sixty, or more days, depending on how much time the buyer and seller need to complete everything and move. Sometimes, as Michelle's story will illustrate, escrow can drag on past the time you agree upon, due to factors beyond your control.

Escrow is the time when the biggest purchase of your life is being carefully negotiated. It is a time for patience, trust, and flexibility. You may, as Rose did, simply let yourself be guided through escrow, showing up when asked, signing where indicated, and allow the process to take its course—but be certain your agent is attending closely to the process. If your agent is not so attentive, you may find, as Colleen did, that many small details can slip through the cracks and cause many headaches in the early years of home ownership.

To survive escrow, you need to keep a cool head and both eyes open. You need to remain present, and flexible. At a time of great transition, this is all harder than it sounds.

What Happens During Escrow

"Escrow," Marie explains, "is when you dot all the i's and cross all the t's." Sounds easy, but sometimes gets complicated.

Escrow is necessary because, when such large sums and high-ticket items are at stake, the sale must be carefully and thoroughly executed by an impartial third party. Money and property must change hands in a timely fashion—so nobody absconds with the dough *and* the deed, or moves in without paying. Escrow ensures that the seller is paid in a timely fashion, the deed is duly recorded.

Escrow exists to make certain that you're getting exactly what you think you are, in terms of the land boundaries and the condition of the home. The escrow agent makes sure that nothing—funds or property—changes hands until all the provisions of the purchase contract have been met. Once all the stipulations in the contract have been met, the escrow company distributes the money and documents, thus completing the sale.

During the escrow period, a number of things happen, some of which are coordinated by the escrow company, some by the real estate agents, and others by the lender.

- A title company is hired to research and deliver a title report on the property to make sure it can be sold without encumbrances.

- An appraiser is hired to do an independent appraisal of the property to verify that the property is worth what is being paid for it.

- An inspector is hired to investigate for termite damage and other possible structural problems. (Buyers may stipulate several kinds of inspections including geological and plumbing or waive the inspection to help their offer get accepted.)

- A comprehensive disclosure required by law is completed by the seller and the seller's real estate agent, detailing things like smoke detectors and environmental hazards.

A good real estate agent and escrow company, working in tandem, should see you through the inspection and disclosure processes.

On the seller's side of the equation, the escrow company works with the seller's lender to arrange to pay off the existing mortgage on the property.

On the buyer's side, the escrow company receives first the final down payment and then, when the loan "funds," receives and holds the rest of the money for the house until it is time to hand it over (usually within a day).

Once the title is clear and all the inspections, disclosures, and money are in place, the escrow agent orders the recording of the property, gives the title to the buyer, and distributes the funds.

MICHELLE IN HELL

My new real estate agent—the one representing the house I decided to buy—was named Tai, and I was clear on what I wanted from him. I wanted the house with as little fuss as possible. The seller asked for—in fact, insisted on—a thirty-day escrow. Fine with me. I specifically asked that the owner *not* do any further "improvements"—wooden closet doors should *not* be replaced with cheap mirrored sliders. More plastic blinds should *not* be hung over windows. He could remove the old bed frames and trash and dog poop in the yard. And if the inspector found any structural problems, he could fix those. Otherwise, please, don't do another thing!

I couldn't have been an easier buyer, or so I thought. I made no demands. I signed the papers I was required to sign as Tai presented them. I shopped for and obtained a loan within my five-day window. I did everything that was required of me.

And thus I embarked on the path straight to Escrow Hell.

Escrow, escrow . . . the word is one I'd heard a thousand times without knowing exactly what it meant. Oh, I knew it was the time between buying a house and being able to move into it. Thirty days, sixty days. I did wonder why on earth should it take so long?

I'd also heard that escrow could be hell, but now that I was in it, I couldn't imagine what could go wrong. (Clearly, I did not imagine far enough.) My loan was approved. Also, a year before, the house had come within a hair's breadth of selling—the last buyers reneged the penultimate day of escrow. So the house had already passed inspection, and all the little odds and ends suggested by the inspector had been completed—all except for the installation of new mirrored closet doors in one bedroom (which is ostensibly why the buyers backed out, though in reality, they'd found another place they liked better and used the mirrored closet doors as a legal excuse). Thanks to those balkers, my inspection went well—my inspector said only that another strap was needed on the hot water heater, and several windows, he noted, were stuck. All I asked from the owner was that he clean some of the junk out of the backyard. Old bed frames. Rolls of hurricane fence. Rotting wood.

So, no problem. In three weeks, then two weeks, I'd be in.

I started packing.

I showed up to sign off on the contingencies.

I brought in contractors to give me estimates on a remodel.

Things were going smoothly, right on schedule. What else could happen?

One couple I knew had to have all kinds of extra geological inspections done on their prospective hillside home. But my lot was as flat as a parking lot. Another friend had lost her financing when her fly-by-night mortgage company went belly-up. But my mortgage was with an established, stolid, nationwide banking institution.

Plus, my seller had demanded a thirty-day escrow. After having his house on the market for a year, and having already come so close to selling it once, he'd virtually moved out, and was itching to shed the place. Where could the hitch be?

Then, the escrow company contacted Tai. The title company had discovered a little problem with the title. During escrow, it seems, something called a title company researches a property, comes up with maps and deeds, looks at the ownership history, and checks for any loans and liens against it.

In my case, liens had been filed against the property.

Filed by the government.

Unpaid child support.

The exact sum of these liens would be determined by a governmental office in downtown Los Angeles. Escrow could not proceed until this lien report was filed. The downtown office was backed up with such matters. The information we needed would take at least three weeks to obtain. No, there was no way to expedite the process.

"Didn't you know about these liens?" I asked the real estate agent. After all, he'd gone through an escrow on the property before.

"They didn't show up in the last title search."

"But surely the owner knew about them. Didn't he tell you?"

"Yes, but we didn't worry about them because they didn't show up before."

"But this means escrow will go forty-five days or more," I said. "And I have a thirty-day lock on my loan."

"Don't worry," said my Realtor. "I'll pay to have the lock extended."

"And if it goes much longer than sixty days, I'll be out of the country!" I already had a plane ticket to Switzerland.

"Don't worry, we'll get it done long before then."

Famous last words.

Transitions are always a time of heightened emotions. These interludes, when we are leaving one way of life, but not quite ensconced in another, are full of anticipation, possibility, and excitement. They're also queasy times, and moods routinely vacillate from grief (at leaving the old) to euphoria (in imagining the new).

After I heard about the liens, I began having intense second thoughts. Perhaps this *wasn't* the house for me. Perhaps this was a little hint from the universe that I should bail while the bailing was good. I had a legal reason to, and to do so would still cost me nothing. Should I hang on? Should I give up? I asked my good friend and long-term spiritual adviser Claire to come look at the property and give me advice.

She drove out with me. In the driveway, before we got out of the car, she said, "It's awfully far from where you live now. Aren't you afraid you'll be isolated?"

"Well, Michele is next door. Though I am afraid I'll be too dependent on her and her husband. I hate being a single person in deep with a couple."

She took this in. "Well, let's see the house."

She was not impressed. "The yard is . . . big," she said. "But the house is, uh, pretty bad."

"I know."

"I seriously urge you to reconsider," she said. "I think it's too far away. And too much work. And you deserve more. Much more. You really do."

She was a former union carpenter and is presently a construction supervisor for a large commercial builder. She knew houses. She owned a house. She wanted the best for me. I had to give serious consideration to her opinion.

When do you hang on?

When do you push?

When do you cut and run?

When do you sit back and let things take their course?

When do you do what's required and then let go?

As always, I took my confusion to the Tao Gals. "Claire thinks I should let it go!" I wailed, and told them what she said.

They said Claire had a point. An excellent point. But I should follow my heart.

My heart said to hold on.

On the day that escrow should have closed, the very day that my loan lock would expire, I called my loan officer to see if Tai had extended the lock. She hadn't heard from him.

I called Tai. "You promised to extend the lock."

"It's not necessary," he said.

"You promised," I said.

Silence.

"I wouldn't have locked in for just thirty days if it hadn't been for you. You're the ones who wanted a thirty-day escrow! I could've locked in for sixty days."

"It's not necessary. If they don't extend the lock themselves, you can always get another loan. But I think they will."

"I'm not in a gambling mood," I said.

"Then you pay for the lock," he said.

I couldn't believe my ears. I was so angry, the air in the room seemed to be pulsing. Darkness lapped at the edges of my vision.

"You said *you'd* pay to have the lock extended." Me.

"It'll be all right if I don't." Him.

"And what if it's not?"

"We can take that chance."

"But you said you'd pay."

We went round and round in this manner, the only variant being the pitch of our voices. Finally, I exclaimed, "You are either a man of your word or you are not. Now which is it?"

A long pause. He agreed to pay, and gave me his credit card number.

I called the loan officer to pay for an extension. I was shaking with an anger hangover. She took all his information and charged his credit card $400. I wanted an assurance that this wouldn't happen again—that we could have the lock until the sale. She consulted with her manager and I overheard their conversation.

"It's the Huneven loan," she said. "Her lock has expired."

"Oh, just extend it," he said. "Don't charge her."

"I already charged her."

"Oh, okay," he said. And that was that.

So Tai had been right. And I, so sure of myself, so pumped up with self-righteous fury, had been wrong. It wasn't necessary to pay for the loan lock. But how was I to know?

The next time I need a loan lock extended, god willing, I'm going to ask to speak to the manager first. At the very least, I'll fight a little bit in order not to pay the clearly waivable fee. And maybe, maybe, maybe I'll listen to my real estate agent, who just possibly may know what he or she is doing.

Another lesson learned.

The next lesson I learned had to do with power of attorney—that is, getting someone to "be me" when I couldn't be present in person.

Yes, my thirty-day escrow was now fifty days and counting.

"I've got this ticket to Switzerland—it's nonrefundable," I wailed to the Tao Girls. "And the sale might not close before the due date."

Marie—beautiful, adept, business-savvy Marie—said, "No problem. Just give me power of attorney. I'll sign your escrow papers for you."

"How do I do that?" I said.

"Some lawyer can tell you, I'm sure," she said.

I called the lawyers I knew, but they were criminal lawyers and whatever distant law school memories they had of such civil proceedings were vague and unhelpful. When I phoned Marie to report on my lack of progress, she said, "That's okay. I already downloaded a form for it. We just need a notary."

That easy. Or almost that easy.

Another side bit of advice for the future homeowner: When you have decided to start house hunting, locate a notary public in your neighborhood, someone you know will be there during business hours. Preferably not someone up two flights of stairs who will be on the golf course even on the two days they say they work. I don't know how many notary offices I stopped at only to be told the notary only did work by appointment, or only two days a week, or whatever.

Chances are, you'll need a notary, and it saves some time and irritation to know where to find one.

Marie assumed power of attorney, which meant she could write checks on my accounts, sell my assets, and, most important, sign my name to legal documents. I left for Switzerland.

Leaving the country proved, in fact, an excellent thing to do. It broke the obsession, the sense of helplessness I'd had since the deal developed kinks. Being on another continent afforded me the serene detachment I had only aspired to previously. If you can manage it, I highly recommend a transatlantic trip in the middle of escrow. (Years later, my boyfriend and I would be in Spain when his escrow closed—and his escrow hell was far deeper and more torturous than mine.) Six thousand miles, a different culture—these things are great salves for a tricky escrow.

In Switzerland, I was part of a house party in a large château not far from Gstaad. There were eight of us being pampered by mutual friends who owned the place. I saw lush green fields, the occasional dark, picturesque chalet, and the Alps from the window of my room. The soft clanking of cowbells filled the air. We hiked during the day, rested, then met before dinner for drinks and conversation. Just as I came down to the cocktail hour one evening, the phone rang throughout the château, then someone said it was for me.

Tai.

The documents had come from the governmental agency—and the news was not good. The full amount of the liens would not be covered by the sale. In other words, once the seller paid off his mortgage, he would not have enough money from the sale to pay off what he owed the state. And a payoff was necessary before the house could change hands. So what did this mean?

"It's not a lot of money," said Tai. "If you kick in another $1,500, that will do it."

I was so tempted to say yes. Just say yes and get it done. And I still felt bad about the four hundred dollars I'd made him pay for the loan lock. But I have learned the hard way that when I do not know how I really feel, I should pause and think things over, take inner stock and, if necessary, seek advice. In this case, I told Tai I'd get back to him in an hour or so, and I phoned Marie.

"Tai asked me to kick in another $1,500," I told her.

"The answer is *no*," said Marie.

"I told him I'd think about it."

"The answer is *no*," said Marie.

"Maybe I should kick in four hundred dollars, because of the loan lock thing."

"The answer is *no*," said Marie. (Please notice how many times I need to be told things before I hear them.) "This is not your problem. This is the seller's problem. And Tai's problem."

"Okay. I guess I'll call him back and let him know."

"You are *not* calling him back. I'm your agent in this transaction, and I'm calling him back. I'm handling this. You enjoy your vacation."

If I had a wish for every woman buying a house, it's that they could have an advocate as forceful and tigerish as Marie.

I didn't hear anything more for a day and a half. Then Marie phoned. "You own a house. I have the keys. Congratulations."

I waited for a feeling—elation, satisfaction, relief—but curiously, I felt nothing.

"I wonder how they came up with the money," I said.

"Who cares?" said Marie. "When I talked to Tai, I asked him why he thought you should have to pay a penny more than the agreed-upon price. He said, 'To prove that she's a nice person.' I told him, probably a little louder than I intended to, 'She doesn't have to prove any such thing. *She already is a nice person!*' "

Me, a nice person. And a homeowner.

ROSE, RIGHT FOOT LEFT FOOT

When it came to moving through the escrow process, Rose was in a blur. The whole deal was just too overwhelming.

Rose's agent directed Rose from one item to the next and Rose simply followed, happy to be guided all the way. First thing was the mortgage.

"I got the loan from a friend of a trusted friend. I had 10 percent down and this fellow asked to see a year's worth of checking account activity. I faxed over my bank statements. He checked my credit rating and said I was over 700, golden. When he offered me a loan with a decent interest rate, I just said yes."

No sense of panic, of shame, of financial undressing in the loan process?

"Either they're going to say yes or no," Rose says. "But I wasn't too worried. Everyone's dying to loan money right now."

In truth, she knew her credit wasn't spotless. She shouldn't have had a "golden" score at all. "I'd paid a few bills late. There were things I was worried would show up. But they didn't."

When it came time to sign the papers—known as "closing"—she went to a place in Glendale. "I was directed there by my Realtor, Alexis. She said, 'This is the title company we use. This is the escrow company we use.' And I said, 'OK.'"

Marie from the Tao group had also helped prepare Rose for each step of the process. "This is what's going to happen next and next and next," she'd told Rose, easing much of her anxiety. Having someone you trust—a friend or real estate agent—in your corner during this process makes all the difference in the world.

"I couldn't have done it without Marie and Alexis," Rose says. "If I had to figure it all out on my own, I'd still be renting."

Throughout the process, Rose was willing for the whole deal *not* to go through. "That's why I don't remember any of it. I didn't care. I was very ambivalent about the whole deal. If, at any point in this process, somebody had said 'this isn't going to happen,' phew, I'd just get to go back to my little rental house and never think about it again."

But no one ever told Rose that it wasn't going to work. "They'd say, here's where you go next, and I kept doing the next thing." In the end: home ownership.

MARIE DOES IT HERSELF, AGAIN

Even Marie, the Gals' real estate angel, ran into problems during her escrow process nearly twenty years ago, thanks to a mess created by her real estate agent and the seller's agent.

Marie and Dennis had completed the transaction with the sellers and were waiting for all the details to be finalized and the property to be recorded—the final stages of escrow. At the time, Marie and Dennis were living out of suitcases.

"We had stuff in boxes. We'd been living in someone else's empty house—it had been sold—and we needed to move. Everything we owned was on a truck."

The purchase of Marie and Dennis's house was set to close in three days. They called the sellers to ask if they might be allowed to store their things in the garage until it was all done. The sellers were fine with the idea.

"All we wanted to do was put our things in the garage. It was empty; it was available."

At that point, things got really mucked up.

"The real estate agents got together and decided we couldn't do that."

There were liability issues, the agents pointed out.

Marie explained to the agents that she and Dennis would resolve the issues with the sellers. "I will indemnify them," she said. "We'll take care of it."

But the two agents kept messing with the setup, afraid that if something went wrong, they'd lose their commission payments.

"I finally told both brokers, 'Don't call me again. I'll let you know when you can pick up your check, because that's all you care about anyway. Don't bother me.'"

Looking back, Marie thinks that perhaps she'd been too involved in the home-buying and escrow processes. But she knew what she was doing. "From being in real estate law, I knew what to look for, how to talk with them, how to make it work, and I did."

She and Dennis moved their things in the garage, and three days later, the house closed without a glitch.

COLLEEN NEEDS A WIFE

When she entered escrow on her house, Colleen was in the midst of divorce settlement proceedings that were not going well. She and Rick had sought mediation to resolve their differences, and though they were paying a fortune for each mediation session (both to their mediators and their respective attorneys), they weren't making any progress. Meanwhile, she was getting ready to start the kindergarten-application process for her oldest child and was figuring out child care for both boys—all this on top of her demanding job in court. Each day was a struggle She'd come to the Tao meetings with the weight of all these concerns settled visibly on her shoulders.

"What I really need is a wife," Colleen told the ladies. "Someone who can just focus on the house purchase details and let me attend to the stuff of my daily life. You know, someone who's focused on what's going on in the home. About the home. With the home. I don't have that."

Though as friends, the Tao Gals tried to pull together for Colleen, still, they didn't quite add up to the wife she needed. As a result, many of Colleen's escrow details were not taken care of. In reality, the real estate agent should have been overseeing the deal, but the market was on fire and the agent had, for the most part, moved on to the next sale.

The seller, for example, was supposed to have fixed the sprinklers on the property, redone the window casements and completed a myriad of fix-it items in the house. Because there was no wife to follow up on these things, and Colleen's real estate agent didn't follow through, nothing got done. She allowed escrow to close, knowing these things weren't done, because she simply needed to move and didn't have the time to sweat it. Colleen moved into the house with all these details unattended.

Eventually, all the details were taken care of, but it was a hassle. Colleen arranged for a repair person to come out and complete the fix-it items. She also arranged for the sellers to pay for these repairs. Still, she says, it was a tremendous headache that she really didn't need at that time. In an escrow that's being tended to, these details would have been completed.

Once she was settled in the house, you'd think the demons of that wifeless time would have been exorcised. But no.

Back when Colleen had bought the property, she'd gone

through her father to make the deal. He bought the house and she paid the mortgage, an arrangement that would stay in place until the divorce was final. Some months later, she got a bill for thousands of dollars in property taxes that she owed. She'd assumed they were part of the mortgage payment. She was wrong. Colleen had to call her father and ask him to bail her out, a situation none of us likes.

Then, once the divorce was final, she took over the mortgage, was put on the title and refinanced the property in her own name, this time requesting that her tax payments be impounded each month. She didn't want to be hit up for a whopping tax bill again.

After getting used to making her mortgage payment with taxes included, Colleen felt that it was all quite doable. Thanks to the lower interest rates, her payment wasn't too high and she congratulated herself on having arranged things so well.

Then she got a call from the lenders.

"There's been a mistake," they said. "We didn't do the impounds."

"What?" Colleen had worked to make sure her payment, including the impounds, remained affordable.

Now, they told her, she'd not only have to pay more to cover the taxes, but also she'd have to pay extra to make up for the months passed in which she hadn't paid the taxes. In that one phone call, her monthly mortgage payment leaped up $600. Ouch!

"I should have paid more attention," she said ruefully.

While the impound account on her refinance was not a detail that could have been ironed out in escrow, it shows the importance of going over every detail carefully, making sure everyone knows what's going on and that all the minutiae are in order. Without that kind of attention, ugly surprises may come home to roost.

And that, after all, is the purpose of escrow—to make sure you're getting what you think you're getting and that everything is in place to pay for it. Escrow takes time and attention, but doesn't have to be a nightmare.

What You Will Learn from the Inspection Report

If you include an inspection as part of your purchase agreement (which is highly recommended), a trained inspector will assess the property for you and provide a report on its overall health. Pay particular attention to ensure that the following have been assessed. If there are any major problems, this is the time to think about if it's worth going forward.

1. condition of foundation

2. condition of roofing, including roof tiles, rafters, and any decks

3. condition of the heating and air-conditioning systems

4. condition of the electrical systems

5. condition of the plumbing

6. condition of house's exterior—wood siding, brick, etc.

7. condition of the attic, basement, and/or garage

WHEN TO WALK AWAY

During this process, there may be numerous points at which you may be tempted to shake your head and say, "This is just too much. Too many things are going wrong. I should probably cut my losses here."

Each of us Gals hit that point. Sometimes, it's evidence that we need to back off and let things fall through. In other cases, though, we may push far too hard because we want what we want when we want it.

BERNADETTE'S IMPATIENCE

When I was buying the new home I subsequently lost, I'd experienced months of things going wrong. Our condo wasn't selling, and then, once it did sell, the house was behind on construction. Even to the end, when the fire insurance policy seemed to go missing, I was determined to make the deal work. In retrospect, I wonder if this was such a good thing.

"At one point, we were a week away from moving in," I tell the Tao ladies. "Our stuff was in boxes, the moving truck was all arranged, when the builders called. The house wouldn't be ready in time, they told me. It was already a month overdue and now they were telling us they needed two more weeks."

I blew my stack. No, I wasn't going to wait any longer! As a journalist and former publicist, I knew how to get the ear of the media and I threatened to do just that.

"I told the builders that they'd better have my house done as promised, or I'd be camping out in front of their model homes with a huge sign, telling of my displeasure, and I'd make sure the press knew about it as well."

The ladies are surprised to hear this part of my story. I'm generally very mild-mannered and they found it hard to imagine me going to such lengths.

"It was not one of my better moments, but I was desperate."

The builders pulled all their construction crew members off the other houses in the development to finish my house. We moved in on the date we had planned.

Looking back at the fiasco that house became, culminating in the foreclosure, I wonder if I should have been more easy-going about the whole thing, if maybe I could have been as laid-back as Rose. If I had had the Tao principles active in my life then, who knows? Maybe I wouldn't have forced events to unfold. Maybe I would have seen the signs of danger that were lurking everywhere.

Hindsight, of course, is 20/20. But during the escrow process, it's good to keep your radar active for signs of trouble. If this deal simply takes too much pushing to work, maybe it's time to back off.

Or not.

Listen to your heart. Confer with your friends—and your agent. A certain amount of buyer's remorse is normal.

Tao Worksheet

1. How do you imagine the escrow and closing processes? What could go wrong? Are you confident your agent can walk you through escrow? Are you able to turn this process over to someone else? What do you need to feel comfortable and safe?

2. Escrow doesn't always follow the plan. What can you do for yourself to be ready for the changes escrow may entail? Write about the virtue of flexibility and how you might culti-vate it in your own life.

3. In just about every escrow, there comes a point when you think about dropping the whole home-purchasing idea. It is

just too much. Write about how you can walk through that process with your heart open to signs of danger, yet not run away at the first little glitch.

4. If you don't have a "wife," is there a friend in your life who might play that role for you? Someone who would shepherd you through and help you make sure all the details are in place? Or, can you talk with your real estate agent about what kind of help you need? How does it make you feel to ask for help? How can you make this a more comfortable process for yourself?

CHAPTER TEN

REMODELING AND SETTLING IN

We hammer wood for a house,
but it is the inner space
that makes it livable.

O F THE FOUR Tao Gals who bought houses so far, every one of them put a substantial amount of money into the house she bought: remodeling, fixing up, and in Marie's case, practically gutting the place and starting from scratch, essentially doubling the size of the home. Rose was the only one to undertake all the repairs she had initially planned before she moved in. The others—Michelle, Marie, and Colleen—did the work as time and money allowed while they were living on-site. And "on-site" means in the middle of the construction site, and dust. In all cases, the hassles could and did at times escalate into enmity, and the bills had a way of expanding exponentially.

The results? In just about every case, the women are happy they took the steps they did to turn what had been just-okay properties into homes that more accurately reflected their spirit and needs.

MICHELLE REMODELS; OR, HOW TO TALK TO MEN

I have a rule when shopping: Don't buy something that needs to be fixed. Don't buy pants that need to be hemmed unless the store can do it right then and there. When yard sale–ing, do not buy a dress with a broken zipper, or a coat missing buttons, or a lamp that needs rewiring. The reason for this rule is that I have bought that dress and coat and lamp—and I have never ever fixed a one.

I do not fix things. I buy the too-big skirt, the jacket with the sagging lining, and they take up closet space until, years later, I give them away.

I know myself. So when I decided to buy a fixer-upper, I did so only by making a stern promise to myself. I'd remodel *immediately*.

My contractor, however, couldn't start for two months after escrow closed. In the meantime, my friend John, a former union stagehand and sometime nonunion set dresser, was embarking on a new career as a self-employed handyman. I volunteered to be his first client. I wanted two things done before the general contractor arrived.

Job #1: I wanted a door put into my garage. The only way in at present was to lift the whole front garage door. My cat, Shirley—formerly an outdoor cat—needed to go inside at night; there were coyotes living in the cemetery across the street and all the lampposts in the neighborhood were cluttered with lost-pet flyers. I'd been keeping Shirley in the house and she, in turn, was keeping me up all night with her hyper nocturnal antics. We'd both be happier with her in the garage after dark.

Job #2: I wanted to rebuild the gate between the front yard

and the backyard—the existing one had to be lifted and dragged to make even a foot-wide opening to squeeze through.

John came over and looked at the two projects, then looked through my house.

I had known him for twenty years. He was an artist and a perfectionist, and had made his own various homes into perfectly functioning, beautifully set-dressed curiosities inside and out. He said, "If you are going to do construction to the kitchen area, you're going to have to make the back wing habitable. That's what I would do first—fix up those back two bedrooms, so you can live in them while construction's going on in the other part of the house." Oh. I hadn't thought of that.

And so he went to work in what we took to calling "the privacy wing." And my privacy continued to be disturbed on a nightly basis with Shirley cavorting through the house in endless moth hunts. By day, John removed the closet in one room, fixed the windows so they went up and down, repaired the closet in the other room—that repair, since he had to fabricate a door, took days and cost, in supplies and his hourly wage, over $500. I objected continuously, but he doggedly persisted. Later, when I was designing the remodel, I wanted to knock out the closet to add space, but felt I had to keep it, since I'd already put so much money into it.

I should've had a plan. But the plan was being made for the general remodel. John just kept working, in spite of the lack of plan. I tried to stop him. John, I said, I don't think the closet needs to be perfect. John, I'm not even sure I want that closet. John, I don't want to put so much money into the closet.

He'd say, That's okay. You'll like it when it's done. It's not that much money. You'll need this closet.

I thought, What is happening here? I didn't want any of this work! The damn cat is keeping me up all night, and I'm still wrestling the back gate every time I want to go in and out of the yard.

One day, I talked to John's wife, another long-term friend. "I hired him to do two things, and he's doing a dozen other things."

She said, "Welcome to my life."

I talked to my shrink about it, who suggested I talk to John. I talked to John. I said, "I really want a gate and a door into the garage."

He said, "Just let me finish the privacy wing."

And I didn't want to insist, to be a bitch, to hurt his feelings, to seem pushy, or demanding or unreasonable—*unfeminine* in a word. Who was I, a new homeowner, to tell a skilled artisan what to do? I was afraid, too, of making him angry and having him say snide things to our mutual friends. I wanted to keep the peace more, it seemed, than I wanted the door to the garage or a new gate.

By the time John was finished with the privacy wing, my contractor was ready to start work on the remodel. John never did get to the gate or the garage door.

Oh, the privacy wing was nice when he finished it. And I did live in the rooms when the rest of the house was undergoing its remodel. But I could've lived in them in their original state, as well. And, if Shirley had been in the garage, slept far, far better.

I wish I hadn't put so much money into the closet, because to this day, I think the shape of the house would've been better if I'd removed it.

A further conversation with John's wife was enlightening. "Actually, John doesn't know how to hang doors," she said.

"And he hates to dig fence-post holes. But our dog destroyed so many closet doors, he was an expert at closet doors."

Thus did I learn the absolute importance of being able to talk to a contractor. Nothing is more important than that.

You need to be able to talk to your contractor.

You need to be able to say what you want done, and not be dissuaded. If they don't want to do what you want, find another contractor who will.

You need to articulate what you like—and what you don't like, and what is gorgeous, and what will have to be done over again.

When you hire a contractor, ask for references. Then, talk to the *women* they've worked for and ask them about the quality of communication. The most incredible contractor-artisan in the world could be a nightmare if he doesn't know how to listen and communicate.

When John left and my contractor, Lucian, arrived, I went from the ridiculous to the sublime. Lucian had worked for architects and museum curators and movie stars. He'd worked with some famously temperamental clients. He worked regularly with one of the better-known Hollywood designers—a designer I'd interviewed at one point for *House and Garden*. Lucian was not a budget contractor. But I got him when he was beginning to downscale. He wanted to take less-pressurized jobs, work only four days a week, with a smaller, less high-end crew. My kind of small, containable job that had lots of room for creativity appealed to him. He was not the least expensive contractor by a long shot—although he might have ended up that way. But after I saw what Rose and other friends went through trying to find inexpensive labor, Lucian, dollar for dollar, and headache for headache was a steal.

Lucian had a degree from an art school, he had a good eye, but no ego about imposing his ideas. We worked together on the plan, and he did the drawings and took them to the engineer. He drove an ancient VW bus that was as intricately packed and organized as a brain—and held as many surprises. He had every kind of tool for every kind of job. Every night, he and his crew cleaned and left a spotless construction site. Meticulous, focused, steady, egoless—Lucian is, as all his clients agree, a saint. He is also a vegetarian, and taught my dog to like tofu and seitan, and eventually had to bring larger and larger lunches so he could share them with her.

His construction values—the standards to which he worked—were very high. To this day, I'll go into new homes or new remodels and see that the doors don't swing so perfectly, that the walls aren't so smooth, carpentry so careful. Most of Lucian's subcontractors—plumber, electrician, wood-floor guy—were excellent professionals without being overly pricey. (Again, I saw friends find people whose quotes were lower, but who ended up costing as much or more.) The electrician was famous for making the smallest mess possible—thus costing far less in wall patching and repainting. The plumber—though he complained nonstop—showed up when promised and finished when he said he would. (I got used to his complaining, and soon found it quite comic.)

Lucian's only fault lay with his small crew. He had taken on one young man, Enrique, as an apprentice and lead worker in what can only be described as a case of blind, paternal love. Lucian really felt he could make an ace carpenter out of Enrique, and Enrique did work hard (when Lucian was around), and he could do everything from plastering and carpentry to masonry and landscape drain systems, albeit with varying degrees of competency. Enrique's main problem was something no teaching could cure: He had no eye, and no sensitivity for details, no sensibility.

At one point, Lucian had to leave for the day and had Enrique put in a window. Enrique did a fine job in many respects—set it in, repaired the stucco, get it so it opened and closed perfectly. The problem was, all the other windows and doors on the back of the house were set in at the same level, and this new window was set a good two or three inches lower than all the others. It was very noticeable. I felt terrible. When Lucian arrived the next morning, we looked at it together. "I don't know, maybe we can make a kind of eyebrow or optical illusion or something to put it in line with the others," I said.

Lucian interrupted me. "It's coming out," he said. By the end of the day, the window was reinstalled at the right level.

That's what a good contractor does.

Then, there was the tile guy. Lucian found him, but this was the first job they'd done together. "He does beautiful work," Lucian said, and this proved true—mostly.

The day he was due, however, the tile guy didn't show up. He came a full day and a half late.

I didn't understand then that many subcontractors actually run three or four jobs at a time, and a snarl-up at one job can throw off the schedules at all their other jobs. The tile guy said he was coming at noon on a Tuesday and I stayed at home waiting for him, too shy to bother him with a phone call. When I needed to go out at night, I phoned him. He said he'd be there the next day at noon. I waited all day for him, and again, at seven that night, I went out. I didn't bother to call. I came home at ten to the following note (which I kept for its phonetic pidgin Spanglish): *I arríb 7:30. No barri joom. Sus tayo man.*

After some puzzling, I translated, "I arrived at 7:30. No-body home. Your tile man."

I phoned him and, very upset, asked him to please call and tell me when he was going to be late. "I've wasted two days waiting for you!" I cried. To his credit, he did phone me frequently after that. But I was his second or third job each day. He and his crew would get one job to a stopping point and move on to the next. I think they slept five or six hours a night. For several days in a row, he arrived at my house around 7:30 P.M. and worked until the neighbors complained about the tile saw screaming after 11 P.M.

He did an absolutely stunning job in one bathroom—subway tiles throughout, and a beautifully executed window indent that served as a shampoo nook.

Next came a hearth with a tile surround where the wood-stove would go. I'd ordered beautiful and heart-stoppingly expensive handmade tiles at one place and even more expensive accent tiles at another. I spent about six hours laying out the design on the floor next to the hearth so the varied colors in the two kinds of tiles flowed together smoothly. I explained it all to the tile man and went into my office to work. When I came out for a look some forty minutes later, I saw he had ignored my design and was laying tiles higgledy-piggledy, in whatever order his assistant handed them over.

In shock, I pointed out that I'd made a design. He seemed remorseful, and translated what I'd said to his assistant.

I was too nice to make him undo all the work he'd just done. Chalk it up to liberal guilt.

Only I look at those tiles today and notice that the careful gradation of tones occurs on only two thirds of the surface. Nobody else notices.

But a very good thing came out of that bad tiling experience.

I still had countertops, backsplashes, and another bathroom to tile. I already knew I never wanted to lay eyes on that particular tile man again.

So my friend Hannah and I went to Home Depot on a Saturday morning and took the free two-hour tile-setting class. I bought an electric tile saw. I bought a book of instructions and helpful hints.

Setting tile is not difficult, I discovered. It's exacting, and if you take your time and are careful, you can do a good job. But tiling is very, very time consuming.

I tiled my kitchen counters. I'd discovered the "boneyard" of the place where I bought my handmade tiles. The boneyard was full of overruns and rejected orders, hundreds of colors. I tiled my counters with some of my findings—at a fraction of the cost. The tiling was easy—flat and straightforward.

Then, I began work on the second bathroom—a tub surround and a floor. When I started the tub surround, I was using these heavy eight-by-eight-inch off-white crackled tiles dug out from deep in the boneyard. Hannah came to help. I got about six of the tiles up when they began sliding this way and that. I looked to Hannah in panic.

"You can always call in the tile guys," she said.

Never! With renewed energy and purpose, I consulted my book and improvised ways of keeping those big, heavy, crackled babies right where I wanted them to be, straight and still. I figured it out. The whole tub surround took about forty hours of work.

Then I moved to the floor. For the record, sheets of one-inch hexagonal tiles are much trickier to set than they look. Again, the project took much longer than I ever dreamed.

But I don't regret a second of the time I invested in tiling. The kitchen and bath both are lovely—the handmade tiles themselves are beautiful and forgiving of small errors—but the fact that I did the work made me intimate with the materials in a way that carries over into how I feel about living with them day to day. A deeper appreciation. A deeper connection. A profound sense of belonging.

By this stage in the game, I'd learned some important lessons—though I was still not able to follow all of them.

Watch. And don't leave the room until you know things are proceeding according to plan.

If a contractor or subcontractor proposes to do something different than the plan, listen to him. Try to determine if the suggestion is really going to make the project better—or if the contractor is just trying to make life easier and more cost-effective for himself.

Don't allow yourself to be talked into anything you're not absolutely sure about.

Don't acquiesce just because you don't understand something.

Don't assume their expertise trumps your amateur ideas. Just because a person can lay tile or paint trim doesn't mean they can design tile work or choose great colors.

Remember, you're the one who has to live with the finished product.

Still, keep a perspective.

When somebody does something substandard to your home, it can seem horrendously, irrationally personal. Your house can seem like a second skin, and any scrape or cut or mangling is going to feel far worse than if it were someone else's skin—or house. Remember, when you're staying up all night because of a badly beveled piece of trim, that may well be completely irrational. Then again, you may have a point.

Remember, some things only you will notice. So let go when it's reasonable to let go.

Remember, some things you'll have to live with for the rest of your life. So stand up for yourself when necessary.

Don't fall into the perfectionist trap. During a remodel, your aesthetics will be allowed full bloom, and you'll be ultra-dilated to beauty and imperfection alike. Try to keep a perspective. I was surprised, during my remodel, to see that some of my wealthiest friends had homes where the tile work was inferior to my own amateurish efforts, where their finish work was downright shoddy—baseboards bowing out from walls, crown molding badly joined. In the decades I'd been coming to their houses, I'd never noticed these things before—and I've forgotten to notice them since.

Remember, it's entirely possible to live happily with imperfection.

Three years after Lucian finished, I still have an unfinished beam in my living room. Smears of white paint soil both sides; big splinters jut off here and there. The wood needs to be sanded, then oiled, or painted, or clad in wood. I can't decide. For months at a time, I forget all about that beam. It sits there, smeared and splintery, and I don't give it a moment's thought. Then I see it, or someone might ask, What are you going to do with the beam? And it returns to consciousness. And fades again. One day, I'll get to it.

In remodeling, it's a struggle to keep any kind of balanced perspective. What is a big deal? What is a little deal? When is it time to stick to your guns? When is it time to let something go?

Shawn, the man who installed my wood floors, was careful

and thoughtful. He ordered the red oak well in advance of laying it to give it time to cure. He spent hours arranging the lengths of wood so that the colors were shown to their best advantage. He installed, he sanded. And when he Varathaned the floor, the Varathane bubbled up in several spots like little rashes. Maybe five small spots, all about 8 inches square. Despondent, he stripped the whole 600-square-foot area. We waited several weeks, thinking the wood needed to cure even longer. Then, he re-Varathaned. Again, bubbles rose up, in some of the same places and some new ones. Shawn looked on the verge of tears. He'd already lost his profit in the extra days of stripping and refinishing. But he was ready to strip the floor again and try something else.

I was the one to say, "Shawn. It's a *floor*! People will walk on it. It's for feet! A few barely visible bubbles are not a tragedy. We'll deal with them in five or ten years, when the floor's refinished."

Indeed, with my furniture in and the rugs down, I haven't noticed a bubble zone in, oh, a good two and a half years.

I found it especially difficult to assert myself when a professional spoke to me with authority.

I mean, here I am, a rank amateur, and here they are, professionals who have been doing this sort of thing for years. How does someone, with their pathetic little hand-done plan, stand up to them?

But it's imperative to stand up to them. Otherwise, you can be very sorry, even depressed about it later on.

I wish I'd learned my own lessons after the first few battles—after John the handyman and the maddening tile guy. But I had more lessons to learn.

Because then came the linoleum installer.

I can't say I wasn't warned about Frank. Frank was famous

for being the best linoleum layer in town—"He can do anything!" they told me at the linoleum store where he picked up a lot of business. Frank's portfolio—on display at the store—was indeed impressive. He laid floors as complex as Persian carpets and Aztec calendars, all cut from lowly linoleum.

Frank was also anecdotally famous for doing things his way, and forcing his opinions on customers. "He's good," my friend Hannah's husband, Matt, said, "just don't let him make any aesthetic decisions." Matt and Hannah had wanted a big checkerboard-pattern floor in their kitchen, only with the checkerboards on the diagonal. Frank showed up to install the tiles and argued against laying them on the diagonal with such authority that Matt and Hannah caved into his opinion—and have regretted it ever since.

It's easier to lay tiles horizontally than it is to install them diagonally. Less measuring. Fewer angles. Less time. Frank didn't adjust his quote after he talked them out of the diagonal design. He just gave himself an easier day for the same pay.

I had heard these stories, and now the talented but infamous Frank was coming to my house. I felt armed and ready to be strong. But I have to admit, I'd liked Frank over the phone. We made each other laugh. He was a loquacious, slightly outrageous gay guy with a lot of enthusiasm for his work. I had labored over my paltry little linoleum design for weeks, changing this and that, laying out paper cutouts on the floor, eyeballing the design from every angle. Basically, it had a chocolate brown outline, a pale guacamole green color field, and two areas (at the sinks) with three big red diamonds in them. I faxed Frank this design, all the measurements and colors, and the linoleum was ordered.

But I'd never really designed a linoleum floor before, and

though I'd looked at a lot of pictures and a few real-life examples, I was far from being an expert.

When Frank showed up to start the work, I still had my paper cutouts on the floor and was determined that he would see and understand my design—you see, I'd learned from the tile man that being clear was important!

Frank frowned. "You really don't want to extend your border out from under the counters' overhang," he said. "Borders should just defend the counters, and no more."

Oh. I'd never heard of linoleum borders defending anything. I didn't know there were rules and guidelines about such things.

"And you really don't want the border in the pantry," he said. "That should be a solid color."

He redrew my design. It didn't look right to me, and I said so.

"Yes, but I know how it will read once it's installed. You'll see. If I do it the way you have it, it will look very lopsided."

Oh. "Yes, but if you just put the borders under the counters, they'll be hard to see."

"They defend the counters; that's what a border is for!"

I was defenseless against this argument. So I let him install the linoleum the way he suggested. Several times, I whispered, "I don't know, Frank, it just doesn't look right to me."

He said, "That's because it's not finished."

I had to stop watching, because each time I looked, it seemed more lopsided. I left the house. I was nervous. When I came home, he was putting his tools in the truck. We went into the kitchen together. He was snapping pictures, proud of his work. I was dismayed. You couldn't see any of the border color and the red diamonds were now totally off-center. I found myself tilting my head at all angles, twisting my body, trying to make the floor balance.

Frank left, and I kept staring at the floor from various contorted positions, hoping that somehow, someway, it would look right to me.

I called Hannah to come over and look at it.

She couldn't believe her eyes. "It's *all* wrong," she said. "Oh my god! It's totally off! How can you doubt it for an instant?"

That night the Tao Gals met at my house. Everybody agreed, the design made no sense.

I felt bad, though, because I'd agreed to Frank's changes. I'd told him to go ahead. I thought—assumed—he knew what he was doing. Then again, I'd been warned expressly against taking his advice. So whose fault was it that the floor was all wrong?

Frank was furious, but he reinstalled the floor according to my plan. He didn't do as good a job as he had the first time. He didn't grind linoleum and mix it with glue to fill in the cut lines. More cuts showed than before. Today, the floor is a dazzler—if you don't look close. It also has buckled in some places, and bubbled in others. I see these flaws as my punishment for defending myself—and not just my counters.

I look at the floor and I still wonder: I was told from the start, Don't let him make any aesthetic decisions.

But I let him.

I let him because he was the professional, and I was the rank amateur.

I let him because he was so sure of himself and I didn't want to cross him.

I didn't want to arouse his contempt.

I liked him and I wanted him to like me.

Jesus—does one have to live out one's neuroses in every damn encounter?

Apparently so.

The good news is, improvement is possible. I have become better—though not perfect—at talking to the people I hire to do work on my home and property. I could go on and on with the stories. I could tell you about the painter with no boundaries, who did gorgeous work but tried to scam everyone who came within hearing distance: he tried to get neighbors, guests, mail carriers, journalists who'd come to interview me, to hire him, to buy his trash pickings, to rent a car or a piece of equipment from him. Long after he finished working for me and was working for my next-door neighbor, I came home and found him in my study using my phone. "I thought we were friends that way," he said. (No amount of careful reasoning, stern talkings-to, or actual yelling penetrated his consciousness, but he could apply paint like an angel at very affordable prices—not affordable enough, however, for me ever to employ him again. However, he still haunts me.)

I could tell you about the arborists who trimmed the giant eucalypti in my backyard, who, no matter how many times I told them, could not remember to cut the logs into twenty-inch sections or less—even though they'd agreed to it ahead of time; even though I was paying them extra to do so; even though I took them inside, showed them the size of my wood-stove and what size logs it would take.

I could tell you about the contractor who agreed to remove the asphalt from a part of my driveway and dispose of it for $300, and then said I had to pay his helper extra.

Now that I'm a homeowner, I keep talking to men. Gardeners.

Fence builders. Manual laborers. Sometimes it really is like talking into the void. Sometimes I'm heard. Often, I'm ignored, and it becomes a game of nerves—how many times can I request/suggest/demand/insist on something?

A designer I know says that she falls apart, cries hysterically, when the men she's hired won't listen to her. She sobs, and they become very paternalistic, and want to help her and take over, and do a fine job because then they are inspired, called, to make it all better.

Not my style, but I have no doubt that it works: Her house is lovely.

Another designer I know has found a way to work well with her workers. She pitches in, side by side, and shows them what she's doing. She is very brave and not frightened, and works harder than they do, and commands their respect. But what if you want someone to do the work, and you don't have the skills to work side by side with them?

My neighbor is a landscape architect who regularly hires dozens of subcontractors—masons, pavers, arborists, gardeners, pool builders, etc.—and swears he has all the same problems I do. "I consider it my job, as the architect, to talk and talk, and talk and talk to these guys, over and over, tell them what's needed, what's right, what's wrong. If I stop supervising, the job almost instantly goes off course. You just have to stay with the job, stay with it, until it's done—to your specifications."

That seems right to me—and also wrong. I mean, when you take your car to the mechanic, you don't have to stay and make sure they're doing their job. When you take your dry cleaning in—your very best clothes—you don't supervise the cleaners step by step. But there is something about having things done to your own home that raises the stakes. And there's often some kind of retro, horrid, but real sexist dynamic at work—sometimes even when you're paying top professionals top price.

One day, I promise myself, I'll be more vigilant. I'll not feel embarrassed to oversee each stage of a project, and ask questions throughout. I'll remember to put in writing what a contractor and I agree will be done, and give each of us a copy.

Someday, I'll talk to contractors without trepidation, without feeling intimidated, or like I'm disrespecting them when they're clearly doing something wrong. We'll see. I still have a lot of landscaping to do, and trees to trim, and exterior walls to paint. And an entire addition to build.

One day, perhaps, I'll figure out how to talk to men.

Finding a Contractor

Ask around. See who your friends have hired. Do they know a good tile person? Someone who's a whiz with kitchens? How did it go? Was the project close to budget? On time?

If you haven't been in town long enough to have a network of friends to ask for referrals, check with your real estate agent or the loan broker; anyone who works in the real estate business should be able to give you a lead. If you're getting referrals from people you don't know very well, be sure to check out the contractor's references and verify that the contractor's license is valid.

ROSE REMODELS ON THE CHEAP, NOT

When Rose bought her house, she decided to have a number of cosmetic things taken care of before she moved in. She wanted the carpets pulled up and planned to install hardwood flooring. (She ended up settling for Pergo, a wood-looking laminate that is less expensive than hardwood and easier to care for.) She liked the idea of French doors in her bedroom. The interior walls of the house were cracked from the previous earthquake, so she'd replaster and paint. And as long as she was at it, it would be nice to take down the partial wall between the dining room and living room. Without that wall, the whole living space would be opened up.

"It was just a small, partial wall," she says, "and even with the prospect of knocking it out, my plans didn't seem like a big deal. A month, tops, I thought, and then I'd move in."

Rose was working on a tight budget and wanted to do these jobs in the most cost-effective manner. Ray, a neighbor, suggested she contact the local community college, which offered classes in house repair and contracting.

Ray had taken its construction class and knew that the students often rented themselves out to help people with fixer-uppers. Sometimes, he said, the class teacher used a house as a class project and then the labor was free.

As it turned out, the timing wasn't right for Rich, the teacher of the class and a licensed contractor, to take on Rose's house as a class project, but she could still hire two students, and Rich would oversee the work.

Rose thought, This is perfect: I'll really have a contractor on the job but not have to pay full contracting prices.

Sounds great, right?

Except that the kids were, in Rose's words, "unbelievably unqualified." They "*so* didn't know what they were doing" and Rich didn't come by nearly enough.

Rose paid each of the workers more than $10 an hour. "They were here twelve, fifteen hours a day for months and months," she said. "And the project itself got bigger by the day."

They began the job by taking out the partial wall separating the living and dining room. As soon as they cut into the wall, they noticed that none of Rose's walls had insulation. They advised her to insulate, which seemed sensible—and also meant that all the walls had to come down, all the way to studs. Everything in the ceiling had to be insulated as well. And then it all would have to be drywalled and plastered. And painted. Of course, once the walls were down, they saw the house had an old kind of electrical wiring called "knob and tube," which is considered a fire hazard. So the wiring was cut out and replaced.

And since she'd taken out one partial wall, why not take down the wall between the entryway and living room, have one great room from the front of the house to the back of the kitchen?

As the job dragged on, Rose's friends raised concerns. "Are these workers just saying these things because they want more money or more business? Is the wiring really such a risk?"

How was Rose to know the answer?

"Who do I ask?" Rose wondered. "How do I find out?"

Rich was not returning her calls.

In addition to being a three-time Olympian, Rose is also a cancer survivor. She's often asked to speak to groups about the will to overcome, to be inspirational and uplifting. Redoing this house, for her, became a huge hurdle to surmount, much bigger than she'd bargained for. The learning curve, for her, was similar to the learning curve she'd experienced when fighting cancer.

Not that she felt particularly sick, though, as the project continued to drag on, she certainly didn't feel well. "The amount of new information I had to take in when I was sick, all about the disease, the treatments, the pharmaceuticals, and how it all worked together, was amazing."

Learning about the house was the same. "At what point does the electricity have to happen? When can the floors go in— before or after or alongside the walls?" Every day she had to learn more and more about things, things she never wanted to know about.

For three months, she lived in her rental house while chaos raged at her new home. She was paying both rent and a mortgage, on top of the various wages and material costs. The project became increasingly costly as time went on. Mistakes added days, days added rent.

For example, there was a problem with a beam, the four-by-four beam that replaced the wall between the entryway and living room.

When the student workers originally placed that beam, they did it in such a way that the beam didn't butt up against the rest of the ceiling.

Rose knew the beam was meant to replace the weight-bearing wall, which meant it had to take on the weight. "Guys, guys," she said to the students. "That big beam has to bear the weight and you have it four inches away from the rest of the roof. What's up with that?"

She started to give the workers instructions on how to position the wood closer to the ceiling, when it dawned on her. "Why am I telling you all this? You're in the construction class and I'm paying you. I shouldn't know more than you do. I know nothing. *Nothing.* But that piece of wood has to go up flush against the roof!"

She let loose an enormous sigh for the Tao Gals. "It makes me so insane. I know that not one single thing is being done right and that the house is either going to burn down or fall down!"

It didn't take Rose long to realize she'd chosen the wrong course of action, but by then, she was in way too deep to do anything about it. She did, however, fire the two students from the class and hire a guy who'd finished the class some time ago, a guy recommended by Rich.

Doug.

"I got Doug to come in and finish the drywalling in the living areas and bedroom."

"This was a better choice?" the Gals ask.

"He was as useless as they were. See that corner down there?" She points to a piece of molding near the door to her bedroom. The wood molding is clearly two or three inches shy of the wall's edge. "This kind of stuff is all over the house. I would come in and I would look at it—every single thing Doug did—I'd look at the end of the day and say, 'Doug, if I was doing this, I might have had that piece of wood come all the way to the white piece of wood.'

"And he's doing this for a living?!" I couldn't believe it.

"He'd be like, 'Well, I'll get to it, stammer, stammer.' There was an excuse for everything. It just blew my mind."

Rose finally had had enough when it took Doug three days to install a bathroom sink. "He had to take some pipes from under the house. The plumbing for the bathroom sink is directly under the bathroom sink, so all he had to do is bring the pipes up through the wall and attach the sink. He took three days. This is the guy who's experienced, who's charging me by the hour."

The toilet for that bathroom still needed to be installed and Rose was going to have Doug do it, when she thought, "How complicated can this be?"

Rose went to Home Depot.

"What do I have to do to put a toilet in?"

"You need these rings, you need this waxy stuff, you unscrew the thing in the back, you take the toilet off, you put the new toilet on, secure it, make sure the thing goes on the thing—you have a new toilet," the Home Depot worker said.

It took Rose an hour and a half.

"Why did it take Doug three days to do the bathroom sink? Phew!," she exhales. "I don't want to go through it again. And there are people who do this rehab thing for fun!"

For Rose, it was simply too much stress. But the house is done now, or as done as anything this complicated can ever be. She likes the funky purple walls and tries to ignore the too-short molding. The Pergo floors, she tells us, have been great.

Still, she needs to replace a fence between her yard and the next-door neighbor's property, and has ideas for other improvements. She just doesn't relish the thought of undertaking another home-enhancement project by herself.

That's what makes it all so hard, she says, doing it alone.

"Say, I decide to build that fence this weekend. If there were two people here and a fence needed to be built, "let's build a fence this weekend" would work for me. But when it's just me, I don't want to build a fence this weekend. I don't want to do it by myself. I don't know how. It's too overwhelming to think about. So . . . I'm not going to build the fence this weekend."

The tasks involved in home ownership are simply endless, Rose says.

"That fence has to get replaced and my neighbors say they're going to help but they don't." The married couple with kids, and untrustworthy dogs, say they can get a discounted price on the labor and promise to split the cost. But nothing moves forward. "If I have to ask them one more time to get a bid . . ." Rose says. "They just blow me off. They were going to pay for the vet bills from the three times their pit bull attacked my dog Bubba and he needed stitches, but they never did." It's times like this, Rose says, that it would be nice to have a partner on hand who could go over there and work these things out.

But the reality is she's alone, and if a fence is going to get built, it looks like she's going to have to be the one to build it. It may not be this weekend. It may not be next weekend. But, Rose is confident, one day or another she's going to go to Home Depot, learn a few things about putting in a fence, and eventually, a fence is going to be built, even if she does all the work herself.

Before You Sign That Contract

When you're ready to get going with a contractor, be sure the contract you're signing is very clear about two crucial details:

1. The scope of work to be done is clearly detailed. For example, "The kitchen floor is to be replaced with linoleum. The old flooring is to be torn out and disposed of." The more details in this document, the easier it will be for both you and the contractor to know what you're getting into.

2. Specifications are also detailed. List the specific materials to be used, how the work is to be done, etc.

COLLEEN, THE RELUCTANT REMODELER
When Colleen was ready to move into her house, she realized that virtually nothing had been done to prepare for her arrival.

Not only had items that were supposed to have been fixed been ignored, but also the house was filthy. The renters had moved out, leaving a disgusting mess. Colleen called her real estate agent and let loose.

"Someone is making a bundle on this transaction and it isn't me!" she'd bellowed. "That house, at the very least, needs to be cleaned before my kids and I move in. And arrangements need to be made for those repairs. *You*"—she growled at the real estate agent—"need to take care of that."

After a brief skirmish, the agent relented and a house-cleaning crew showed up the next day, scrubbing down the kitchen, the bathrooms, cleaning the oven. Bernadette stopped by with a bottle of industrial-strength orange-scented cleaner Marie had told her would sterilize anything.

Though the house was far from paradise when the cleaning crew left, at least it was no longer a health hazard. Eventually, the promised repairs were completed and Colleen settled in. The living and dining room areas were still much too dark for her taste, and the kitchen was antiquated, missing the one appliance Colleen could only dream about: a dishwasher.

"I *hate* the kitchen," she said to everyone who asked about her new house.

Six months later, the main window in the living room, a window that had been rotting in its frame, blew out during a winter storm. Colleen learned a lot about replacing windows in a short period of time. After dealing with window-replacement contractors and getting ridiculously high bids, she made a visit to Home Depot. Their custom department was able to do exactly what she wanted, and the fabulous wood-framed windows she selected made a vast improvement in the room. In fact, those windows, which span the east wall of that part of the house, are

now a showpiece. The success in the window department moti-
vated Colleen to do more. She'd got the bug.

Watching Michelle transform her little box of a house had
inspired Colleen to buy the house in the first place. Now she
was game to go. She undertook minor repairs and cosmetic
touches herself, but she had to save up to remodel the kitchen.
After two years, she was able to refinance and cash out equity
to afford the work.

She called contractors and asked them to come over and bid
on the job. Being a single woman, she found, proved a distinct
disadvantage, both with the refinancing and the remodeling.

"It's just a nightmare," she wailed to the Gals when her first
loan application was turned down. Apparently her appraisal
didn't come in high enough. "Which is unbelievable in this
market, where properties are leaping up practically overnight."

The appraiser had come over on a day when the house was a
mess. Colleen has two small boys and they'd done what small
boys will do to a house on a weekend morning. Those circumstances added up, Colleen believes, to a low ball appraisal. She
doubts that the appraisal would have been so low had a man
been there, even a single man with kids.

By the next meeting of the Tao Gals, however, she'd obtained another loan showing a very high value on the house,
thanks to a different appraiser.

But the appraisal hassles were nothing compared to the
contractors and their aggressiveness in trying to get her to
hire them. The men answered her questions evasively,
condescendingly—not the right tack to take with a district
attorney.

One man kept saying, "I will do whatever you want, any way
you like it. Sixteen thousand dollars. Any kind of tile, sink."

"What if I want a five-thousand-dollar sink? And a five-thousand-dollar countertop?" Colleen demanded.

He waved her away. "I make it beautiful in here. You don't worry."

"Thank you for coming," Colleen said. "I'll let you know what I decide."

"Okay. Sixteen thousand, sign here."

"No, I'm not signing anything tonight," Colleen told him.

"No, you don't understand," the contractor replied. "This is a great price, a great deal. You'll get just what you want. I need you to agree."

"I'm not going to sign anything tonight." Colleen was adamant.

"No, you don't understand . . ."

This went on and on. He wouldn't leave.

"I had to get angry and mean, and I *do* know how to get angry and mean." Colleen and the Tao Gals laugh uneasily. "Yeah, it was *not* pleasant."

All the time she was getting bids on her kitchen, Colleen was thinking about a friend of hers from the equestrian world, Amanda, and what she'd been able to do with the investment houses she'd bought.

"Amanda did what Michelle did," Colleen says. "She was the first person I saw who bought an absolutely hideous house and redid it entirely. She's an artist and photographer, and the house she first bought was the same kind of shit stucco box as Michelle's. She's got a knack for getting people to do things for her—for a song. People call her Demanda."

In Amanda's first house, the floor was covered in hand-laid slate with black grout. The living room had vertical skylights, and the ceiling was painted a light blue-white. The walls were a green that tied into the outside foliage. "You walked into her little house and you felt in the presence of the mountains."

Since then, Amanda had been buying houses, fixing them up, and renting them out. By her sixth house, she'd really developed a way of tastefully rehabbing houses on a lower-end budget.

As they rode their horses together, Colleen unofficially consulted with Amanda about the contractors she interviewed and the prices she was being quoted.

"That's just too high," Amanda would say. "That's just too vague." Or, "It's just too much money."

Colleen hit on an idea.

"Why don't you take the money I've budgeted," she suggested to her friend, "and see what you can do? Just, please, please get me a dishwasher!"

They formalized an agreement. Amanda could use the budgeted allotment however she saw fit and, so long as specific work was done, she was welcome to keep whatever cash was left over. With the bids Colleen had been getting, she knew she was going to pay an arm and a leg for the most basic, blah kitchen anyway. At least with Amanda, she figured, she'd get some style along the way—and not have to deal with an overbearing and/or unresponsive contractor.

"Her biggest thing is the design," says Colleen, explaining her decision to trust Amanda's abilities. "And she'll make the design decisions for me. I really don't care which fixtures I get, so long as they're tasteful and *I don't have to spend the time looking for them.*" In essence, Amanda would serve as the wife Colleen dreamed about.

The Tao Gals drive over to Colleen's on a cool October morning to see her new kitchen. Work had started a month and a half ago. Her voice on the phone, when inviting the Gals over, revealed she's happy with the results. "My cabinet pulls are made out of horseshoes!" she bubbles, as only a serious horsewoman could.

Walking into the house, it's apparent that a huge transformation has taken place. Her "dark, dark, little house" now is flooded in light. Walls that previously sealed off the kitchen from the dining and living areas have, in one case, been removed and, in the other, cut to a partial wall with a countertop.

The kitchen itself is painted a bright cheery green that Colleen calls "apple."

A dramatic new window has been added in the kitchen. Colleen had wanted a greenhouse window, but it would have jutted out into the backyard walkway, knocking in the head anyone who happened to take that path. Instead, Amanda made a fabulous deep wooden frame for a plate glass window so there's a ledge for plants, giving the visual effect of a greenhouse window without the unwanted dimensions or expense.

"It's just a normal window in that great frame."

Where one of the walls used to be, there's a breakfast bar where the boys can eat and do their homework.

The openings are now edged in exposed wood, which has been impressed with horseshoe shapes—workers literally pounded horseshoes into the beams to make those impressions.

Overhead, exposed wood beams were an inexpensive way to support the wall and, together with the sturdy cast-iron support hardware Amanda selected, add a great rustic barn-flavored feel to the place

The floor was a soft wood, actually subflooring, which Amanda had sanded, then applied two coats of clear polyurethane. It looks like the kind of rustic plank floor they pay big bucks for in fancier neighborhoods. Colleen kept her original stove, a near antique, but it's been moved to a different place in the kitchen, its former location now taken up by . . . a dishwasher!

Budget constraints made them go low-key with the cabinets and countertops. The cabinets, all new, were "just the boring white laminate ones Lowes sells." But Amanda spiced them up with a crackled-surface milk crate paint, a nontoxic paint that's like dairy: it needs to be refrigerated or it goes bad.

The recessed lighting is new and, Colleen demonstrates, can be dimmed. The counters are Formica, "boring but functional." The ceiling is a paler apple green than the walls. "Originally, the plan was for Amanda to stencil in red-and-white-striped gingham between the cabinets and the counter to offset the bright green. I loved the idea in concept, but I didn't like it in practice. Too bright. Too hip. Very cool looking. We painted over it."

Next, we all sit at the table and Colleen takes us through the process. She has photos.

"First, everything was 'demo-ed'—demolished out," she says, showing pictures of what looks like a postearthquake, postvandalized nightmare. "They did this in, like, two days. It was horrible."

Then came drywall and the new cabinets: a white world with ragged edges, no counters. She and the kids were able to walk through the area and lightly use the space again after just two and a half weeks. But she and the boys relied on take-out food, and had numerous picnics in the back room. "Or we'd eat in restaurants and come home to shower and do homework in the bedroom."

In some regards, she says, it wasn't as bad as she thought it would be, even with the kids. "For me, it was the construction dust on my work clothes that was the hardest part. The briefcase, everything. Every time I'd pick something up, it was covered in dust."

Now that it's done, Colleen loves the way it turned out and loved working with Amanda. "Amanda was very straight with me. She would tell me what was what. What could and couldn't happen."

Plus, this house transformation, she tells the ladies, has changed how she feels about living here.

"Before, there was an anxiety I felt, not being able to see the kids when I was in the kitchen. I was always having to check, leave what I was doing. Now, I don't have to do that. I'm just a part of it, standing in my kitchen," she raises her arms as if she's a queen surveying her lands. "I feel a part of my house."

"Yeah," she nods her head and looks around, "I'm going to be real happy here. I didn't feel that when I bought it. I didn't want to live in it. It would be a good investment and a safe neighborhood for the kids, but I didn't want to live here. And now . . . a green kitchen with horseshoes on the cabinets . . ." She laughs. "It's definitely my house."

"Actually committing to doing the work was very scary," she confides. "I had no clue how to do it. I trusted Amanda, and put up with the inconvenience, and everything worked out. And now I can say, this is one of the most empowering things I've ever done."

Tao Worksheet

1. What promises have you made to yourself about the property you're considering buying (or have already bought)? How can you help make them come true?

2. Keeping in mind that a dream deferred is not a dream denied, make a plan on how you can accomplish what you want without breaking yourself or the bank. Remember, in Colleen's case, it just took new windows for her to start to see the possibilities.

3. How can you be content to see the possibilities and not have to jump into action now, if now's not the time? For all Michelle's changes in her house, there's still much to be done. The exterior, for instance, is painted in different colors and needs an overhaul. Imagine the end product and working your way there, slowly, slowly, slowly. Write about how you might do that.

CHAPTER ELEVEN

WHEN THE WORST HAPPENS

Failure is an opportunity.

I F BUYING AND remodeling their houses were the most empowering things Colleen and Michelle ever did, Bernadette's
experience of losing her house in foreclosure was downright
devastating.

When you look at buying a house or undertaking any huge
change of that magnitude—moving to a different state or country, say, or changing careers midlife, divorcing or marrying—you
can't help but wonder, what if it doesn't work out? What if we
think we can swing this mortgage payment, handle this commute, live with this decision, but in the long run, we discover
we can't? What happens then? For most buyers, they'll never
face that reality. Thankfully, all will work out as planned. But
for some, the path may turn rocky and the choices available,
thorny.

In previous times, people bought a home, settled down, and
made their payments until the mortgage was paid off and the
mortgage papers burned. There was no fear the house value
would plummet, but neither was there the hope that one might
make a fabulous killing on a house purchase timed just right.
Buying real estate, in much of the country, has become a kind

of speculation, like buying stocks or investing in something where your return is not guaranteed. Though many people have made a lot of money buying real estate, some have lost their shirts—and homes. When markets get this hot, it's a risk you take by playing the game.

The story of Bernadette's loss is a sobering reminder that the American dream does not always materialize the way we intend, and yet, that doesn't mean the dream is not worth pursuing. It means simply that it's best to be prepared in case things go wrong. And to learn to let go.

Because our culture attaches such shame to financial loss, we don't usually hear friends and family members talk in detail about how they have made it through hard times. It's as if those who've experienced misfortune are meant to go and hide themselves until such a time as they're back in the game, and the problems that beset them can be relegated to the distant past.

One of the joys the Tao Gal group has experienced is the ladies' ability to share fearlessly with each other about their misfortunes, to learn from each other that it's okay to come out from under the mantle of shame, to cry communally and share the burden. It's okay, the Gals learned, to start late in life, or to start over. More than okay. It's fabulous. What courage it takes! What joy may be found, especially in light of past disappointments.

By confronting their fear and shame, the Tao Gals were freed from the power those despairing feelings held over them. As long as Bernadette feared financial insecurity, she was a tightly wound ball of nerves. Once she experienced financial insecurity and loss firsthand, she realized it wasn't as bad as she'd feared.

Here, then, is her story of failure and loss, offered in optimism and faith. Should the unthinkable happen and your dreams of the perfect home come crashing down around your head—due to an earthquake, a fire, a hurricane, a natural disaster, a job loss, a chronic illness, or any one of any number of reasons that can destroy the dream—the Tao Gals want you to know that you're not alone. Contrary to what society tells us, financial setbacks are not a sign of moral weakness or poor character. This is life: It just happens. And when it does, it's important to remember what we've learned about knowing ourselves and to climb aboard the "broad back of the Tao" (as Michelle likes to say) and know that life goes on.

BERNADETTE'S SLIGHTLY USED DREAM

Fifteen years ago, I wanted a house, pure and simple, for the protection it would afford me. Like most of us, I grew up in an age focused on fulfilling the precepts of the American dream: Get a good education, buy a house, give your children opportunities you never had. As a young professional, a new mother and wife, I knew it was my duty to shore up my family's financial coastline, to create a world and life for my child that was superior and safer than what I'd known. If I could arrange all the facts of my life, get those real estate ducks all in a row, I could wrest good fortune from wherever it had been hiding and make it mine.

Many of us set out on the home-buying journey with similar thoughts. If it weren't for the desire for protection, to ensure future security for ourselves and our loved ones, would we go to all this trouble? Buying a house can be a long and ugly haul, but usually, we make the trek because the rewards promised are so great: long-term safekeeping for our money, a refuge for ourselves, something that's ours. A place to call our own.

My parents were immigrants. They came here from Ireland

looking for a better life and found it in the sun-warmed haze of Southern California. My parents struggled and bought a 1910 home—with built-in mahogany bookcases and china cabinets, hardwood floors in every room, two huge palm trees on the front lawn—in Glendale, then a sleepy suburb of Los Angeles. My parents were able to convince the sellers to give them a break on the price—$35,000—and to carry the mortgage for them. Seven of us lived in a three-bedroom, one-bathroom home, a place I loved dearly and mourned when it was torn down in the mid-1980s to make room for a condo complex.

Times were tough, though, growing up. My mother was ill most of my life and my father often worked two jobs to make ends meet. Neither of my parents had gone to college and it was vital to them that we did. Education and home ownership, they told us, were the stepping stones to the American dream.

Throughout our college years, my siblings and I paid our own way, working internships and side jobs. I read textbooks in the university library because I couldn't afford to buy my own. Those efforts paid off. I made a good career for myself as a corporate writer, and soon married a man from the Midwest with a business degree from Marquette University.

When John, my husband, initially proposed marriage, my father's primary concern was whether we should marry if we couldn't yet afford a home. Home ownership, he made clear, had to be our first priority. In 1988, at the age of twenty-five, married less than a year, John and I signed on the dotted line and became homeowners. Well, condo owners to be exact, but it was real estate and a step closer to the white picket fence. At last we had a tax deduction, solid credit history, and a good employment record. We were on our way.

A year and a half later, after our first child was born and I quit my day job to be a freelance writer, our two-bedroom condo seemed to shrink. Our son's bedroom doubled as my office during working hours; he was the only infant I knew with a fax and computer in his bedroom. John and I looked into moving up into a "real" home. Thanks to the strong real estate market, we thought we could parlay the condo into a tidy profit—plenty of cash for a down payment on a house. Untrue! The cash profit we would attain, we soon realized, wouldn't buy much—not unlike people today who have made a profit on their earlier real estate investments, only to find it nearly impossible to parlay their profits into anything else since prices have risen accordingly.

Since my earliest days, I had been indoctrinated into the belief that home ownership was the American way. My immigrant father's lectures made clear that home ownership was the dividing line between those who made it in life and those who didn't. Stories in the media confirmed that opinion. The real estate section of the paper, weekly newsmagazines, and television programs on personal finance all echoed the same thought: A house was your three-bedroom piggy bank. Stop throwing your money away on rent. It's the best investment you'll ever make.

It was 1989, the height of the previous real estate frenzy in California. The story is the same one you'll hear today: The few homes for which we could qualify flew quickly out of reach as the market heated up. Just as we made an offer, we were outbid by someone else. (Interest rates then, though, were hovering at 10 percent. Part of what's fueling the current real estate frenzy is the long-standing record-low levels of interest.) One house we seriously considered buying had been vandalized, and tar poured over the carpets. The roof leaked. The backyard swimming pool was so damaged, it would need to be filled in. It was typical of the choices we were facing.

The geographic area we were considering was not even near the heart of Los Angeles, where real estate was ridiculously high; it was more than forty-five miles outside of the city. Places closer in, like Glendale, where I'd grown up, we didn't dare look. Unable to find a workable situation, we began to consider farther outlying areas. Friends of ours had recently moved to Palmdale and invited us up to come look.

In the shadow of Edwards Air Force Base, in the Mojave Desert, the Antelope Valley is home to sister cities Palmdale and Lancaster, a community built on the backs of the aerospace and defense industries. The weather there is harsh for California—freezing temperatures in winter with a touch of snow, and summer days that routinely reach 110 degrees. The commute to jobs in the city is an hour-plus.

It wasn't the ideal solution.

But the homes: they were breathtaking! Four, five, six bedrooms. You want land? No problem. Many lots were half an acre and those who wanted more land could easily find two- and three-acre parcels. We couldn't believe what we were seeing: homes for nearly half of what we had been considering closer to LA.

Horse country. No smog. Four seasons. And booming. In 1980, the combined population for Lancaster and Palmdale had been sixty thousand. By 1990, the year we bought, it was edging up toward two hundred thousand. The outlook was bright. And with the way prices were skyrocketing, what an investment! We could even pick the color of the carpeting.

We wrote a check as earnest money on a house in Lancaster.

At that time, the house wasn't even built yet; it was just a lot, an expanse of land on which we could project our dreams. We envisioned it. The place where our son Jarrod's playhouse would go. Where we'd put the swing set. The covered patio where we'd have friends over for a barbecue. We'd have an actual street address and be thrilled to check the "home owner" box when filling out questionnaires.

John's employer, a lending institution, operated a branch office in the Antelope Valley and agreed to transfer him to the Lancaster facility once we moved. He could walk to work if he wanted. He wouldn't be part of the vast number of tortured souls who made the grueling commute each weekday.

Late at night in our condo, as our house was being built, we dreamed. Where we'd put the furniture. What type of window coverings to get. How we'd make one bedroom into a guest room so that when our family members made that long trek—eighty-five miles from where they lived—we'd be able to offer them hospitality and a place to stay. We learned about xeriscaping so that our yard would be in sync with the natural surroundings. I kept hearing people talk about the beauty of the desert and I tried to conjure up as much beauty as I could.

In April of 1990, our little family had finally made it. The American dream was ours.

WE STARTED OUT by meeting the neighbors—other expatriates from the city—walking the suburban sidewalks in the late-afternoon twilight, talking about what type of shrubs did best in the heavy clay soil, how to stake the roses against the wind, where to get a discount on lawn furniture. We planted trees, tinted windows against the coming heat, painted rooms, installed garage-door openers; we bought a lawn mower. The Antelope Valley Mall—the first "real" shopping mall in the area—prepared to open and talk swelled of a new outlet mall that was going to be built. Los Angeles International Airport, we kept hearing, was planning to turn to Palmdale Airport as an annex and a high-speed rail line would eventually connect the two. Jobs, shopping, and prosperity, with easy access to the big city, were just around the corner. John came home from work during lunchtime to play with our son and I hired a nanny so that I could get my writing work done.

We did the math and found that if we paid an extra sum each month on our mortgage, we could own the home in twenty, rather than thirty, years. We tightened our belts and made the payments, knowing how glad we'd be later when our equity was so high.

Within six months, we heard rumors. It was now late 1990 and the price of real estate, we learned, wasn't holding. Gangs were turning up in Palmdale, moving to the outskirts of the Los Angeles basin, just as we had, for the affordable housing. But you hear rumors no matter where you live, we reassured ourselves. At the time, the entire Southern California economy was being decimated by a recession set off by cuts in the aerospace and defense industries. It wasn't just us. Don't pay any attention. It'll get better. We were shocked by the extreme weather and hadn't planned to spend so much money heating and cooling our dream house, but we'd adjust. What's a little wind? What's a little heat?

Neighbors began to frequent other new-home developments and came back with disturbing evidence. Homes were being sold at $10,000 under last month's price. Then $20,000 less. In our little subdivision of some fifty homes, the second phase of development was put indefinitely on hold. The sound of construction ceased.

So it's a downturn. We've just got to hold out long enough for things to get better.

Summers came and seemed to last forever. Plants died. Kids begged to stay indoors, where it was cool. Applying sunscreen in the morning was as routine as brushing teeth.

In January 1991, John was laid off from his job with no notice—part of the economic downturn. We had some money in savings and my work was steady. We let go of the nanny and cut all inessential spending. Our house was our first priority. We continued to pay the extra on our mortgage every month, though living now on a greatly reduced sum. Like using library books to study, working two jobs to make ends meet—it was one of the sacrifices you made to get ahead.

Shelling out an additional $500 a month for health insurance, we made it through the birth of our second son and twenty months of John's unemployment. And we kept the house. Never once a late payment. Our credit was spotless.

When John finally found a job in September 1992, it was in Pasadena, a sixty-five-mile one-way commute over a treacherous forest highway. The cost of gas initially shocked our budget to the tune of $220 per month. And, there were no more weekday lunches as a complete family—or, for that matter, breakfasts or dinners. He left the house before six A.M. and got home after seven P.M. But he had a job and we had a house.

Almost imperceptibly, the neighborhood began to change. People who had moved in planning to make the commute to LA were getting tired of the drive. It'll wear anyone down after a while. Some couples left and rented out their homes, willing to eat the difference between the rent they could charge and the amount owed on the mortgage. A number of couples divorced. Was there a correlation, I wondered, between the drive and disintegrating marriages?

The home developer that had started the neighborhood abandoned the project altogether and left empty lots perched on little rises, complete with their concrete foundations broken by intrusive weeds, shattered glass littering the area. One couple talked of a "short sale"—getting the bank to agree to take whatever the house could be sold for in the soft real estate market in exchange for letting the owners out of the mortgage. We were shocked. Hadn't we all worked so hard to get here?

When our oldest son was four, our corner fence was targeted by taggers. He began to have nightmares. "Will the bad guys who wrote on our fence come back and get me?" Our guest room remained vacant; family members said the drive was just too long.

One neighborhood couple decided to milk the situation. They stopped paying their mortgage and, with the help of a local attorney, stayed in the home for nearly two years. Every week during this time, their kids were showing up with new playthings—motorcycle-looking bicycles, hip new clothes—all the things they couldn't afford when they'd been paying the mortgage. Even with their spending sprees, they were able to save a small fortune. When they were finally removed from the house, they just rented another one (actually, a nicer home) for $800 a month less than what their mortgage payment had been, having netted at least $35,000 during the free ride.

We shook our heads. How will the market ever improve with people pulling stunts like that? We would stick it out.

Meanwhile, John's employer moved its offices to Simi Valley, extending his one-way commute by another 10 miles. But when you're driving 130 miles a day, what's another 20?

When our oldest was ready to start school, we looked into the local elementary school and were appalled. Built in the heart of a deteriorating neighborhood that abutted our once-nice little enclave, the school was antiquated and neglected looking. Talk among neighbors focused on the low expectations in the school system. If kids made it through high school, that was considered a good thing, as though people living here shouldn't hope for too much. Some of the local kids I spoke with told me they'd never been to the city, had never seen the beach, couldn't picture themselves going to college.

We enrolled our son in a private school and quit ordering pizza or going out to the movies.

Resale prices and rents continued to plummet. One neighbor, a military couple reassigned from Edwards Air Force Base to Oklahoma City, were fortunate to rent out their four-bedroom, three-bathroom home for $800 a month. A single mother of two, tired of the drive, settled on renting her house, complete with a brand-new pool, for $500; anything to get out. Others just left and let the banks deal with the homes. The street was littered with abandoned dreams.

My husband, a sports fan beyond imagination, used to tell me how, when the kids were old enough, he'd coach them in basketball and baseball and go to all their games. Soon, I was sitting alone on sidelines watching strangers coach our kids because John would be home too late for practice.

As these little irritations built up, I began to see the truth: I had been hoodwinked by all the talk of home ownership and the beauty of the American dream. The idea of going to these lengths for a piece of property that had become a millstone around our necks was ludicrous.

Yet how do you walk away from a dream you've invested so much in?

We tried to leave. Three times I called my Realtor friend, cleaned the house until my hands were raw, yelled at the kids to keep their rooms neat, and prayed that someone would want this slightly used dream. A good asking price, I was told, would be half of what we'd paid. After making extra payments on the mortgage to reduce our loan debt, we'd be lucky, our Realtor explained, to pay only $25,000 to get out of the house.

We didn't have $25,000. We'd sunk every dime into the house.

Meanwhile, the media began running pieces about how much strength the real estate market was regaining. Bidding wars were starting up again. Just not where we were.

For eight years we put up with winds that never stopped and summers that turned us into moles. We went through two cars with the commute. And there was no relief in sight. The new outlet mall declared bankruptcy and Ralph's, the grocery store we favored, left town. A tattoo parlor opened around the corner.

The final straw was an article about the Antelope Valley in the *New Yorker*. In this sixteen-page exposé on the woes of my children's hometown—the high rate of child abuse, the epidemic of methamphetamine use, the alarming rate of teen pregnancy, and the propensity for neo-Nazi skinheads—the reporter noted many disturbing statistics. Among them was one I couldn't ignore. "In 1996, Palmdale High School, out of a graduating class of about four hundred, sent exactly six students into the University of California system. Less than 10 percent of the graduating class went on to any four-year college at all."

I was done. I'd worked too hard too see my children lose all the advances I'd gained.

I tallied the numbers. We put more than $40,000 in cash down on the house. Over eight years, we'd paid $122,000 in mortgage payments, another $13,000 in property taxes, and $2,800 in fire insurance. We'd come up with gas money for the commute, tuition money for school; I couldn't even bear to register what we'd paid to heat and cool our dream home.

We were responsible, I knew, for the choices we'd made. Had we been willing to settle for less—a smaller house, carpeting we didn't choose—maybe we wouldn't have made some of the mistakes we did.

We let the bank foreclose against us and we walked away.

By the time we pulled our U-Haul truck out of the Antelope Valley and headed back to Los Angeles, to a cute little rental house I'd found, we had nothing left in savings, three kids to raise, and a credit report we were ashamed of.

Fast-forward six years. John and I are happy most of the time with the decision we made, and looking back on it, we don't know that we could have done anything else. We might have been able to stick it out and regain our original investment— the house we walked away from is now worth nearly double what we'd paid—but at what cost? Time together as a family, living in a neighborhood that feels like home, without the pressures of that financial squeeze—those elements have come to mean more to us than the return on our investment.

Still, it pains me when our kids talk about the old house as if it were Disneyland, a place with a massive yard, more room than we needed, pure abundance made manifest. The old house, they think, was heaven.

"Can't we move back?" they sometimes ask, nearly breaking my heart. But John and I know the truth. Our kids' lives have been immensely enriched by the move. As a family, we're happier here.

We're still renting the same 1910 Craftsman house we moved into when we left Lancaster. It's in Glendale, where I grew up, the very area we couldn't afford to buy in all those years ago. We still can't afford to buy here, but we've established a life I wouldn't trade for all the real estate deeds on this block. This afternoon, John will be attending our son's basketball game. Hope, our youngest, has only a hazy memory of the previous house with the swing set and trampoline. She's taking gymnastics, though, at the local Y and it seems to me she's not missing out on much. We have dinner together as a family most every night. My oldest is fortunate to attend the LA County High School for the Arts, a tuition-free public school that offers top-notch conservatory-style arts education. Ninety-four percent of the kids from that school go on to college.

Still, when I look at the way we lost out and how we're now stuck thanks to skyrocketing prices, I feel angry and victimized by a real estate market I could do nothing about. But that's the nature of life sometimes. We can't control the outcome. We make choices and then we live, as best we can, with the results.

John and I have money in the bank again, a down payment for when the market cools off. Analysts are saying that won't happen any time soon. For today, we're fine. No one's asking us to leave. Our landlord seems to like having us here. When we're ready to buy again, we'll do it differently. We'll look for a place that's part of the community in which we live and work, not shunted off in a separate world. A place where we can walk to the market and sit outside to read on a gorgeous Southern California afternoon. A neighborhood with good schools.

Extra bedrooms and a sunken bathtub in the master suite? No thanks. Room for a trampoline in the backyard? That's okay; we can do without.

I don't know yet how the story will end, but I have faith. And a bit of hard-earned wisdom paired with a scaled-down, life-size dream.

Before You Go the Foreclosure Route

If you find yourself in the position Bernadette did, don't opt for a foreclosure unless you've exhausted all other avenues. And be sure you talk to an attorney or other real estate expert in your state, since the rules vary from state to state. At the minimum, be certain you've considered the following:

A short sale A short sale is when you sell your house and the proceeds from the sale fall short of what's required to pay off the mortgage. In some cases, the lender may agree to accept the proceeds of a short sale and forgive the rest of what is owed on the mortgage when the owner cannot make the mortgage payments. By accepting a short sale, the lender avoids a lengthy and costly foreclosure, and the owner is able to get out from under the mortgage burden.

A deed in lieu of foreclosure If a homeowner can't make the mortgage payments and can't find a buyer for the house, the lender may accept ownership of the property in place of the money owed on the mortgage. Even if the lender won't agree to accept the property, the homeowner can prepare a quitclaim deed that unilaterally transfers the homeowner's property rights to the lender.

Understanding Foreclosure

Foreclosure is a legal process by which a homeowner in default on a mortgage is deprived of interest in a property. The lender forces the sale of the property, typically at a public auction, and the proceeds are applied to the mortgage debt. Consequences of foreclosure may include (but are not limited to):

Loss of property After foreclosure, you no longer own the home and will be obligated to vacate.

Spoiled credit rating A foreclosure on your credit record will damage your credit rating and may impair your ability to get credit in the future.

Possible liability to the lender After foreclosure, if the proceeds from the sale of your property were less than the amount you would owe the lender, you might, under certain circumstances, be liable for that difference.

Tax woes If you were not to pay the lender what was owed, above and beyond what the property sold for, the IRS, in certain circumstances, may consider this unpaid debt to be part of your taxable income.

Tao Worksheet

1. Walk yourself through the worst-case scenario in your mind. Write it out. Look at it. That which seems horrible can often be the doorway to something wonderful. Can you find an upside to the scenario you've drawn?

2. Write about financial failure—does this engender shame or disgrace for you? When has failure been a good thing in your life? Tell a story about the time a seeming disaster turned into something good.

3. We often believe that financial security can protect us from difficulties in life. When has financial stability failed to protect you? Write about a time when all the money in the world couldn't fix something you desperately wanted fixed. Tell a story.

4. When we start over, we know more about ourselves and what we really need and want out of life. What have you learned about yourself when you've had to back off and start again?

5. In an earlier chapter, Bernadette wrote about her desire to be free from fear, and how that desire was greater than her desire to be free from want. What does freedom from fear mean to you? Write about a time you were free from fear. Now write about freedom from want. Have you ever not wanted? Did you then fear losing what you already had? Sometimes, the more we have, the more we fear. How has this dynamic played out in your life?

WHAT WE TALK ABOUT WHEN
WE TALK ABOUT HOME

Do your work, then step back.
The only path to serenity.

ROSE, ON FENCES AND NEIGHBORS

"WHAT ABOUT YOU, Rose?" Colleen asks one Tuesday night when the Tao Gals are meeting at Rose's place. "Of all the things you feared, going into this real estate decision, did any of them come true?"

"Well . . ." Rose pauses to think. "They may not have come true, but most of them are still there. I'm still fearful, two years later." Rose had hoped that buying a home would give her a sense of security, but in many ways, it hasn't. Instead of worrying that her landlord would sell her rental house and she'd be on the street, Rose now she worries that the winter storms we're having will destroy her roof, or stews over problems with her next-door neighbors.

And they are among the worst kind of homeowner.

Her neighbors to the west are an extended family; a couple with four kids, and various grandparents, aunts, uncles, and other children passing through. The household also had three dogs: a chow, a pit bull, and a golden retriever. The dogs live in the backyard, are never walked, and bark constantly, at every-thing, especially at Rose's dogs, Bubba and Bella.

Good fences make good neighbors, and a prominent item on Rose's list of must-do home improvements was the fence—it rose to the top of the list after the chow and pit bull broke through the flimsy wood fence and attacked Bubba the first time, sending him to the vet with deep puncture wounds and gashes that required stitches.

Rose shored up the fence and the next-door neighbors, deeply apologetic, promised to pay the vet bills and fix the fence. "Don't do anything yourself, we know people who will fix it inexpensively, and we'll split the bill."

The four children who lived next door made friends with Rose—and her dogs. Rose's dogs were friendlier, and much cleaner than any of their three. Bubba and Bella were leash-trained, could perform many tricks, were wonderfully obedient and affectionate. The children's chow, pit bull, and even the golden retriever were squirrelly, almost wild. Not suitable pets for children.

One morning, Rose and Bubba were getting into her car—which was parked just four or five feet from her front door. As they crossed this small space, the pit bull, who was out loose, shot in and attacked Bubba again, sending him to the vet for more stitches, leaving Rose with another $300 bill.

Again, the neighbors were contrite, apologetic. "We don't know how the dogs got out!" they said. "We'll fix the fence! It won't ever happen again!"

This time, Rose reported the attack to the animal regulators in Los Angeles.

The fence was not fixed. And the dogs were often out.

The neighbors' dogs were out so often, Rose was terrified to go out of her front door with her own dogs. She came out first, looked up and down the street to make sure that the pit bull and chow were not loose, and only then took her dogs from the front door to the car. Bubba was attacked yet again. Rose called the authorities again and reported the attack.

The dogs attacked other animals up and down the street. The pit bull bit a child. The authorities, who deal with thousands of dog bites a year, duly noted each of the attacks, but did not act.

Rose's neighbors remained contrite, and constantly promised to fix the fence. If Rose went out and worked on the fence, they told her to stop, that they would help her soon. Nothing came of it. Rose fixed the fence to the best of her ability, repeatedly asked for money for the vet bills, and they continued to promise, to apologize, to explain they had no money, to insist they'd put in a new fence as soon as they did. Nothing they promised ever materialized.

"I didn't want to get harsh and nasty with them, or take them to court, because I have to live next door to them," Rose tells the Gals. "I kept giving them the benefit of the doubt. Plus, the kids were over all the time, they liked me, they liked the dogs, I didn't want to jeopardize that relationship."

Rose came home one day and found the oldest boy, a thirteen-year-old, and a friend of his inside her house, stuffing their pockets with her things. She yelled at them, and told their parents. The parents were horrified, contrite, apologetic, promised it would not happen again. At their pleading, Rose did not call the police.

Bubba was an older dog, and when he passed away, Rose looked high and low for a puppy. After about six months she found a funny little dachshund-spaniel pup she named Shemp after the fourth Stooge. Bella, Rose's other dog, loved Shemp. Michelle, who watched him when Rose went to track meets, adored Shemp. The neighbor kids especially loved Shemp. They were at Rose's house constantly, wanting to play with the puppy—while their own dogs were neglected in the backyard, or terrorizing the neighborhood.

Rose remained vigilant, checking up and down the street every time she left her house to see if the neighbors' dogs were out.

And then, of course, one day she checked, and didn't see them, and brought Shemp out. The pit bull raced out of nowhere, grabbed the puppy, and killed him. Right under Rose's nose.

A nightmare.

Rose called Michelle, who came over. This time, animal regulation came when called and took the chow and pit bull away. "Why did you come now?" Rose asked them. "Why this time? Why didn't you come before?"

"Well, we looked at the file"—the officer showed with his fingers how thick the file was, over two inches—"and decided it was time."

While Michelle drove Rose to the police station to make a report, Rose turned to Michelle. "Why did you let me buy this house?" she asked. "Why didn't you warn me against it?"

Michelle, who of course had minced no words about Rose's house, was speechless for once.

Rose patted her knee. "Sorry," she said. "My idea of a joke."

Home ownership, the Gals have learned, is not an answer to all life's problems. Learning to be at peace with life, even when there are worries and mishaps, is what they're after now.

Plus, Rose says, it's sometimes a drag to be a sole homeowner.

All of the burden falls on your shoulders and there are days when you just don't want to worry about it. She thinks the real question is this: Does it feel different coming home to a house you own?

And the answer, for Rose, is no. "I *do* feel like I'm saving for the future—and that's important. But owning a house hasn't given me any overwhelming sense of fabulousness that I'd heard came with the territory. I keep waiting for it to arrive, and in little ways, how I feel about it is changing a bit, softening. I feel good about coming home. But I did at my rental house too." Rose thinks for a bit about how her life is different.

"I can have people over for dinner now," she announces, having stumbled across an overlooked benefit. The Tao Gals look at her quizzically. We're seated around her dining table at this very moment. What's so special about that?

"I lived among *a lot* of people until I was thirty-four."

As a child, Rose tells the Gals, she'd grown up in a family of six. Then, as a young adult in the 1970s, she'd lived communally. "I was cooking for people. I was paying rent for all these people. I was the one doing everything." Finally, the day came, at age thirty-four, when she was done sharing her space with others. "I was so done with having people in the house, I was sure I never wanted anyone in my house again!" Rose moved into her little rental house in the hills and the first thing her father bought her for that house, she says, was a dining room set.

"I gave it away the next day," she explains. "I thought, if I don't have a dining room set, nobody will ever come over for dinner."

She didn't want anyone coming over at all. Ever. She didn't want to cook meals for anyone. She just wanted to be left alone. And she was. "It became my cave."

Eighteen years later, Rose realized she missed having people over. "I should be in the world," she thought. But how do you do that?

"That was part of what went into buying the house," she says as the Gals sit around her dining room table, munching on the lavish snacks she's prepared. "It wasn't just about security or savings or tax advantages. I decided I'd have a dining room—and rejoin the world!"

GAYLE, CONTENT TO RENT

Gayle, like Bernadette, continues to rent and most of the time feels good right where she is. It would be nice to own a home, she says, still, "it's more important to me to feel at home." And she does feel at home in her apartment. Sure, she has to pull out the couch to get access to the bookcase, but she can live with that. "There's all this crap, gifts and stuff, and it's all got meaning for me. I don't think I'll ever do one of those neat-and-tidy *House and Garden*–type homes, but when I think about having a home, I just think, it would be nice to build bookshelves." The whole house, if Gayle had her way, would be bookshelves.

"I like houses where you go in and you feel the soul of the family. It's really apparent. It translates into a real welcoming. I could just go and sit down on the couch and be there all day; I could read a book. I feel that at your house," Gayle says to Bernadette of her rental in Glendale. "Your place feels like a home to me."

So, maybe the idea of "home" is not tied into ownership, after all.

"Sophie and I," Gayle says, "we don't have the bookshelves I'd like. No washer and dryer. But we do have the spirit. Sophie says to me, 'Mom, this is our home.' And she's right. I like it where I am. The cat likes it too."

MARIE'S LONG-TERM ADVENTURE

Marie thinks of her early house purchase as something that has supported her lifestyle and can't imagine her life being any other way.

That's not to say she hasn't gone through rocky times with home ownership. When she and Dennis were remodeling, doubling the size of their home, they stayed at friends' houses, moving from couch to couch, living out of suitcases. But they managed. "We had no kids, no pets. We could fend for ourselves."

Once the hassle of the remodel was finished, the market bottomed out and Marie and Dennis found themselves owing much more on the house than it was worth. Dennis took more of an emotional hit than Marie did during that time. "I'm more of a Scarlett O'Hara," she says. "La-de-da, it'll all work out." And it did.

"I knew buying real estate's a long-term investment," she says, and then corrects herself, "a long-term adventure!"

She allows that the adventure is not always happy. "Life is filled with stories like Bernadette's. Real life happens. And you do have to make adjustments. But that's the cool thing about the Tao. Action and inaction are littered through those writings. The trick is being conscious enough to act when you need to act, sit still when you need to sit still, and otherwise being willing to be in flow."

Still, owning a home may have prevented her from impulsive actions. "There are times when I think that having my house has forced me to stay married when otherwise I might have walked," she admits, surprising the Gals with the comment.

"Is that a good thing?" Rose asks.

"Today it seems so. There are plenty of days when it doesn't seem like a good thing. There are plenty of days when I say to myself, 'God, if I had just not been so responsible, so obligated, etc., my whole life would be different today.' And of course, *different* means *better*!" Marie laughs at this grass-is-always-greener mind-set. "Life would definitely be different if I hadn't bought the house. Or, if I hadn't stayed married. Today, selling the house would not be the answer to every problem—or any problem—I have."

COLLEEN, HANGING ON

Colleen, especially after the kitchen redux, is happy enough in her house. "I don't think it was a bad move," she tells the Gals. In fact, Colleen thinks she was very fortunate to get into her neighborhood at all. The house, in itself, is really not all that special, but the strength of the neighborhood, she believes, will maintain its value, whatever might come.

"In that regard, I don't regret it. I'm not going to sell it right away so it doesn't matter what the real estate experts say it's worth. The thing that I learned from past experience is that it's all smoke and mirrors. Unless you're in a position to be flipping houses, or actively investing in the market, what you're doing is that you're just living somewhere. And you hope that it will retain some value. I hope I'll get my down payment out of it. Other than that, I'm fine here."

The truth is, though, that it's still a financial burden for this single mother. "The payments are a lot," she says. "And I'm not being as responsible as I could be. I'm making interest-only payments right now, not paying on the principal. I don't know if it's because I've lost a house before, but, you know, fuck them, is my feeling. Is it prudent? Probably not. Should I be paying down on this? Probably."

The last time Colleen was in this situation, she says, she was diligently paying down her principal and it didn't help. "And the value of the house? Well, you know that situation." If you're paying on a $400K loan, Colleen says, and your house is only valued at $250K, "who's the fool?" She's not in a position at the moment to pay down the principal, so she's not. Still, she believes it will all turn out okay.

"If there's a nutshell version of the Tao, it's that home is where you are," she tells the Gals. "You need to be where you are, and that's where home is."

BERNADETTE PONDERS THE SOCIAL CONTRACT

> *When rich speculators prosper*
> *while farmers lose their land;*
> *when government officials spend money*
> *on weapons instead of cures;*
> *when the upper class is extravagant and irresponsible*
> *while the poor have nowhere to turn—*
> *all this is robbery and chaos.*
> *It is not in keeping with the Tao.*

"It's just greed, pure and simple," my friend Bonnie, who's also priced out of the market, said to me the other day. "I won't buy a house right now out of spite. The spite may end up hurting me in the long run, but so be it. I, for one, won't participate in this."

Her words echo as I drive to an open house for a property about which I am very interested, thanks to what I've already read online. It's exactly the right neighborhood with the schools

I want for my kids. It's small—perhaps too small for my family—but it's priced right and a portion of the garage has been made into a bonus room. With that extra space, we'd manage. This may be it.

It's raining today and though I would have thought the damp might keep lookers at bay—this being California where the slightest hint of bad weather freaks most people out—there's a constant stream of potential buyers moving through the tiny house. The house is boxy, not well cared for, but shows promise. I notice immediately a wheelchair perched on the front porch.

The living room is in near darkness when I enter, the air clotted with the smell of industrial-strength disinfectant. Huddled together at the corner of the sofa in the dim room perch an elderly couple. A pair of walkers rest before them.

"Hello," I say, trying to be friendly. "How are you?"

They don't answer but make grunting noises, clearly unhappy to have people tromping through their house. The Realtor, a woman in her late fifties wearing a lot of makeup and a plastic rain bonnet, quickly ushers me toward the bedrooms, trying to get me away from the old couple. They must be in their eighties at least. Maybe their nineties.

After pointing out details of the nondescript bedrooms, the Realtor directs me to the house's sole bathroom, which is only memorable for the handicapped appliances that fill the small space. There are handrails for the shower stall, a place to sit while bathing, special equipment on the toilet.

The kitchen, where she whisks me next, is cramped with potential buyers who've been herded here until the other Realtor—the two women are working as a tag team, I learn—is ready to lead the procession through the rainy backyard to gaze upon the bonus room.

"See that wall," one man says to his companion as he waits in the overcrowded kitchen. "I'd tear that down and open the space up."

"The heater needs to be replaced," a woman is saying to her friend. "And I hear there's asbestos in the ducting."

"Do the washer and dryer come with the place?" another person asks the "inside" Realtor, who's busy trying to corral the group, which I have now somehow joined.

Ms. Outside, a more friendly looking Realtor, meets us at the kitchen door and leads us out to see the bonus room. We sprint through the drizzle.

The bonus area is huge—almost the size of an apartment. But much of it is inaccessible. Sofas have been upended and squeezed into a tiny entryway that leads, the outside Realtor tells us, to a makeshift kitchen and bathroom. We have to take the Realtor's word on it, though, since there's no way past the sofas. I look around. The workmanship of this added living space seems shoddy. Windows are not firmly in place. The air-conditioning unit looks like it might topple out of its cutout in the wall. The walls themselves are Sheetrock; the floor, cement.

"Is this space permitted?" one potential buyer asks.

"No," Ms. Outside answers. "You take your chances that if the city finds out about it, you could be asked to convert it back."

The questions keep coming.

"Can we arrange an inspection or is the house as-is?"

"What about the asbestos issue?"

The shoppers poke through the couple's things, tilting the sofas aside to peek into the hidden space. One by one, after they get their answers, they make a tributary toward their cars and leave. When it's quiet, just the sound of the rain hitting the porch overhang, I approach Ms. Outside.

"What's the story?" I ask. "The old couple."

"It's a bankruptcy sale. Been a nightmare to organize, let me tell you." She nods conspiratorially toward the living room and the now-silent couple. "But I think we've got them all straightened out now. There'll be no more delays. We'll start taking offers in three days," she tells me, "but none before then."

I leave the open house feeling sick.

"Sylvia," I say, when I call my Realtor to report my findings. "It was a little old couple. They're being forced out. Bankruptcy. The house would have fit us, sure, but I can't bid on that."

"You know," she tells me, "if you don't buy it, someone else will."

"What's happened to the social contract that tied neighbors to each other?" I wonder aloud at the Tao meeting after relating my story. Don't we have a responsibility to help each other? It's a bankruptcy sale, probably brought on by medical expenses. Sure, the old couple could be complete profligates for all I know, but the whole scene strikes me as bothersome and immoral. Where has this booming real estate market taken us?

"Look at all the people who are sitting pretty thanks to equity gains," I go on. "In reality, they're stuck. Unless they want to cash out and move somewhere else where prices are still reasonable, they're caught in a trap. A new place is going to cost them that much more, and add sky-high property taxes on top of it. How is this a good thing?"

The Tao Gals shake their heads. No one argues the point.

But what's to be done about it?

"I read an editorial in my local paper last week," I tell the Gals, "written in response to complaints about the high cost of housing in Glendale. 'If people don't like it,' the writer, who obviously owned his own house, had written, 'they can just move to Lancaster.' Lancaster! That's where I lost the previous house. Is this really the kind of world we want to live in?"

Still, I'm checking the Web sites every day, driving the neighborhoods, looking for a place to buy, trying to make the best of a difficult situation. Some days, I want to give up. Not only because it's hard on me, but also because I think of all those who've lost in this game. Compared to many, I'm one of the lucky ones.

The looking process is no longer filled with promise and excitement. After encountering those Caltrans homes sitting empty and then meeting the old couple on their way to who knows where, I see that this booming market has taken a toll. It reminds me of all those people who lost their retirement savings in the Enron scandal. How is this any less damaging?

But it's the market, I'm told. It's the way things are.

THE DECISION COMES after I've done everything I can think of: polled friends, talked with the Tao Gals, researched the market, gone to open houses. Just as there comes a tipping point at which a potential buyer turns into a homeowner, there's another tipping point: the moment you decide you can't do it. At least, not now.

For me, the tipping point comes after an e-mail exchange with my real estate guru and friend, Thom. For years, he's been urging me to buy. The time is right. Do it now.

Finally, I'm starting to find properties that might work, I write to him. There's this one little Craftsman in the hills of La Crescenta. It has one bedroom too few, but maybe we could make it work. The listing Realtor will start accepting offers tomorrow. If I want to do this, I need to get moving. "What does your crystal ball say?" I ask Thom, fully expecting him to nudge me forward, over the hump.

He doesn't.

For the first time since I've known him, he tells me to wait.

"All I know is that prices have to come down. HAVE TO!" he writes back. "The fundamentals are screwed up." Thom, who's a professional real estate investor, says he can no longer invest in income property and make a decent return. "In fact," he writes, "in 'good' areas, my return is negative in the short run. As for houses, they are more like the prices of fine artwork. There is nothing that can support their prices such as rents, etc., unless you make long-term, absurd assumptions."

It's not at all what I was expecting to hear and it takes me a moment to digest his words. After years of Thom telling me to jump, he's now telling me to wait. I swallow hard at that thought of giving up and yet a feeling of relief swells in my chest. There's a part of me—in fact, a huge part, I now realize—that's utterly tickled by this news. I don't have to jump into this mess right now. I don't have to do anything! Oh, happy day.

"I think you have the luxury of being indifferent toward either buying or renting," Thom's e-mail goes on. "In other words, I don't think it matters what you do. You may come out the same financially either way."

I sit still and listen to my heart. When big decisions beckon, an old friend's advice always comes to mind. "If you picture the scenario and it gives you peace, it's the right choice. If the scenario only makes you more anxious, maybe you should just hold still." When I picture myself letting go of this real estate–search burden, if only for a month or two, I feel great. I could just drop this weight here and now—I can always pick it up again later.

I consider my life as it currently is: I love where I live. I'm comfortable with the rent I'm paying. The only reason I want to buy now is fear that I'll be unable to do so later on. I remind myself of the old adage I'd hung on to when I lost my last house: *Freedom from fear is more important than freedom from want.* That still matters to me most, I remind myself: freedom from fear.

Over the next few days, I feel magnificent. I'm in a position to buy if the right property presents itself, but I'm no longer battling with myself and I'm not at war with the market. I tell the Tao Gals about this feeling. They don't try to dissuade me.

"You know what's best for you," Gayle says.

Meanwhile, Thom mails me an article from *Money* magazine in which a Yale economist (the guy who predicted the bursting of the tech-stock bubble) warns that the "irrational exuberance" of the real estate market cannot be sustained. The bubble will end, he maintains, but no one knows when.

Whenever the fear starts to rear up again, I reread Thom's e-mail. "Of course, I could be completely wrong," he'd written. "Maybe because of terrorism, exposed weaknesses in our securities policies (screwed-up stock market), growing urban populations, land shortages, and a need to shield/ hedge against inflation, real estate could become the new 'gold standard.'"

I can live with that risk, I decide. I've made it this far without owning a house; I can make it further.

"That said," Thom's missive continued, "I'm still looking myself. But I haven't found ANYTHING that makes sense. I get on the MLS, search, search, search and print, print, print. Maybe the best investment is in Boise Cascade."

Like Thom, I'm still looking and I imagine I'll be at it for some time to come. If the landlords decide to sell the house we're living in (along with the rental units), we'll think about buying it. Likewise, if a little house in the La Crescenta Valley area comes up for sale at a price we can afford, we may move on it. But I don't have to do anything now. I don't have to act out of fear. I can be still and quiet and calm. And for that small fact, I'm extremely grateful.

MICHELLE, AT HOME

Finding a home and moving, then remodeling—I did these things because I had to. They were the problems to be addressed, the next-indicated items on my to-do list. I approached these tasks with a stolid pragmatism. I never expected that buying a home would transform me or give me a better life. I'm a little too old—and a little too steeped in the Tao—to allow myself much in the way of expectations. My goal was to provide myself with the best dwelling I could afford—with a bit of beauty thrown in—and live there.

I didn't expect buying a home to elevate my status in the world, or make me more comfortable.

I knew that buying a house was financially sound and could be emotionally satisfying, but I did not count on these benefits.

By my forties, I had long since given up expecting happiness from externals. Happiness, I knew, was an inside job. A house would give me shelter, perhaps refuge (assuming the neighbors were tolerable), and a yard for my garden and pets.

I'd had my share of Great Expectations in regard to Great

Undertakings—and I'd seen the gap between what I hoped would happen and what reality delivered.

I'd published my first novel in 1997, and like so many first-time novelists, I had countless expectations about what that one slim volume might accomplish in my life. I hoped it would make me, if not famous, at least known and respected in certain circles. I hoped it might bring me a certain amount of gravity and respect—literary heft, in other words.

And there were the quiet, slightly unconscious expectations I hardly dared articulate: I hoped it might bring me new friendship, love, wealth. I hoped this one little novel might change the essential depressive and lonely nature of my life.

I was disappointed, of course—in almost all categories.

And I was gratified too—almost all in ways I didn't expect.

I didn't expect people to be so dear, to give me presents just for having written a book, to write me thoughtful, insightful letters, to love my characters. I didn't expect such generous and sweet reviews.

I also didn't expect the weirdness of old friends who assumed my life would change and I would ignore them. I didn't expect the envy-tinged comments and behavior of professional colleagues, or the strange fawning friendliness of people who liked me because of my book.

I *didn't* expect to get clinically depressed after the book's publication—despite the lovely reviews. I didn't expect to feel so incredibly lonely, the loneliest I've ever felt, the year my novel was published.

If achieving that lifelong dream was so fraught with unexpected emotions, I didn't even dare anticipate what buying a home would feel like.

Years of Tao Gal meetings and therapy made it clear that expectations, especially the barely conscious ones, can be deadly. I knew:

Thou shalt not expect.

Happiness does not come from "out there." Happiness is an inside job.

SO IMAGINE MY surprise when the workmen cleared out and I had my new home to myself and, instead of feeling emptiness or a postpartum letdown, or loneliness at the sudden silence in every room, I experienced a gradual but steady upswell of well-being.

My home was making me happy, and in ways I never expected—hadn't dared to expect.

People say, home is where the heart is. Home is where they can't throw you out.

But I had no family in my home, nobody drew me there except for the pets. (Although one should never underestimate the joy-producing powers of a welcoming tail-wagging, smiling dog.) Home, to me, was definitely not other people.

I had wanted—demanded—something beautiful in a new home, because I had been oppressed by the starkness and plainness of my last home. But I had not really grasped how much I had hungered for beauty, and now that my new home was sweetly appointed and on a truly beautiful piece of land, that beauty had a powerful effect on me. To this day, I can't look into my vast backyard shaded by huge trees, and up to the mountains, and the vast sweep of sky, and not feel grateful and enlarged and filled up with beauty.

All those countless decisions and little leaps of imagination made in the remodel phase had resulted in a tangible, concrete, deeply appealing reality—in which I now dwelled.

The black-coffee brown melamine light switches, the garden glimpsed through the doors, this and that paint color, all my rugs—in assembling these items, I hadn't tried to please anybody else. I wasn't even consciously trying to please myself. I was just making decisions based on my eyes and my gut and my own preferences; the result was an environment that provided constant aggreeableness. Faucets, drawer pulls, floors, doorknobs, all the things my hands grasped on a daily basis were chosen because some part of me, some internal part of me, was drawn to them. And so, in fact, they *fit* me, and are pleasing and subjectively beautiful to me. I don't mean to sound too solipsistic here, but I live in a space that accommodates me. And in some part that's what makes me happy.

Somehow, too, I'd managed to land in an area populated by simpatico people. Who knew that the small unincorporated scrap of a town where I was born would fifty years later be attracting precisely the kind of people I like?

I soon made friends among my neighbors. The gay guys two doors down in one direction, the married philosophy professors three doors in the other direction. And, of course, my old friend from high school, Michele, with whom I shared a fence. I live surrounded by friends.

And the story gets happier.

Two years after I moved into my house, my second novel was published. The day it hit the shelves, I gave a reading in a Hollywood bookstore. Afterward, a man approached me.

He had a warm, wide-open face, big brown eyes, killer eyelashes. He'd liked my first book, he told me. Also, we had friends in common. "And I have to confess," he went on, "I've been inside your house. You weren't home."

Our common friends were the philosophy professors. I vaguely remembered how, about a year before, when I was out of town and the professors were watching my pets, they'd taken a friend over to see my house. This friend was remodeling his apartment, they told me, and needed ideas.

As a little joke, I signed his book, "For Jim, The House-breaker of Altadena . . ."

The next day or so, I asked the philosophy professors about him.

He asked them about me.

A few weeks later, they had us both over for dinner.

Two weeks after that, he asked me over for dinner . . .

The upshot is, we're getting married. He already lives here.

But the point I want to make is, he saw my house before he met me. And it made an impression. He not only used bolder colors in his own apartment, he went out and read my first book. Then he came to a reading . . .

So that's another way homeownership has made me happy.

I look out my window right now, and see the patio I designed, the garden I planted, the mulch-covered property still waiting to be addressed. It's February and the yard is full of color—purple iris, red toyon berries, chartreuse euphorbia blossoms. I can't believe I live here, and get to see this much beauty right outside.

The yard is private, vast, calm, and, at present, frightfully messy—so many roses to prune and weeds to pull! Wild parrots squawk overhead, crows convene seventy feet up in the eucalyptus. The rufous-sided towhee—is it the same one who shows up every February?—is kicking up compost like a tiny dust devil; if I watch him long enough, I see the sun glint in his bright red eyes. Truth be told, however, I don't get much pleasure from the squirrels burying their acorns in holes dug all over my backyard; at least the dog and the cat have great fun chasing them.

If I hadn't been given an eviction notice from my long-term rental, I doubt that I would ever have bought a house. I didn't want to buy a house.

I didn't love this house when I saw it, not the first time, not the fifth time.

I didn't want to remodel, particularly. It was just what I had to do so I wouldn't move in and die from depression.

But I think it was not wanting to move, not being in love with the new house, not expecting anything, that helped things work out.

I did not overinvest in this house, emotionally or financially. It wasn't the house I loved, it was the least-expensive property I looked at.

It was nothing special.

But then I invested myself in it, reasonably and slowly, and it became a part of me and I of it.

As a person who is home all day, who cares deeply about her surroundings, home is a place where I can be myself, a place that fits me, that welcomes me and the people and pets I love.

Who knew that owning a home would bring this chronic depressive and perpetual malcontent not only happiness, but love?

As we say at the end of each Tao meeting: So be it. So may it *ever* be.

GLOSSARY

401(K) A type of retirement plan, sponsored by an employer, that allows an employee to save for retirement while deferring income taxes on funds saved and interest earned until funds are withdrawn.

AMORTIZATION Loan payments are calculated so that the borrower pays off the debt, including interest, by the end of a fixed period. Typically, with mortgages, a large part of the monthly payment will go toward interest in the early years of the loan. As the loan period continues, a larger percentage of the payment goes toward principal rather than interest.

AMORTIZATION TABLE A chart showing what monthly payments would be, based on the amount borrowed, the term of the loan, and the interest rate.

ANNUAL PERCENTAGE RATE (APR) The cost of credit expressed as a yearly rate, which includes the interest rate plus points, broker fees, and other credit charges you may incur—the interest amount you will actually pay.

APPRAISAL An estimate of the value of a piece of property made by a professional appraiser.

APPRECIATION The amount by which a piece of property increases in value over time.

ASKING PRICE The suggested sales amount for a property. The seller is under no obligation to sell the property for the amount listed. If other potential buyers start offering higher prices, the property can sell for much more than the asking price. Likewise, it can also sell for less.

BACKUP OFFER An offer made by a potential buyer to purchase a property for which an offer has already been accepted. Since the first offer may fall out of escrow, this allows the sellers to have a backup buyer lined up.

CASH AVAILABLE The amount of money a borrower has on hand for the down payment, closing costs, and cash reserves.

CLOSING A meeting between buyer, seller, and lender (or their agents) at which the property and funds legally change hands.

CLOSING COSTS Costs involved with the transfer of property, typically including loan origination fees, points, appraisal fee, title search, insurance, taxes, deed recording fee, credit report fee, survey, and other costs assessed at closing. Typically, closing costs will total between 3 and 6 percent of the mortgage amount.

COMMISSION Real estate agents earn a commission, computed from the selling price of a house. Typically, the commission is 6 percent, and the seller's agent determines how that commission is divided with the buyer's agent. Commissions are negotiable.

CONDO Short for *condominium*. Individual ownership of a portion of a building—typically a unit—with common areas shared by all owners. Fees, called "assessments" or "homeowner dues," are paid to the condominium association for repairs, maintenance, and improvements on the property.

CONTINGENCY A condition that must be met for a contract to be legally binding. In home purchasing, contingencies may include, for example, that a satisfactory home inspection report be received from a qualified home inspector for the contract to become binding.

CONTRACTOR A tradesperson who does construction work and is under contract with the owner of the property.

CREDIT SCORE/RATING A report of a borrower's credit history and current credit standing.

DEBT-TO-INCOME RATIO A ratio, given as a percentage, that indicates how much of a borrower's gross monthly income is going to be allocated to long-term debts.

DEPRECIATION A decrease in the value of a property.

DISCLOSURE Important information that must be revealed to the buyer about the property prior to a sale. Disclosures may include facts affecting the value or desirability of a property.

DOWN PAYMENT An amount of money paid to make up the difference between the mortgage amount and the purchase price.

EARLY PAY-OFF When the borrower pays back the mortgage debt prior to the maturity of the term. Some lenders may charge an "early pay-off penalty."

EMPLOYMENT RECORD Proof of your job and employment history.

EQUIFAX A company that provides access to your credit report for a fee.

EQUITY The value of the property, above what the borrower owes on it.

ESCROW An account in which a neutral third party holds the documents and money in a real estate transfer until all conditions are met. After the buyer's offer is accepted, the buyer does not immediately move into the property. During the escrow period, the neutral third party holds the buyer's down payment and documents until the sale closes. The term "escrow" can also mean an escrow or impound account. See IMPOUNDS, OR ESCROW ACCOUNTS.

EXCLUSIVE AGREEMENT An agreement real estate agents may ask clients to sign, indicating that the client will work only with the specified agent.

FICO SCORES A credit score, calculated by Fair Isaac Corp., commonly used in mortgage loan transactions.

FORECLOSURE A legal process by which a homeowner in default on a mortgage is deprived of interest in a property. The lender forces the sale of the property—typically at a public auction—and the proceeds are applied to the mortgage debt.

GOOD FAITH ESTIMATE A written estimate of projected closing costs. A lender must provide this estimate within three days after a prospective buyer submits a mortgage application.

GROSS INCOME The amount of money a person earns from all sources, before taxes are deducted.

HOMEOWNERS (OR HAZARD) INSURANCE A form of insurance required by lenders that protects the insured from losses due to specific risks, such as fire, flood, earthquakes, etc.

IMPOUNDS, OR ESCROW ACCOUNTS An account in which money for property taxes and insurance is held until the obligation is due. When a borrower uses impounds, money from every mortgage payment goes into the account to ensure funds are available when the fees are due.

IMPROVEMENTS Money or effort put into a property to increase its value or desirability.

INSPECTOR A trained professional who assesses current and potential problems associated with a property.

INTEREST RATE The amount of interest charged on a monthly loan amount, usually expressed as a percentage.

LENDER The person or institution that lends money to the homebuyer for the purchase of a house.

LIEN A debt that is attached to ("secured by") a specific piece of property. Liens must be paid off before the property can change hands.

LISTING AGENT The real estate agent under contract to the owner to market ("list") and sell the owner's house.

LOAN LOCK A guarantee, often for a fee, that the rate of interest on a loan will not change for a specified number of days, often thirty or sixty days, usually the length of escrow. Loan locks are important to get in an unstable market, or when rates are rising.

LOAN/MORTGAGE BANKER A person, mortgage company, or bank employee who can lend you the money for your home.

LOAN/MORTGAGE BROKER A person who will shop (among individuals, banks, and mortgage companies) and find the appropriate mortgage for you.

MAINTENANCE The general care and repair necessary to keep a house in good condition.

MARKET PRICE/VALUE How much a house is worth at a particular moment in a specific housing market.

MONTHLY PAYMENT The amount of money paid each month to the lender; the payment typically includes principal, interest, and sometimes impounded home insurance payments, private mortgage insurance (PMI), and property tax payments.

MORTGAGE The sum of money that's borrowed to buy a house and uses the house as collateral.

MULTIPLE OFFERS When several offers are made on a house by various interested buyers.

NET INCOME How much money you make after all deductions are subtracted from your gross income—how much you get to take home.

NEW HOME DEVELOPMENT A tract or development that consists of newly constructed homes.

NO DOCUMENTATION (NO-DOC) LOAN A loan for which you do not have to provide any documentation of income (specifically tax documentation). No-doc loans are typically allowed when the buyer can make a large down payment. No-doc loans also cost slightly more at the outset.

NOTARY PUBLIC An individual licensed by the state to give a legal imprimatur to a document. Notary publics record the date of the document, the signatures of the parties, and their fingerprints in a record book, and stamp the necessary document with an identifying, state-issued imprint.

OFFER An official document presented to a seller that declares how much you are willing to pay for a house and how you intend to finance the purchase.

POINT A point represents 1 percent of your loan amount. If your loan is $400,000, one point is $4,000. Points are often the price you pay for various stipulations in your loan; for example, a no-doc loan may cost a quarter of a point to a full point (in our example, $1,000 to $4,000). The borrower can pay for points when the loan is made or can "roll" them into the overall loan and pay for them over time—with interest of course. Remember, when you're talking points, you're talking real money!

POWER OF ATTORNEY Authorizing someone to act on your behalf in financial matters. If you can't be in town when your escrow closes, for example, you can give a trusted associate power of attorney to sign all your documents.

PREAPPROVAL An assessment of a potential borrower's ability to pay for a home that is based on a credit check and a review of earnings and other relevant financial information. Preapproval is a more thorough process than prequalification, which is often based on a verbal interview and does not require any credit checks or documentation. Preapproval is still an intermediate step in home financing and the completion of a lend application is necessary to close the loan.

PREAPPROVAL LETTER A letter obtained from a lender after they have assessed your ability to pay for a home; it will state the amount that lender is prepared to lend you for the purchase of a home.

PREQUALIFICATION This is the preliminary assessment made by a potential lender of a buyer's ability to pay for a home. It is usually based on a verbal interview and does not involve credit checks or other documentation. Prequalification serves as a rough, undocumented estimate of how much the buyer could borrow. In a hot, fast market, prequalification carries little weight; many real estate agents won't accept an offer without preapproval, a more thorough assessment of your ability to pay.

PRIME RATE, OR PRIME LENDING RATE The minimum short-term interest rate charged by commercial banks to their most creditworthy clients—in other words, most of us will never see this rate! For our purposes, it serves as a "base" rate, a starting point for lenders. Home loan rates are usually priced several percentage points above the prime rate.

PRINCIPAL The amount of money originally borrowed in a mortgage. Be aware that the principal does not include interest or other costs.

PRIVATE MORTGAGE INSURANCE (PMI) A kind of insurance required by a lender when the borrower's down payment or home equity is less than 20 percent of the selling price. When the buyer has made enough payments so that equity in the home reaches 20 percent, the insurance can be dropped. This insurance protects the lender only, however, and while PMI may enable a buyer to enter the housing market with less cash, it has no other benefit to the buyer, does not add to the value of the home, and should be avoided whenever possible.

PROPERTY TAX Tax paid on privately owned property. Property taxes are usually paid in twice-yearly installments. Sometimes, if the lender requires it or the buyer chooses to do so, these taxes are "impounded" with monthly mortgage payments and therefore are paid monthly (see IMPOUNDS, OR ESCROW ACCOUNTS). The amount of tax owed is based on local tax rates and assessed property value.

REAL ESTATE AGENT A person licensed by a state to represent a buyer or a seller in a real estate transaction. Unless they are also brokers, agents must work in association with a real estate broker or brokerage company. Agents are paid by commission.

REALTOR A real estate agent or broker who is a member of the National Association of Realtors.

RECORDING The act of entering (filing) titles and other property-related documents with the appropriate government agencies so that they become part of the public record.

REFINANCING The process of paying off your older mortgage with a new mortgage that—presumably, ideally—gives you better terms. However, some people refinance to "take money out," or borrow against their equity, to remodel or repair their home, or for other reasons.

RENTAL UNITS Apartments or rooms on a property that can be rented out for income.

STRUCTURAL PROBLEMS Defects in the structure of a house (in the foundation, walls, roof, windows, for example) that can threaten its overall physical integrity. Structural problems are more serious than cosmetic problems, which tend to be more superficial, visually apparent, and displeasing in nature, and often much less expensive to repair.

TAX DEDUCTION The amount the government allows you to take off your taxes for specific costs and expenditures. Property taxes, certain escrow fees, loan points, and a percentage of mortgage interest are all tax deductible.

TITLE A legal document that asserts or confers ownership of a property. If you "have title" to a property, it means you have legal ownership.

TITLE COMPANY A firm that performs title searches (and thus ensures that the property title is clear) and also provides title insurance.

TITLE SEARCH The process of reviewing all recorded transactions in the public record to determine whether any title defects or risks exist that could interfere with the clear transfer of ownership of a property. Title searches are performed by title companies in the course of escrow. An increasing number of real estate agents request title searches before contracting to sell a property to avoid surprises further down the line.

TOWN HOUSE A home of two or more stories that is attached (shares structural walls with other units), individually owned, and not a condominium. You may ask, what, then, is a "town house condominium?" Well, it's a town house that *is* a condominium!

INDEX

INDEX

INDEX

A NOTE ON THE AUTHORS

Michelle Huneven is an award-winning fiction writer whose novel *Jamesland* was shortlisted for the *Los Angeles Times* Book Award for Fiction and whose previous novel, *Round Rock*, was named a *New York Times* Notable Book and a *Los Angeles Times* Best Book of the Year.

Bernadette Murphy is a literary critic for the *Los Angeles Times* and has written for *Newsday*, *Ms.*, the *San Francisco Chronicle*, and the *LA Weekly*, among other publications. She is the author of the best-selling *Zen and the Art of Knitting*.